AGGRESSIVE TAX AVOIDANCE FOR REAL ESTATE INVESTORS

By
John T. Reed

John T. Reed
342 Bryan Drive
Danville, CA 94526
510-820-6292

ABOUT THE AUTHOR

John T. Reed is a small landlord and real estate writer.

His real estate work experience includes home, land, and investment property brokerage and residential and nonresidential property management. As a property manager, he managed apartment complexes, office buildings, industrial space, farms, and single-family rental houses.

He has invested in New Jersey, Texas, and California.

He is the editor and publisher of *John T. Reed's Real Estate Investor's Monthly*, a national newsletter—and the author and publisher of ten books on various real estate investment subjects.

Mr. Reed has been interviewed about real estate by Morley Safer on *60 Minutes*, by David Hartman on *Good Morning America*, and by Larry King on *Larry King Live* as well as other television and radio programs. His analysis of real estate investing has appeared in *The Wall Street Journal*, *Newsweek*, *U.S. News & World Report*, *Changing Times*, *Money*, and various real estate journals.

He holds a Bachelor of Science degree from West Point and a Master of Business Administration degree from Harvard Business School.

OTHER MATERIAL BY JOHN T. REED

- *Distressed Real Estate Times—Offensive and Defensive Strategy and Tactics Special Report*
- *High Leverage Real Estate Financing* (cassettes)
- *How to Buy Real Estate for at Least 20% Below Market Value, Vol. I and II* (cassettes)
- *How to Buy Residential Property* (cassettes)
- *How to Do a Delayed Exchange Special Report*
- *How to Find Deals that Make Sense in Today's Market* (cassettes)
- *How to Increase the Value of Real Estate* (book)
- *How to Manage Residential Property for Maximum Cash Flow and Resale Value* (cassettes or book)
- *How to Save Tens of Thousands of Tax Dollars by Exchanging* (cassettes)
- *How to Use Leverage to Maximize Your Real Estate Investment Return* (book)
- *John T. Reed's Real Estate Investor's Monthly* (newsletter)
- *Offensive and Defensive Strategy for Distressed Real Estate Times (cassettes)*
- *Office Building Acquisition Handbook*
- *Residential Property Acquisition Handbook*
- *Real Estate Investor's Monthly on Real Estate Investment Strategy* (book)
- *Single-Family Lease Options Special Report* (book or cassettes)

For more information, see the order form in the back of this book or contact John T. Reed, 342 Bryan Drive, Danville, CA 94526, or call 800-635-5425.

THANKS TO...

Leigh Robinson, author of *Landlording*, for his invaluable assistance in publishing and marketing this book...Bob Baldassari, CPA of Brown, Dakes, Wannall and Nobrega of Fairfax, VA, for pointing out some technical errors...Bill Tappan, Jr., author of *Real Estate Exchange and Acquisition Techniques*, for pioneering the idea of putting legal references in a book for laymen and for his comments on this book...Bob Bruss, real estate columnist, for his generous assistance and favorable book reviews...Tom Kurkjian, for his proofreading and comments on the first edition...John Whitman for his suggestions on book design...Jack Campbell, tax attorney in Albuquerque, NM for his help with deals and tax questions...Brooke Gabrielson, tax attorney with Howser, Gertner and Brown in Newport Beach, CA, for his advice on deals and answers to questions...Apple Computer, Inc. and Microsoft Corporation for producing the hardware and software I used to write, "typeset," and produce this book...those who have attended my seminars for increasing my ability to get my ideas on taxes across and for correcting my errors...the intrepid tax pioneers who boldly went where no man had gone before and won; thereby giving us many of the tax breaks we enjoy today...Marty Tunnell for painfully proofreading; thereby allowing perfectionist readers to concentrate on the content rather than the presentation of this information.

To my mother,
Marion T. Reed

Copyright © 1981, 1982, 1983, 1984, 1985, 1986, 1987, 1988, 1989, 1991, 1992 by John T. Reed

First edition	August 1981
Second edition	December 1981
Third edition	February 1983
Fourth edition	February 1984
Fifth edition	February 1985
Sixth edition	February 1986
Seventh edition	August 1987
Eighth edition	November 1988
Ninth edition	November 1989
Ninth edition, second printing	March 1990
Tenth edition	January 1991
Eleventh edition	January 1992

Published by Reed Publishing
342 Bryan Drive
Danville, California 94526

Manufactured in the United States of America by Delta Lithograph Co., Valencia, Ca.
Library of Congress Catalog Card Number: 90-092056
ISBN: 0-939224-26-7

AGGRESSIVE TAX AVOIDANCE FOR REAL ESTATE INVESTORS

Contents

Introduction

The taxes you pay are too high.

What's worse, you probably pay **more** than you have to.

Why do the vast majority of real estate investors pay more taxes than the law requires? There are 8 major reasons:

1. **Ignorance** of favorable parts of the tax law.
2. **Bad advice** from tax advisers who are either incompetent or placing their own interest above their clients.
3. Inordinate **fear** of the IRS and the courts.
4. **Erroneous notions** about losses, "shelter," deductions, and so forth.
5. Lack of understanding of the **judgmental nature** of many aspects of tax law.
6. Lack of understanding of the **time value of money.**
7. **Human inertia** as in reluctance to exchange rather than sell.
8. Failure to **think through** the "old wives tales of tax law."

In this book, I aim to make sure that **you** don't pay more taxes than the law requires. To do that I'm going to :

1. Tell you about tax breaks which investors often **overlook.**
2. Show you how to tell when you're getting **bad advice**—and how to find a good tax adviser.
3. Give you a **more accurate picture** of the IRS and the courts so you fear them less.
4. Correct your **erroneous ideas** about taxes.
5. Explain the **judgmental** nature of many tax questions—and tell you the **aggressive** way to deal with those questions.
6. Show you how the **time value of money** should affect your tax decisions.
7. Help you overcome the **human inertia** which causes you to pay thousands of dollars more taxes than you should.

This book will **not**:

1. Tell you how to start **your own church** or become a minister in someone else's.
2. Recommend that you put everything you own in **family trusts.**
3. Reveal that income taxes are **unconstitutional.**
4. Ask you to become a **tax protestor.**
5. Tell you how to **cheat** and get away with it.
6. Show you how you can write off **vacations to Hawaii.**

I have never been accused of fraud by the IRS (or anyone else for that matter).

I tell you these facts because some of those who give tax advice have been convicted of various illegal activities. And by using the word "aggressive" in the title of my book, I cause some people to wonder if the book's advice is legal. It is. My approach to taxes is to go over the law with a fine tooth comb making sure I'm not paying one more cent than I have to. **That's what this book is about—legal ways to minimize taxes.**

One other thing about this book: I am not **obsessed** with avoiding taxes. You shouldn't be either. At the end of this book, I'll step back and look at the whole idea of avoiding taxes—and how tax avoidance should fit into the grand scheme of your life. I'll point out that while paying zero taxes is possible, it may not be worth the effort and risk required. Your goal should be **maximum after-tax income—not minimum taxes.**

But if you're willing to take a whole new approach to earning your living, **I can** tell you how to become invulnerable to taxation. No gimmicks or untested legal theories. Just a straight-forward look at what gets taxed and what does not.

I used to give seminars on this subject. I also write articles on taxes. As a result of both activities, I have discussed taxes with hundreds of real estate investors all over the United States.

From those discussions I learned that the vast majority of real estate investors are making a bunch of mistakes. The cost of the smallest mistakes is hundreds of dollars per year. The biggest mistakes cost tens of thousands in the typical case—hundreds of thousands or even millions if your holdings are large enough. And most investors make just about **all** the mistakes if they make any. If you're the typical investor and you follow the advice in this book, I believe you'll probably **save tens of thousands of dollars** in taxes. All that from a book that costs less than $25.

John T. Reed
Danville, California

PART ONE:
<u>THE AGGRESSIVE PHILOSOPHY</u>

1

Who Makes the Law—and Who Doesn't

You should understand where tax law comes from

The way to make sure you don't pay more tax than the law requires is to **know the law**.

The first step in knowing the law is to understand where the law comes from. Tax law comes from:

1. The Internal Revenue Code (IRC) and
2. Court decisions.

In some cases, Congress delegates its law making authority to the Department of the Treasury. That's where IRS regulations and rulings come from.

Tax experts use the word "Treasury" a lot when talking about tax law. But most laymen use the letters "IRS" to refer to the entire government tax enforcement operation. Since this book was written primarily for laymen, I'll use the letters IRS the way laymen do. So don't any of you nit picky tax experts write to tell me that you can't use "IRS" to mean "Treasury." My goal is to make sure my readers **understand**. Not to win the pedantic law professor award.

The Code is Congress's version of the law

According to the Constitution, Congress makes the laws. When it comes to income tax, the law

Congress made is called the Internal Revenue Code of 1986. (Income taxes came into being in 1913. It's called the "Code of 1986" because that's the last time there was a revision big enough to warrant a name change.)

The Internal Revenue Code must, of course, conform to the Constitution. But don't waste any time looking for Constitutional loopholes. The courts invariably dismiss such suits as "frivolous" and fine the taxpayers who filed them.

You're probably not aware that state and local laws sometimes have federal income tax ramifications. The *Wise* case is an example. Benjamin Wise had a building contractor build a home for him. He paid the contractor $5,000 plus all expenses. Among the expenses was the sales tax the builder paid on the building materials. Wise reimbursed the builder and deducted the sales tax on his federal income tax return. But the Tax Court said he couldn't do that because Michigan **state law** imposed the sales tax on the contractor. In other words, the **state** law in Wise's state determined how the **federal** tax law would apply to him. (*Wise*, 78 TC 19)

Under California law, an interest in a cooperative apartment is real property. But under New York law, it's personal property. In community property state, the ability of married people to file separate returns may be impaired.

On the other hand, sometimes federal income tax law is beyond the reach of state law. For example, the IRS has tried to ignore **verbal** contracts where state statutes of fraud say only **written** contracts are enforceable. In *Charlotte Union Bus Station, Inc.* (209 F2d 586), the court said only parties to a contract can invoke the statute of frauds.

You have to stay up to date continuously

Buying a tax book once a year may not be enough to keep you up to date. The tax law changes continuously. New developments affecting real estate investors come out at a rate of about once a month. Of course, sometimes we get a burst of new developments in the form of a new law passed by Congress (like the Tax Reform Act of 1986) or a burst of real estate court decisions.

By buying this book, you've really bought a "subscription" to a twice-a-year real estate tax "magazine" (counting the Update booklet you get after you send in the postcard bound into the front of the book). If you want to be brought up to date more often than that, you might want to subscribe to my *Real Estate Investor's Monthly*. That's a national newsletter I write and publish. The newsletter covers all aspects of real estate investment, not just taxes. But I tell my readers about almost every tax law development pertinent to real estate investors.

If you want more depth, you may want to subscribe to the *Real Estate Tax Digest*. The information it contains is generally excellent. It's aggressive. But it's hard to read. I could earn a good living if Matthew Bender would sell me the "plain English translation rights" to *Real Estate Tax Digest*. They could go on publishing it. Meanwhile, I'd translate it to plain English and outsell their version 10 to 1.

For a broad, weekly loose-leaf, tax update service, subscribe to the *Report Bulletin* portion of Maxwell-MacMillan's annual *Federal Tax Guide*. (Commerce Clearing House publishes a parallel loose-leaf service.)

NOTE
Full names and addresses of these and other publishers are listed in an appendix in the back of this book.

If you're just a part-time real estate investor, this book and its update are probably enough. If you're a more serious investor, you ought to subscribe to *Real Estate Investor's Monthly*. (There's an order blank for ordering that and other books of mine in the back and front of the book.) If you are a professional real estate investor, you ought to subscribe to the *Real Estate Tax Digest* and *Federal Tax Guide* in addition.

Another book you should get is J. K. Lasser's *Your Income Tax*. Don't get the yellow and red version sold in every grocery store around tax time. Get the "professional edition." It's advertised in the back of the yellow and red one. You have to buy the professional edition by mail.

Another book you might want to get is *Federal Income Taxation of Real Estate*. Gerald Robinson writes it. And Warren, Gorham & Lamont publishes it. WG & L is stodgy. But their books are good, if a bit expensive. Robinson's book is aggressive and creative.

Here's a summary of who should get which books:

If you're a...	You should get...
"Hobbyist" investor:	• *Aggressive Tax Avoidance for Real Estate Investors* • *Your Income Tax* (Professional Edition)
Serious investor:	• All of the above and • **Real Estate Investor's Monthly**
Professional investor:	• All of the above and • *Real Estate Tax Digest* • *Federal Income Taxation of Real Estate* • *Federal Tax Guide*

Court decisions

Here are the courts which decide tax cases:

Appeals Courts:	• U.S. Supreme Court • U.S. Court of Appeals
Trial Courts:	• U.S. District Court • U.S. Claims Court • U.S. Tax Court

When you are challenged by the IRS, you can either cave in or fight. After the audit, IRS will either agree with you or disagree. If they disagree, and you want to fight, you get to pick the court. You can fight them in any of the three trial courts. The main difference between the three is when you pay the tax if you lose. This table explains:

Court	When you pay
District Court	Pay tax then sue to get it back
Claims Court	Pay tax then sue to get it back
Tax Court	Don't pay until you lose

If you choose either the District Court or the Claims Court, you have to pay the tax first. Then you file for a refund. When the refund request is denied, you sue to get back the money you claim you should not have paid—plus interest.

If you choose the Tax Court, you don't have to pay anything until you lose the case. That's one heck of an advantage. I'll discuss choosing the best court in more detail later.

There is a "small claims" Tax Court. This table shows the main differences between the "big" and "small" Tax Courts.

Item	'Big' Tax Court	'Small' Tax Court
Maximum amount	No limit	$10,000
Attorney common?	Usually	No
Appeal allowed?	Yes	No

If you lose in the trial court, you can appeal to the Court of Appeals. If you lose in the Court of Appeals, you can appeal to the Supreme Court. Don't laugh. Rowan Companies appealed all the way to the Supreme Court in 1981. They finally won and their decision meant over two billion dollars in tax refunds. A large part of the refunds went to real estate investors. The diagram below shows the structure of the courts for appeals.

Organization of the federal courts for tax cases

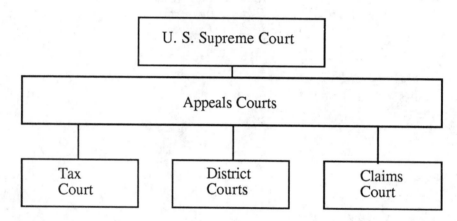

The government also has the right to appeal if it loses in any court other than the "small claims" Tax Court.

Here's a diagram from an IRS publication (modified by me because the IRS publication was out of date.) It shows the paths you can take in fighting the IRS.

Income Tax Appeal Procedure
Internal Revenue Service

At any stage of procedure:

Agreement and payment may be arranged.

Requests for issuance of a notice of deficiency to allow petition to the Tax Court may be made.

The tax may be paid and a refund claim filed.

Examination of income tax return
District Director's Office

Preliminary notice
30-Day Letter

Protest
(when required)

Appeals Office

If no response or the time of issuing a Statutory Notice becomes short, then

Statutory notice
90-Day Letter

Preliminary notice
30-Day Letter

Consideration of claim for refund
District Director's Office

Pay tax and file claim for refund

CHOICE OF ACTION

No tax payment

Petition to Tax Court

Protest
(when required)

Appeals Office

Appeals Office
Settlement opportunities if T/P has not yet been to Appeals

No agreement

District Counsel
Preparation for Trial

Statutory notice
Claim Disallowance

Tax Court
No Appeal Permitted in Cases Handled Under Small Tax Case Procedure

CHOICE OF ACTION

District Court

Court Of Appeals

Claims Court

U.S. Supreme Court

There is just one Supreme Court. But there are eleven regional circuits and two federal circuits and each has a U.S. Court of Appeals. In the district courts and Tax Court, which circuit you appeal to is determined by where **you live**, not where the property you own is. If the case is tried in Claims Court, appeals must go to the Federal Circuit. Each regional circuit is further broken down into districts. There is at least one district in each state. More populous states have more than one district. The map below shows the boundaries of the circuits and districts.

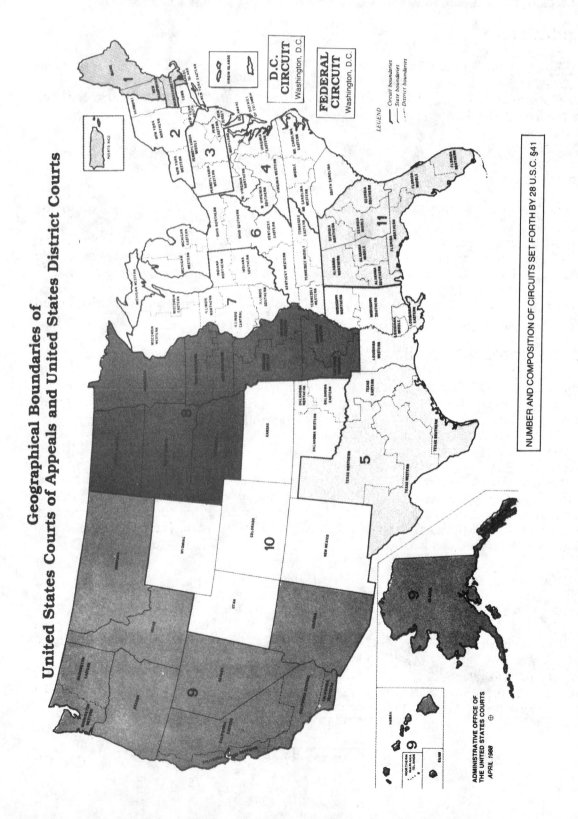

Geographical Boundaries of
United States Courts of Appeals and United States District Courts

NUMBER AND COMPOSITION OF CIRCUITS SET FORTH BY 28 U.S.C. §41

ADMINISTRATIVE OFFICE OF
THE UNITED STATES COURTS
APRIL 1988

The Tax Court is a "national" court with no geographic divisions. But you can appeal Tax Court decisions to the circuit courts of appeals. So to the extent that they know which circuit is looking over their shoulder, the Tax Court is sort of divided up the same as the circuits. There are about 23 Tax Court judges. They live in the Washington, DC area and travel around the country to hear cases. They hold court in major cities on a regular basis.

The Claims Court is similar. It's also a "national" court. Its cases can be appealed to the Federal Circuit Court of Appeals. There are about 17 Claims Court judges.

IRS regulations

Section 7805 of the Internal Revenue Code authorizes the Secretary of the Treasury to "...prescribe all needful rules and regulations for the enforcement of the Code..."

That does not mean that whatever the Secretary of the Treasury says goes, however. The Treasury's regulations are law **unless** they:

- Exceed the Treasury's authority
- Violate the law
- Are unreasonable.

Would the Secretary of the Treasury ever exceed his authority, violate the law, or be unreasonable? You bet he would. Here's an example.

Treasury Regulation sections 31.121 (a)-1(f) and 31.3306 (b) said that you had to pay social security and federal unemployment tax on the value of a free or partially free apartment given to a resident manager. The U.S. Supreme Court declared those regulations to be illegal on June 8, 1981. (*Rowan Companies v. U. S.*, 48 AFTR 2d 81-5115)

In *Langstaff v. Lucas*, 13 F2d 1022, a taxpayer followed an IRS regulation. IRS challenged him and said their own regulation was wrong! And the IRS won!

Another example of an illegal IRS regulation

It's bad enough that IRS sometimes comes up with a regulation which is later thrown out by a court. But sometimes they even produce regulations which clearly go against court decisions which have already come down! That's what happened in the *Curphey* case.

Section 280A of the IRC says you may deduct the cost of a home office if you meet certain tests. IRS doesn't like the home office deduction. Since Congress makes the laws and IRS just enforces them, you may wonder why IRS has an opinion on the subject at all. Good question. But the fact is, the IRS does not like the home office deduction.

Doctor Edwin R. Curphey is a Honolulu dermatologist. He's also a small real estate investor. In 1976, he lived in a two-bedroom condominium. From one bedroom of the condo, he managed six rental units—rental condos, town houses, and a single-family house. He called that condo bedroom his home office and deducted it.

The doctor said he had two businesses

"Oh, no you don't," said the IRS. They pointed out that one of the tests you must meet is that the home office be your "principal place of business." "You're a dermatologist," IRS said. "Your principal place of business is Kaiser Permanente Hospital in Honolulu where you practice dermatology."

Dr. Curphey protested that he had **two** businesses: dermatology and rental management. He agreed that the hospital was the principal place of business of his dermatology practice. But he said that his condo bedroom was the principal place of business of his rental management business.

IRS wouldn't buy it. So Dr. Curphey took IRS to Tax Court. He acted as his own attorney. And he won. (*Curphey*, 73 TC 61) (By the way, in the early '80s, this book was favorably reviewed in the Honolulu newspaper. And guess who sent me an order for a copy? Dr. Curphey himself. I added a note of thanks on behalf of all real estate investors for his fighting IRS.)

Now if the IRS were good sports, they'd have said, "Guess we were wrong. We won't do that again." But they didn't.

They proceeded to issue both rulings and a regulation which tried to "overturn" the Tax Court's Curphey decision.

IRS cannot overrule a court decision

In two letter rulings, IRS told two college professors they couldn't deduct home offices—because the home offices were for secondary businesses. That's precisely the same reasoning the Tax Court **rejected** in the Curphey decision. The Letter Rulings in question were #8030024 and 8030025.

Another letter ruling, #8048080, involved almost the exact same circumstances as the Curphey case— a doctor with rental properties. IRS told the doctor he couldn't deduct his home office.

The IRS also put out a proposed regulation [Section 1.280A-2(b)]. It said you could only deduct a home office if it was the principal place of business of your **overall** business activity. If the home office was used for a secondary place of business, it continued, you could not deduct it.

Congress to the rescue

Congress makes the law, remember? Congress wrote Section 280A of the IRC. It says nothing about "overall business activity." It says nothing about "secondary businesses." The IRS made all that up. Now it's OK for IRS to fill in the "gaps" in laws—as long as they fill them in the way Congress would have if they had known the gap existed. By putting out all these rulings and new regulations, IRS was saying, in effect, "This is what Congress really meant to say."

"Like hell!," said the Congress upon learning what the IRS had been doing. On December 29, 1981, the President signed into law the Black Lung Benefits Act of 1981. It says, in part, that the home office can be the principal place of business for "any trade or business of the taxpayer." So much for IRS's "overall/secondary business" interpretation. In other words, the interpretation of Dr. Curphey and the Tax Court was the one Congress meant. Only at that point—faced with both a court decision and a new law—did IRS throw in the towel.

It doesn't have to be a separate room either

That wasn't the only "we know what Congress really meant" that IRS pulled on home offices. IRS also decided that a home office had to be a separate room.

Does it say "separate room" in the IRC? Nooooo. The exact wording of the law is "...portion of the dwelling unit..."

Along comes Mr. Weightman. He deducted part of his bedroom as a home office. "You can't do that," said IRS. "See you in court," said Mr. Weightman.

Weightman lost the case because he didn't meet the principal place of business test. But in part of the decision the Tax Court pointed out that there's nothing in the law about separate rooms. Part of a room is OK. (*Weightman*, paragraph 81,301 P-H Memo TC)

IRS rulings

An IRS ruling is a promise to challenge or not challenge the way you plan to report a particular transaction on your tax return. There are two kinds of rulings:

1. Revenue rulings
2. Letter rulings

All rulings are responses to requests from taxpayers or their tax advisers. Everyone can rely on a revenue ruling. But only the addressee can rely on a letter ruling. That's the standard line. In fact, rulings are only slightly more reliable than a screen door on a submarine.

The government can use many loopholes to get you when you think you've been protected by a ruling. Here's a list.

Ruling loopholes

- Rulings may be retroactively modified, revoked, or suspended.
- Rulings are not binding on the courts or the IRS.
- No law says even the IRS has to be bound by rulings.
- IRS can claim that your facts are different from those in the ruling.
- IRS can claim that you didn't give them all the pertinent facts.

When should you request a ruling—and how do you do it?

I doubt that I'll ever request a ruling (except when you do a lease option; see my Special Report #1 on *Single-Family Lease Options*). You probably shouldn't either. Seems to me that a favorable ruling addressed to you has only one benefit—a slightly increased probability that you will not be hassled over the transaction in question. What's that worth? Not much.

Now for the disadvantages of ruling requests. Ruling requests are not free. Preparing them takes time if you do it yourself—money if you pay someone to do it. In addition, the government charges for rulings. Here's a list of disadvantages.

Disadvantages of requesting a ruling

- Cost
- 2-4 month wait until ruling arrives—**if** it arrives (IRS can decline to rule)
- They may rule against you
- You "red flag" the transaction. Remaining anonymous probably provides more protection than a favorable ruling.

There are some questions on which IRS consistently refuses to rule. As you've probably guessed, they are precisely the questions on which you'd like to have rulings. Here's a list.

IRS will not give rulings on...

- Part of a deal
- Factual questions like:
      Value of land versus improvements
      Value of personal versus real property
      Useful life (still applies in some exchanges)
- Whether you're a dealer
- A deal which you might do but haven't scheduled yet
- Criminal penalty matters
- Something you're being audited on
- Shared appreciation mortgages on commercial property.

My observation is that rulings are primarily obtained by limited partnership promoters (to calm the limited partners' fears) and by taxpayers whose tax advisers want to cover their behinds. That's right. Your tax adviser may recommend that you get a ruling **not** because it's in **your** interest—but because it's in **his** interest. Unfortunately, when it's **his** interest, it's still at **your** expense. You also suffer the other disadvantages of requesting a ruling: "red flag," delay, and the risk of an unfavorable ruling.

If your tax adviser recommends that you request a ruling, question him carefully as to **why**. If he can't give you a satisfactory answer, it's probably for **his** benefit. If that's the case, let **him** pay for it. But even then, it's still **your** return that gets "red flagged."

If, after all that, you still want to request a ruling, there's an excellent explanation of how to do it in *IRS Practice and Procedure* by Michael Saltzman (Warren, Gorham & Lamont).

Do rulings mean anything?

So much for the question of your requesting a ruling. Now suppose you (or your tax adviser) research a tax question and come across a pertinent ruling. If it goes against what you want to do, does the ruling mean you can't do it? And if the ruling agrees with you, does that mean you're home free?

If the ruling supports you, use it to the hilt.
If the ruling is against you, ignore it. (except that all unfavorable rulings are followed up by an audit of the ruling issue according to Maxwell-MacMillan Federal Tax Guide ¶85,202.)

Frequently, an investor will ask his adviser, "Can I do such and such?" "No," the adviser answers. "That was prohibited by letter ruling # so and so." He may even show it to his client. The typical investor thinks, "Well, there it is in black and white—an official IRS ruling. I guess that's that."

Rulings are not law

Rulings are not law. Don't you forget it! If your tax adviser, or an IRS agent, or anyone else trots out a ruling to prove that you can or cannot do something, tell him you're not convinced. Stay unconvinced until he shows you that either an Internal Revenue Code section or a court decision proves his point. If it ain't in the Code or a court decision, it ain't law.

If a tax adviser wanted to talk you out of a home office deduction prior to December 29, 1981, he could have shown you three letter rulings and a proposed regulation—all official, IRS, U.S. government documents—and all garbage. Garbage because of the Curphey decision. Further certified as garbage by the U.S. Congress in the Black Lung Benefits Act of 1981.

Sometimes even IRS people and tax advisers are not up to date

In August of 1981, IRS sent Senator Armstrong a letter. He was one of the sponsors of the law to allow home office deductions for any business. In the letter which was made public, IRS said, in effect, "We give up. We will rescind our proposed regulation and issue a regulation which conforms to the Curphey decision." Yet in the **Fall** of 1981, a guy who had read my book called and told me an IRS agent had just told him he couldn't claim a home office for a secondary business. That's several months **after** IRS headquarters agreed you **could**.

A lot of tax advisers and a lot of IRS agents talk a lot of trash—and they point to rulings and regulations as proof that they're right.

Rulings have more precedent value than officially admitted

Use anything which is in your favor to the hilt. That includes rulings. If you're being challenged by IRS, and you've found a ruling—letter or revenue—that supports, "hit 'em over the head" with it.

In the case of *Hanover*, 369 US 672, the court said rulings can serve as a "guide." Government agencies are required to be **consistent** and to treat everyone **equally**—or have a good reason why not. A bunch of cases say that. *Secretary of Agriculture v. U.S.* is one. So IRS cannot completely hide from their rulings—in spite of the many loopholes they have.

The reliability of other IRS publications

Regulations and rulings may have some legal weight. But other official IRS publications have none. Except possibly to help you avoid negligence and fraud penalties. In the April 11, 1983 *Wall Street Journal*, IRS admitted that its pamphlets "Tax Guide for Small Businesses" and "Deductions for Bad Debts" were wrong. And if you did what those pamphlets said to do, IRS would **reject** your tax return.

Summary on who makes the law

Congress **makes** the tax laws.
The courts **interpret** the tax laws.
IRS **enforces** the tax laws.

IRS is often not satisfied with the role given them by the Constitution. So they frequently exceed their authority or violate the law.

When they do that, you have the legal right to ignore them. IRS agents and tax advisers often point to IRS rulings, regulations, instruction booklets, news releases, etc. as proof that their interpretation of the law is correct. IRS documents are **NOT** law. If the IRS agent or tax adviser you're talking to cannot show you either pertinent parts of the Internal Revenue Code or relevant court decisions to support their position, it is probably an incorrect interpretation of the law. In that case, **you do not have to abide by it.**

2

How to Research a Tax Question

Most people research tax questions by looking them up in J.K. Lasser's *Your Income Tax* and/or calling their accountant. That's fine **if** the question is one which Lasser adequately covers and/or one which your accountant properly researches.

But *Your Income Tax* doesn't go into fine points. And it doesn't provide citations. So it's only adequate for basic questions like how long do you have to hold a property to qualify for long-term capital gains treatment (more than one year).

Before you rely totally on your accountant...

Two things concern me about relying on your accountant. First, he may be incompetent. Second, he may know the **right** answer to your question, but give you the **wrong** answer because it's in **his** interest to do so.

Why would it be in his interest to give you the wrong answer? He may want to be super **conservative** to minimize the chances he'll have to argue with IRS over your return. He may believe that he's telling you **what you want to hear**—and that's easier than telling you the truth. He may feel that if he tells you the right answer, you **won't understand**. Then either he'll have to "waste" his time explaining—or he'll lose you to another accountant who **does** tell you what you want to hear.

I could go on. Fact is, you cannot totally rely on any adviser—at least not until you've looked over his shoulder closely for a while. If you go over his work carefully for some time, and find that he's doing the right thing, **then** you can rely on him. The primary way you check on your tax adviser is to research tax questions **yourself** and see how your adviser's advice compares.

An example tax question

When you have a tax question, you want to know what the three major tax law groups have said about it:

- Congress
- the courts
- IRS

...in that order. Let me pose an example and show you how to look up the answer.

You're planning to do an **installment sale**. (I recommend that you **not** do installment sales but most of you do, so I cover them in the book.) You've owned the property for some time. And you refinanced once. The amount you owe on the property is **more** than your basis. Whoever buys the property will take over your loan because it's assumable and at low interest. You've read somewhere that that creates a tax problem. But you also read that you can get around it by using a **wraparound land contract**. You want to find out if your recollection is correct and the details of how to get around that problem.

Start with Lasser

Your Income Tax has a chapter on installment sales. Reading one edition of it, we find the following in paragraph 6.17.

> *Payments in the year of sale include mortgages which the buyer assumes or takes subject to only to the extent the mortgage exceeds the basis of property.*

There's the tax problem. The excess of mortgage over basis is considered a payment received in the year of sale. Let's say your figures are as follows:

Sale price	160,000
Mortgage balance	100,000
Basis	60,000

In this case, the mortgage the buyer will assume will exceed your basis by $40,000 ($100,000 - $60,000). So the law says you received a "payment" of that much in the year you sell.

The tax law's logic is that if you **owed** $100,000 **before** the deal, but not after, you're $100,000 better off. True. But you have to give up your $160,000 building to get rid of the $100,000 mortgage.

The law says, "True. But as far as **we're** concerned, it's only a **$60,000** building. You bought it several years ago for $75,000. Since then, you've told us every year on your tax return that it's been **depreciating**. $75,000 minus the depreciation you've claimed is $60,000. So you've given up a $60,000 building to get rid of a $100,000 mortgage. Therefore you're $40,000 better off. So pay up."

In fact, you've received no such **cash** payment. And if the payments you **do** receive on the $60,000 of equity are not very large that year, you could owe more in taxes that you received in cash. So that edition of Lasser's *Your Income Tax* reveals the **problem**. But what about a **solution**?

Lasser said 'no' to the land contract solution

Reading further, we find mention of the land contract solution. The Lasser book did not use the phrase "land contract." But it talked about a transaction in which "title does not pass." That's a land contract. Here's what Lasser said.

> *A wraparound mortgage is treated as if the buyer had assumed or taken the property subject to it, even though title does not pass to the buyer in the year of sale and the seller continues to make direct payments on the wrapped-around mortgage. This will increase the taxable gain in the year of the sale.*

By the way, each of these quotes was followed by an illustrative example in *Your Income Tax*

Lasser's statement that the wraparound land contract would **not** let you get around the excess loans over basis problem suggests that something happened since you heard it **would** get around the problem.

You should get *The Professional Edition of Your Income Tax* It has the same **text** as the regular book store edition. But in the back are the citations **behind** what they say in the text. That's **not** in the book store version.

Here's what they said about the wraparound technique in the back of that *Professional Edition* under ¶6.17:

> *Tax Treatment of Wrap-Around Debt Received in Installment Sales Under Temporary Installment Sale Regulations,* Gary E. Friedman, 60 *Taxes* 439 (1982)
> *Wrap-around mortgages*
> Temp. Reg. § 15A.453(b)(3)(ii)

The first item is a law journal article on the subject. You'll find it at your local law library in volume 60 of the magazine named *Taxes* on page 439. It's not a 500-page magazine. They number the pages of each issue consecutively so that the January issue starts with page 1, February may start with page 51 and so forth through the year.

"Temp. Reg." refers to a temporary regulation issued by IRS. More about that temporary reg later.

The next place you would look for the answer to a tax question on real estate would be this book, *Aggressive Tax Avoidance for Real Estate Investors*. I'll skip that source in this example because it would be "cheating."

Next we look in the *Federal Tax Guide*

Lasser said we can't solve the problem the way we thought. Let's look further to see if Lasser was wrong or if there is another way to get around the problem. For a bit more depth, we go to Maxwell-MacMillan's (M-M) or Commerce Clearing House's (CCH) *Federal Tax Guide*.

Where do you get a copy of the *Federal Tax Guide*? For one, you could **subscribe** to it. The address is in the back of this book. If you do **not** subscribe, you can go to a library. I just called my local library. They did not have it. That's in a town of 15,000. The reference librarian recommended the **county** library. I called there. They have the Commerce Clearing House version. You'll probably have a similar experience tracking down a copy in your community.

I subscribe to the CCH version. A Prentice-Hall salesman told me once that some of his accountant clients were mad when they heard that Prentice-Hall sold the *Federal Tax Guide* to laymen. They were concerned the people who bought it wouldn't need accountants. No kidding.

I don't think you can replace a good tax adviser with that book or any other. But their concern shows how close some accountants think you are to knowing as much as they do. If you follow my advice to research tax questions yourself **before** you ask your tax adviser about them, **many of** you will be surprised at how little your adviser is able to add to what you find out. In fact, **many of** you will find that you know **more** about the question at hand than your adviser.

Federal Tax Guide says...

Looking up "installment sales" in the index of the *Federal Tax Guide* we find a bunch of listings. As we leaf through the main section, we learn that the section of the Internal Revenue Code pertaining to installment sales is 453. We make note of that because we may want to read the actual wording of the code before we're through. (You can buy a copy of the Internal Revenue Code from M-M or CCH or get one in the library.)

CCH's *Federal Tax Guide* has an index entry "wrap-around mortgages." Turning to paragraph 4138 we find a full page of discussion. The CCH discussion pretty much agrees with the Lasser version. The only citation is the same temporary regulation Lasser mentioned.

Try the *Real Estate Tax Digest*

The 1981 "Year in Review" (a year-end feature of the *Tax Digest*) mentions the same temporary regulation as Lasser with rules on "wrap-around" mortgages. We need a copy of that temporary regulation. But first, a look at *Tax Notes*.

Tax Notes: a periodical and a research service

I didn't mention *Tax Notes* in the chapter on what you ought to subscribe to. *Tax Notes* is a bit esoteric. Its main article each week seems to focus on tax law as **policy**. The kind of stuff you'd read if you were on the staff of the House Ways and Means Committee. But *Tax Notes* also does a good job of keeping you up-to-date on the latest court decisions and IRS pronouncements. You may have to call around to a few libraries to find one with a subscription.

Or you can just call *Tax Notes*. The number is 800-955-3444. If you're in the Washington, DC area, call 532-1850. Tell them what you want and they'll try to track it down for you. When I've used them, the bill was usually in the $20 to $30 range. *Tax Notes* also has Westlaw.

Computerized legal research

Here are the five computer legal data bases I'm aware of:

Westlaw: West Publishing Company
Lexis: Mead Data Central
TAXRIA: Maxwell-MacMillan
ACCESS Commerce Clearing House
Varilex: Bancroft-Whitney

The data they contain is primarily legal cases, rulings, and regulations. If you have a computer terminal and you're a member, you can search for cases and IRS material pertinent to the question you're interested in. You type in a few key words, tell it which kind of cases to search (e.g. tax, patent, etc.), and it will read **every word of every case** you told it to look at. When it's done (in a few minutes), it gives you a list of the cases in which your key words appeared. You can then look the case up in a law library or call it up on the computer screen.

Being a member of these services is expensive: in the neighborhood of $5,000 per year minimum. Plus it takes some **skill** to search efficiently. You can use these services in some law libraries. Or you can have *Tax Notes* do it for you. In that case, you're charged for the researcher's time and the Westlaw time. A recent question I had was researched using Westlaw as well as library work and a call to a Congressional committee. The cost was $24.97.

I recommend that you try *Tax Notes* next time you have a tax question you find particularly difficult to answer. See how you like it. Because of the cost, you may want to use it sparingly. But travelling to libraries and asking your accountant isn't free either.

Continuing our research

The July-December 1981 *Tax Notes* index lists two items on "installment sales, wraparound mortgages." One is a letter to IRS suggesting a better way for them to achieve their objective. Interesting, but not law. The other is from before my subscription starts. A little realism there. When have you ever tried to look something up and found that the library had all the issues you wanted? No matter. *Tax Notes* will send you a copy of any tax document they cite for a small fee plus a per page photocopying charge.

Federal Income Taxation of Real Estate

We next find material on our question in *Federal Income Taxation of Real Estate* (FITRE) by Gerald Robinson under "Wraparound Mortgages" (¶12.02[3][b]). In one paragraph, we learn that there is some disagreement between the IRS temporary regulation and the Tax Court. Robinson cites two cases: *Hunt*, 80 TC 1126 and *Frank Hutchinson*, TC Memo. 1981-513.

How to interpret citations

Hunt is the name of the taxpayer in the case.

TC = Tax Court and in the law library you'll find a large set of books labeled "Tax Court." It's like an encyclopedia set.

The number between the name *Hunt* and TC is the volume number. So you would pull Tax Court book number 80 off the shelf.

The last number—1126— is the page number. Turn to page 1126 of volume 80 of the Tax Court books and you will find the beginning of the Tax Court's opinion in the *Hunt* case.

In a minute, I'll tell you how to get copies of those decisions. But first, let's check the supplement to FITRE. Each year FITRE owners receive a supplement telling about new developments. This is in the form of pages which are used to replace the old supplement. So before you leave FITRE, check the supplement under the same subject.

In the 1986 Cumulative Supplement No. 2, under the same paragraph number as the main discussion, Robinson has the following:

> *An article cogently challenging the validity of the Temporary Regulation has asserted, "The IRS used the enactment of the Installment Sales Revision Act of 1980 to attempt to accomplish through the regulatory process what it had abjectly failed to do in court." Dickens & Orbach, "Installment Reporting: Wraparound Mortgages After The IRS's Temporary Regulations and Hunt"* [12 J. Real Estate Tax'n 137 (Winter 1985)]

Aha! There is more controversy about this than Lasser or CCH let on.

Reading the decisions

Tax law is based on the Internal Revenue Code and court decisions. Therefore, if you **really** want to get to the bottom of a tax question, you have to **read** the **code** and the **decisions**. I already told you how to get a copy of the code. It's extremely difficult to read. But it's the final word. So it's worth the trouble.

To read the court decision, you've got to get a copy of it. There are several ways to do that. One way is to go to your local law library, take the appropriate volume off the shelf, turn to the cited page and begin reading. Court decisions are not as well-written as, say, the *Reader's Digest*. But they **are** written in English. You don't have to be a lawyer or an accountant to read them for the most part.

How to use the law library

How do you get into a law library? Call your local **non-law** library. Ask for "Reference." When the reference librarian comes on the phone, tell her you're interested in looking up some tax law cases. She'll probably say they don't have such things (unless you live in a big city) and she'll tell you where you need to go to find them.

Most counties have a law library which is open to the public. Most major metropolitan areas have law schools. All law schools have law libraries. To find the law schools in your area, look up "Schools--Universities and Colleges (Academic)" in the *Yellow Pages*.

Some law schools don't let non-students use the library. Call in advance and ask if the library is open to the public.

When you get to the law library, show the librarian the citations you want to look up and she'll point out the book-shelves where you'll find those cases. One bookcase will have the TC volumes; another, the TC Memo volumes; another, the Supreme Court volumes; and so forth. That's about all the help you should need.

Getting cases by phone

I've already told you one way to get cases by phone; call *Tax Notes*. I've also generally been able to get them by phone from my local **Maxwell-MacMillan office**. They ask only for the citation. They copy the decision and send it in a day or two. Generally, they have not charged me. Presumably because I subscribed to one of their fairly expensive services. By the way, M-M and CCH have **libraries** of their own law books in major cities. If you're one of their customers, you can use their library. As a general rule, you can probably get a copy of any case from the company that publishes the set of books which contain those cases.

Finally, if you have an **accountant** or a **tax attorney**, you can probably get him to send you a copy. Any tax adviser worth his salt will either have the necessary tax books on the premises or he'll frequent a library where they have them.

John T. Reed's Real Estate Investor's Monthly

Real Estate Investor's Monthly is the newsletter I write and publish. Each month I scan a number of tax bulletins for developments of importance to real estate investors. In the November 1988 issue I wrote,

IRS Gives Up On *Stonecrest*

The *Stonecrest* decision (24 TC 659) said you could avoid tax on excess loans over basis in an installment sale by using a wraparound. IRS fought that decision by 'nonacquiescing' to it and its successors and by issuing temporary regulation 15A.453-1(b)(3)(ii). But the Tax Court kept shooting them down—most recently in *Professional Equities*, 89 TC 165.

Now IRS has run up the white flag by acquiescing (IRB 1988-37) to the *Professional Equities* decision.

In general, checking *Real Estate Investor's Monthly* will get you answers to tax laws which have changed during that publication's life. I cover new laws like the Tax Reform Act of 1986, court decisions, and IRS rulings, regulations, news releases, etc.

How the various sources answered the question

This question revealed some interesting information about how the various sources provide tax information. J.K. Lasser, which is probably the most used tax reference, took sides. The conservative, IRS side.

As *Real Estate Tax Digest,* and *Federal Income Taxation of Real Estate*, revealed, there is a controversy on this question. In **many** controversial questions, the Lasser book makes note of the controversy. It usually says something like, "In one case, a court said you could do such and such." If you have the Professional Edition, you can get the citation of the case in question.

But in **this** case, that edition of Lasser didn't give the slightest indication that there was a controversy. Apparently, they simply decided to go with the IRS temporary regulation as if it came down from Mount Sinai. They presented one side's opinion as if it were law. Poor show if legal aggressiveness is your goal.

Another poor show, on this question, was put on by CCH's *Federal Tax Guide*. I was surprised by that. Usually, the *Tax Guide* does a pretty good job of covering a controversial tax question.

Real Estate Tax Digest and *Federal Income Taxation of Real Estate* did well on this example. Both alerted you to the controversy and gave clues to the solution. Of course, my book— *Aggressive Tax Avoidance for Real Estate Investors* covers the subject best of all. But since I chose the example, I'll not claim that proves my publications are the best of the bunch.

Lasser best for most questions

You should note also that only a few questions would produce such different answers from the different references. I deliberately chose a controversial question to make it a tough test. For most tax questions, J.K. Lasser's *Your Income Tax* would be the best source because of ease of use. If you want to be aggressive—or at least fully informed, the best would be Robinson's *Federal Income Taxation of Real Estate*. And, of course, I'm kind of partial to the book you are now reading.

Summary of how to research a tax question

Generally, the following sources, roughly in the order indicated, will work best.

1. *Aggressive Tax Avoidance for Real Estate Investors*
2. *Federal Income Taxation of Real Estate*
3. *Federal Tax Guide*
4. *John T. Reed's Real Estate Investor's Monthly*
5. *Real Estate Tax Digest*
6. Call *Tax Notes.*
8. Read the code, cases, regulations, and rulings you found in the above sources.
9. Check with your tax adviser. Yes, I really mean for this step to be last. At least until you become convinced that your adviser is doing the job properly. But last does not mean least. And you should not omit this step, even though it's last, if the question is an important one (lots of money or possible fraud).

If you want to be aggressive, J.K. Lasser's *Your Income Tax* is inadequate. That's because it is not aggressive. Nor does it alert you often enough to controversies—which offer opportunities for aggressiveness and the resulting lower taxes.

For further information: There's a paper back book for laymen on how to do legal research. It's called *Legal Research*. The address is in the back of this book.

3

What the Law Allows—
and Does *Not* Allow

The diagram below shows the law and your taxes. The law allows anything to the left of the vertical line. To the right of the line is illegal. The scale at the bottom shows what happens to your tax bill as you move from left to right.

Clear-cut tax question

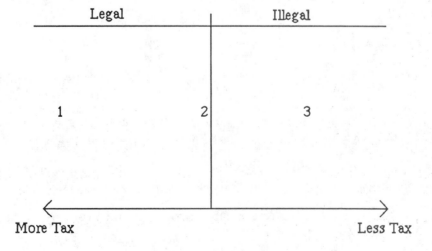

The farther to the right you go, the lower your taxes. But if you go **too** far, you've crossed the legal/illegal line. Position 3 represents an **illegal** entry on your tax return. An example would be not reporting the sale of a property for a gain. Not reporting the sale reduces your taxes—if you don't get caught. But it's clearly illegal. This book is **not** about illegal ways to reduce your taxes.

Look at the left (legal) side of the diagram again. Note that there is room for movement on the left side. Position 1 is legal. And so is position 2. The only difference between the two is that you pay **less** taxes if you choose position 2. The farther right you go, staying on the legal side, the lower your taxes.

Therefore, **when you have a choice between two legal alternatives, choose the one which results in the lowest tax**. That sounds obvious. But **most** real estate investors make the wrong choice in many common situations. Two prime examples are:

- Failure to take advantage of **first-year expensing** when you buy eligible property, and
- Failure to **separate personal property** from real property when first setting up the depreciation schedule on a building you've bought.

In the diagram above, taking advantage of first-year expensing would be represented by position **2**. **Not** taking advantage of it when you are eligible is position **1**. Both are perfectly legal choices. But choice **1** makes you pay **more tax**.

Not all tax questions have clear-cut answers

The diagram above showed your choices in areas of the law where the answer to a tax question was clear cut. Do you have to report a gain on the sale of a property? Yes. Can you use the 200% declining balance depreciation method on personal property? Yes.

But the answers to tax questions are not always clear cut. Suppose the question is,

What is the proper improvement ratio on this property?

That's a question a real estate investor must answer in order to fill out his tax return. The improvement ratio is the percentage of the value of real estate represented by the improvements on the property. "Improvements" means the man-made stuff like buildings, landscaping, pavement, underground utilities, and so forth. You may not depreciate the cost of the land that comes with the property. Here's an example:

Improvement ratio example

Land	$150,000
Improvements	$850,000
Total value	$1,000,000

Improvement ratio = $850,000 ÷ $1,000,000 = 85%

The higher the ratio you choose, the less tax you'll pay. Because a higher ratio increases the size of your depreciation basis and therefore increases the size of your depreciation deduction. Is there a limit on how high you can go? Yes.

The ratio you use is supposed to be based on the **market value** of the land at the time you buy the property. That requires that you or someone else appraise the land. An appraisal is an **opinion** of value.

As you know, three different knowledgeable people would probably come up with three different opinions of value on the same property.

Because different, honest, knowledgeable people would differ as to the correct value, there is no clear-cut answer to the question, "What is the proper improvement ratio for this property?" Nor is there a clear-cut answer to many other questions you'll run into when you do your taxes.

'God' and conservatism at tax time

I call these no-clear-cut-answer questions **judgmental** areas of the tax law. Some questions have clear-cut answers. Others are judgmental. Most laymen seem not to know that. When they have a question about the tax law, they ask their accountant or attorney. And they expect a clear-cut answer. "Yes, you can." "No, you can't."

Some tax advisers explain when the question is judgmental. Others respond as if **all** tax questions had clear cut answers—because they know that's what their client **wants** to hear. Many clients believe their advisers are wizards who know all and are always right when it comes to the tax law.

Among professionals, succumbing to the temptation to encourage clients to believe the adviser knows all is known as having a "god" complex.

Any tax adviser who always gives clear cut answers to your questions is playing "god." But in order to play "god," he has to be **ultra**conservative. Conservative advice causes you to pay more taxes than you should. **Ultra**conservative tax advice causes you to pay a **lot** more than you should.

How to treat judgmental areas of the tax law

This book advocates **aggressive**, not conservative, tax advice. What should an **aggressive** taxpayer do in judgmental areas? The diagram below illustrates a judgmental tax question.

Judgmental tax question

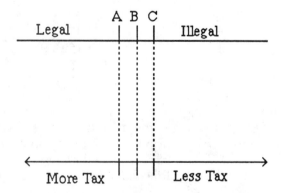

As with the clear-cut diagram, moving to the right reduces your taxes. And as with the clear-cut diagram, moving **too far** to the right puts you in illegal territory. But how far is too far?

The difference between the clear cut and judgmental diagrams is that the line separating legal and illegal is not clear in judgmental questions. To represent that in the diagram, I've used multiple dotted lines.

Two kinds of judgmental areas:

• Questions of **fact**.
• Questions of **law**.

You have a judgmental question of **fact** when there is disagreement as to what the facts are.

You have a judgmental question of **law** when there is disagreement as to what the pertinent law requires. I've already given you examples of both. The legal research problem we did in the last chapter was a judgmental question of law before the IRS acquiesced to *Professional Equities*.

"Could you use a wraparound mortgage or land contract to get around the excess loans over basis problem? The IRS Temporary Regulation said, "No." The *Hunt* Tax Court decision said, "Yes." The *Hutchison* decision said, "Maybe."

Relating those three indicators to the diagram,

Line A =   the IRS temporary reg
Line B =   the *Hutchison* decision
Line C =   the *Hunt* decision

Which was legal? I believed the *Hunt* decision. If you agree, you would be foolish if you did not defer tax on an installment sale by using the *Hunt* approach (assuming there are no non-tax factors in favor of another course of action). That's the aggressive—but legal—approach. IRS would argue that only A is legal. But you'd only need to haul them into Tax Court to get them their comeuppance.

A judgmental question of *fact*

"Which is the proper improvement ratio for this property?" is a judgmental question of **fact**. Let me flesh out the example with a few more facts.

You bought a property for $1,000,000. According to the property tax bill, the local tax assessor shows the following breakdown:

Tax assessor's breakdown

Land	$180,000
Improvements	$335,000
Total	$515,000

That means the assessor thinks the improvement ratio is $335,000 ÷ $515,000 = 65%. You may have noticed that the purchase price was $1,000,000 but the total assessment was only $515,000. Doesn't that mean something's wrong? Yes. The assessment's out of date. But that is not generally pertinent to the **ratio** which is the main thing here. Typically, IRS would multiply your purchase price by the assessor's improvement ratio in order to arrive at the value of the improvements. In this case, $1,000,000 x 65% = $650,000.

Let's say that you have other evidence of the value of the land: an appraisal done by the lender's appraiser. It shows the following breakdown:

Bank appraiser's breakdown

Land	$200,000
Improvements	$800,000
Total	$1,000,000

Finally, your insurance agent says the replacement value of your building is $870,000.

You now have three different facts:

Improvement value according to three experts

Assessor	$650,000
Appraiser	$800,000
Insurance agent	$870,000

On the judgmental tax question diagram, the three positions would be represented as follows:

Line A =	Assessor
Line B =	Appraiser
Line C =	Insurance agent

Line C, the insurance agent's $870,000 would be the most aggressive choice—the one which would cause you to pay the **least tax**. Line A, the assessor's $650,000 would be the most conservative choice—the one which would cause you to pay the **most tax**. Should you pick the middle to be safe? **NO!** Read on.

Here's a list of some judgmental questions of law and of fact in real estate investing.

Judgmental questions of *law*

- What's the definition of a dealer?
- Are reverse Starkers okay?

Judgmental questions of *fact*

- What's the improvement ratio?
- Is it personal or real property?
- How much of the value is land improvements?
- Are you a dealer?
- What's the value of personal property which comes with a building and is included in the purchase price?
- Do you meet the tests to qualify for a home office deduction?
- Did you constructively receive boot when you did an exchange?
- Is a lease option really a sale?

I realize that I used some words you may not understand in that list. Appendix C gives definitions or you can check the index for more detailed discussion. Also, you may have noted that dealer status is in both lists. That's not a mistake. The categories are not mutually exclusive. In dealer disputes the parties usually argue over **both** the definition of a dealer and the intent of the taxpayer. The definition is **law**; the intent, **fact**.

'But if I'm aggressive, won't they throw me in jail?'

No. In some, not all cases, aggressiveness will increase your chances of being audited. But your chances of being audited are quite low whether you're aggressive or not. And being audited isn't the end of the world. Many aggressive and other taxpayers are audited every year. And almost every year, they pay a little more as a result of the audit. But even that is still far less than the nervous Nellies who overpay by huge amounts every year to avoid audit.

Being aggressive does not increase your probability of being audited in some cases. For example, an aggressive improvement ratio will **not** increase the probability that you get audited—because it does **not** appear anywhere on your tax return. Only the amount you allocate to improvements appears on your return. The only way IRS can find out your improvement **ratio** is to **ask** you for it.

Being aggressive also increases the chances you'll lose if you are challenged. I suspect that the increased probability of being audited and the increased probability of losing if challenged have many of you thinking, "Forget being aggressive." Wrong conclusion. Read on.

Three levels of dispute with IRS

There are three levels of dispute with the IRS:

1. Deficiency
2. Negligence
3. Fraud.

It's important that you understand each well. Because the definitions of each determine how far you can legally go in judgmental areas.

What a deficiency is

A deficiency means that you didn't pay enough tax. If IRS says you didn't pay enough tax, you can agree and pay or take them to court. The IRS does **not** have the power to make the final determination about your taxes unless you let them. Only the courts or you can make the final determination.

If you fight with IRS over a deficiency and lose, you pay the tax plus interest. No penalties.

To the average taxpayer, that sounds terrible. He's scared of the IRS and wants nothing to do with them. He's even more afraid of the courts. The idea of being "dragged into court" by the IRS and then told to pay up by a judge sounds shameful and terrifying. It shouldn't.

Why you shouldn't fear a dispute with the IRS

First off, if you're honest, you have little to fear from the IRS. That's not to say you should welcome their coming. Audits waste your time at best. And frequently, you have to pay more tax. So I'm not saying you should **want** to be audited. My point is that many people go too far in the **other** direction—they see audit as a fate worse than death.

Secondly, IRS isn't hauling **you** into court. You're hauling **them** into court.

When you fight IRS in District court, the United States of America is the defendant, not you. **You** are the plaintiff. In Tax Court, you're the "petitioner"—the guy who petitioned or asked the court to hold the trial. IRS is the "respondent"—the guy who has to answer your petition.

If you're familiar with the law, you know that the guy whose name comes after the "versus" is the guy who is being sued. In Tax Court, the case is known as *You versus the Commissioner of the Internal Revenue Service*. In District Court, it's *You versus the United States of America*.

Sounds like terrible odds, doesn't it? Not to worry. As we proceed through the book, I'll tell you about a number of intrepid little people who took on either the Commissioner of the Internal Revenue Service or the United States of America—and won!

It's when the case is titled *the United States of America versus You* that you're in trouble. That's how fraud cases are captioned.

Would you like a government loan?

The most important reason for not fearing a deficiency is this. Losing a deficiency dispute does not mean that you were "guilty" of wrongdoing. A deficiency is an **honest mistake**. That's why there's no penalty. You did nothing wrong.

If the judge says you owe the tax, that means you mistakenly borrowed money from the government. You did that by not paying as much money as you should have on your tax return of several years ago (decisions usually come several years after the tax year in dispute).

If you lose, you have to pay the money back. Same as any loan. And, as with any other loan, you had the use of the money, so it's only fair that you should pay interest.

The interest even was deductible for itemizers until 1987. Starting in '87, interest on tax deficiencies is "personal interest" and its deductibility is treated the same as car loans, etc.

How much interest?

It depends on what years. The following table shows the interest rates that apply to tax deficiencies since July 1, 1975:

Interest Rates on Tax Deficiencies and Overpayments		
Starting	**Underpayment**	**Overpayment**
1-1-87	9%	8%
10-1-87	10%	9%
1-1-88	11%	10%
4-1-88	10%	9%
10-1-88	11%	10%
4-1-89	12%	11%
10-1-89	11%	10%
4-1-91	10%	9%

That interest is compounded **daily**.

The underpayment rate is the rate **you** pay IRS on a deficiency. The overpayment rate is the rate the government pays **you** when they keep your money improperly. Their rate's lower because they have a higher credit rating? Before '87, the rates were the same.

There's one other difference. The government's interest meter begins to run the day you owe the tax—typically April 15th. But the interest meter on what the government owes you does not begin to run until you **tell** them they owe you money. You do that by sending them an amended return. And then they pay no interest at all if they pay you within 45 days. And they don't have to pay interest on your money during the last 30 days they have it—no matter **when** they pay you. Yes, fellow taxpayers, it's a double standard.

Interest the government pays to you is taxable **income** same as if a bank paid it. Although an argument could be made that it is **not** taxable on your **state** income tax return.

So a deficiency is, at worst, a low interest rate loan from the government. What's so bad about that? Especially when you remember that only a tiny fraction of those who "borrow" are ever called upon to repay the "loan" at all. Actually, there's a little more to it than just interest. Depending on how hard and long you fight, you incur court costs, attorney fees and such.

Negligence

A deficiency is an honest mistake. Negligence is one step beyond that. Negligence is **not** an honest mistake. If you are negligent, **you broke the law**. Don't break the law.

There is no guilt or wrongdoing in a deficiency. There is guilt and wrongdoing in negligence.

If you are judged "deficient," you pay the tax and interest. If you are judged negligent, you pay the tax and interest **and a penalty**. The interest will be partially deductible for the next four years. The penalty **never was** deductible.

The negligence penalty
20% of the amount you owe attributable to the negligence

There are a number of other no-no's which trigger penalties:

Other penalties

Late payment	.5% per month up to maximum of 25%
Late filing of return	5.0% per month up to max of 25%; if more than 60 days late, $100 or amount of the tax due, whichever is less
Bad check	1.0% of check amount; minimum of $5 or amount of check, whichever is less
Substantial understatement	20.0% of the underpayment
Overvaluation	
200% or more and tax underpaid at least $5,000	20.0%
400% or more	40.0%

I'll define and explain these various penalties and what triggers them shortly. For now, back to negligence.

The definition of negligence

An **error** is **not** negligence **if** there was a **reasonable cause** for the error. What's reasonable? That's a question the courts have been trying to answer for centuries. There is no hard and fast definition.

An **honest misinterpretation** of the law is **not** negligence. If you made the error because you relied on the **advice of an otherwise competent tax adviser**, you have **not** committed negligence. But the advice-of-a-tax-adviser excuse only works if you have **given the adviser all the material facts**.

You are negligent if you

- Do not have a **good excuse** for the mistake you make
- Are **unreasonable**
- Make **no effort** to fairly approximate your taxes

- Don't keep **good records**
- Don't pay **on time**
- Intentionally **disregard** valid rules and regulations.

You may not intentionally disregard IRS rules or Treasury rules or regulations **unless** you have a **reasonable basis** for believing that the rule or reg is **illegal**. In Chapter 2, I gave you an example of a reg I thought you had a reasonable basis for believing was illegal—the temporary reg regarding wraparounds and excess loans over basis. Your reasonable basis would have been the *Hunt* decision before the IRS acquiescence to *Professional Equities*.

I get the impression that the courts are reluctant to zap anyone with negligence penalties unless they have no basis whatsoever for what they did—or some kook reason like taxes are illegal because currency is not backed by gold or silver.

The different standards for the different penalties

To avoid	You must have (who says so)
Negligence	"reasonably debatable" (*Foster*, 756 F 2d 1430)
Overvaluation	"reasonable basis" and "good faith" [IRC § 6659 (e)]
Substantial understatement	"substantial authority" or "adequately disclosed facts" to IRS [IRC § 6661(b)(2)(B)]
...in **tax shelters**	"reasonably believed...more likely than not" [IRC § 6661 (b)(2)(C)]

Overvaluation penalty

The overvaluation penalty is covered by section 6659 of the Internal Revenue Code. To avoid it, you have to prove that you had a **reasonable basis** for the value you chose (like the value of the improvements in a land/improvements breakdown)—and that you used that value "**in good faith.**" The authority (where it says reasonable basis and good faith are required) is § 6659 (e) of the Internal Revenue Code.

Important: You do not trigger the overvaluation penalty unless you flunk **two** tests:

1. You must exceed the right value by **at least 200%,** and
2. The overvaluation in question must cause you to underpay your taxes by at least **$5,000**.

In the 31% bracket, you have to exaggerate value by at least $5,000 ÷ .31 = $16,129 to trigger the penalty. And then you'd only trigger the penalty if the right value were $16,129 or less. (200% x $16,129 = $32,258 which is $32,258 - $16,129 = $16,129 too much and will cause you to pay $5,000 more taxes in the 31% bracket.) So it's not going to happen on a single used refrigerator or some such.

Substantial understatement penalty

Section 6661 of the Internal Revenue Code spells out the substantial understatement penalty. In order to trigger this penalty, you must underpay your taxes by at least $5,000 or 10%, whichever is greater.

You are off the hook, however, if you can prove the underpayment was based on a position you had "**substantial authority**" to believe was correct.

What's the definition of "substantial authority?" Regulation 1.6661-3 says you have substantial authority if:

> *the weight of the authorities supporting the position is substantial compared to contrary authorities.*

Translated into plain English, that means you'd better have a good legal citation or two on your side. And if the IRS can cite other legal citations that say you're wrong, yours had better be stronger. Strength in legal citations is like the hierarchy in cards: an ace beats a king. A king beats a queen. And so forth. In tax law,

- An Internal Revenue Code section beats a court decision.
- A U.S. Supreme Court decision beats an appeals court decision.
- An appeals court decision beats a trial court (Tax, District, or Claims Court) decision.
- Any court decision beats a regulation.
- A regulation beats a revenue ruling.
- A revenue ruling beats a letter ruling.

Then comes miscellaneous authorities like congressional committee reports, IRS publications, committee explanatory statements, proposed regs, etc.

The following are **not "authorities"** at all for the purpose of this penalty:

- legal treatises (books about the law written by lawyers and law professors)
- articles in law journals
- tax adviser opinions
- Congressional explanations written **after** a bill becomes law
- Private letter rulings unless addressed to you
- "actions on decision" (I don't know what that is.)

So says regulation 1.6661-3(b)(1),(2). Future court decisions may eliminate one or more of the items on this IRS list—like letter rulings.

Adequate disclosure

You can avoid the substantial understatement penalty if:

> *…the relevant facts affecting the item's tax treatment are adequately disclosed in the return or in a statement attached to the return.* IRC § 6661(b)(2)(B)(ii)

What does "adequately disclosed" mean? As far as I know, there are no court decisions on the matter. It's too new. This was put into the Internal Revenue Code as part of the Tax Equity and Fiscal Responsibility Act of 1982.

The IRS has issued their pronouncement as to how "adequately disclosed" is defined. And I'm about to give it to you. But I remind you to take IRS stuff with a grain of salt. The courts may decide that the IRS standards are stiffer than Congress intended. And therefore invalid.

If you "adequately disclose" by attaching a statement, you should use Form 8275. The IRS's version of "adequate disclosure" is in Reg 1.6661-4(b). It says

- A **caption** like the following:

> *The following is disclosed in accordance with IRC § 6661.*

- The pertinent **facts**.

In other words, they want you to **red flag** your own tax return. You'd probably be better off playing the **audit lottery**. That is, disclosure enables you to avoid the substantial understatement penalty. But so does having "substantial authority" or not getting questioned about the item in question at all.

This is not illegal or even shady. Remember IRC § 6661 gives you the **choice** of avoiding the penalty either by having "substantial authority...**or**...adequate...disclos[ure]." "Adequate disclosure" is **not** the **only** way to avoid this penalty. It's one of **two** ways. Therefore, it is **incorrect** to say that the law **requires** "adequate disclosure."

Fraud

Fraud is the Big Time. Commit fraud and you may end up in the Big House. Some frauds are misdemeanors; others, felonies. The minimum penalty is 75% of the fraudulent part of the underpayment. (It used to be 50% of the **entire** underpayment even if only one dollar of underpayment was due to fraud.) You can also be assessed fines of $5,000 to $10,000 and/or prison terms! Fraud convictions don't happen often. But they happen.

Bill "Tycoon" Greene was a Mill Valley, California real estate investor, seminar speaker, and book author. He was especially big on tax avoidance. In 1981, he was convicted of tax evasion, fined, and sentenced to serve two years in prison.

In non-fraud cases, IRS is presumed to be correct at the beginning of the trial. The burden of proof is then on **you** to prove IRS is wrong by a "preponderance of the evidence." But in fraud cases, you are innocent until proven guilty by "clear and convincing" evidence in civil fraud and "beyond a reasonable doubt" in criminal fraud cases. Furthermore, the government must prove that you **intended** to break the law, not just that you did.

According to the 1985 IRS Annual Report, 00.69% of the tax returns that were audited were referred by the auditor to criminal investigation. And the investigators recommended civil fraud penalties in 5,568 cases or about 60% of those referred.

> **WARNING**
> If you ever get a hint that you may be the target of a fraud investigation, **get a top notch criminal tax lawyer quick**. And refuse to say **anything** more to the IRS or Justice Department personnel or show them anymore documents until you consult with your lawyer.

Aggressiveness and judgmental areas

Here are the clear-cut and judgmental diagrams again.

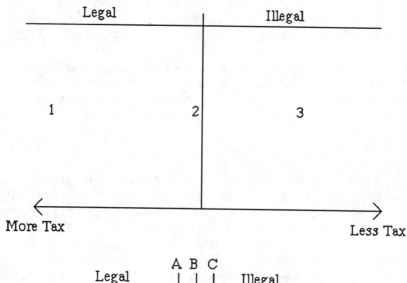

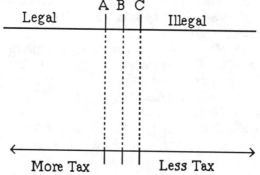

In clear cut areas, 2 is the only correct choice. It's neither aggressive nor conservative. Just correct. Number 1 is just dumb. Number 3 is illegal which is also dumb.

In judgmental areas, anything to the left of line A is dumb—just like number 1 in the clear cut diagram. Here's a list of dumb moves that would fall to the left of line A.

Dumb moves

- Not claiming a home office when you are eligible and not moving
- Using a recovery period other than minimum when it will save taxes
- Not breaking out the personal property
- Not using first-year expensing when eligible
- Taking back a mortgage
- Selling instead of exchanging

In each of the "Dumb moves," you may choose from two or more legal alternatives. In each case, none of the alternatives can be described as "aggressive" or "conservative." If all the alternatives in question are perfectly legal, how can any be aggressive? Only when the legality is arguable can the word "aggressive" be used.

Line A is conservative; line C, aggressive, and line B, in between. Anything to the right of line C is **illegal**, right?

Not so fast.

But, you say, anything to the right is clearly in the illegal area, isn't it?

Not necessarily.

Are you a lawbreaker or a pioneer?

T.J. Starker was confronted with a judgmental area. Crown Zellerbach Corporation wanted to buy some timberland he owned. Starker wanted to **exchange** instead. He would have had to pay **tax** if he sold. There's no tax on an exchange.

To make a long story short, Starker ended up in a situation where he had to do a **delayed** exchange—or none at all.

If you had taken a poll of professional tax advisers at that time and asked them if a delayed exchange was legal, most would have said, "No."

Delayed exchanges **had** been accepted in a couple of cases. But those involved **losses** which taxpayers were trying to take advantage of; not gains they were trying to avoid paying taxes on. And they didn't involve real estate. That's why most tax advisers would have said you couldn't do a delayed exchange. The only ones which had been approved were too different.

Starker was a law-abiding pioneer

Starker decided to go ahead and do the delayed exchange. Given the lack of court decisions saying it was OK, a point to the right of dotted line C on the diagram above represents his position best.

Was he violating the law? No. He and his attorney concluded that they had a **reasonable basis** for believing a delayed exchange was legal. (The Starker deal was done before the "substantial authority" criterion was required.)

Starker **did not report** the exchange (whether you have to report is another controversy I'll cover later). But IRS found out about it while auditing him on **another** matter. IRS said no dice. So Starker paid some $300,000 in taxes plus interest. Then he sued to get the money back. He lost in district court. But when he appealed to the Ninth Circuit Court of Appeals, he won.

So those who thought he'd be breaking the law if he did a delayed exchange were **wrong**. And if Starker had believed them, he'd be over $400,000 poorer. (Starker got back the tax he paid, the interest he paid, and interest on both.)

What does the Starker decision mean for the point to the right of dotted line C on the diagram above? By "boldly going where no man had gone before," Starker took a chance. Not a chance of being sent to jail or fined. Not a chance of being declared guilty of negligence. Because he had a **reasonable basis** for what he did—in spite of its novelty.

By winning, Starker established a "new dotted line." Now it looks like this as far as delayed exchanges are concerned.

What's legal shifts according to court decisions

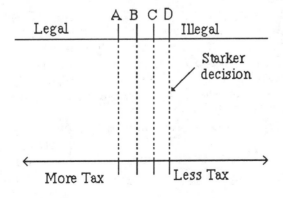

Starker was a "swinger." He was willing to take a chance—to pioneer a new trail in the tax law. IRS, however, still clung to dotted line C. After the Starker decision, they issued a Letter Ruling (#8046122) which rejected a delayed exchange arrangement similar to Starker's.

In 1984, Congress passed the Tax Reform Act of 1984 which says that you can do delayed exchanges. As a result, the question of whether you can do a delayed exchange is no longer a judgmental question. It's now clear cut. In other words, the Tax Reform Act of 1984 collapsed all four dotted lines into one solid line.

If you're aggressive, two things are certain

If you take an aggressive position on your tax return, two things are certain:

1. You'll pay less tax **that** year.
2. IRS won't say anything the **next** year either.

That you'll pay less tax is illustrated by the improvement ratio example. Let's say you bought a $100,000 property. An aggressive 87% improvement ratio gives you a depreciable basis of $87,000. The first year cost recovery deduction would be 3.64% of that or $3,166.80.

But if you used a conservative 65% improvement ratio, the first year deduction would only be $100,000 x 65% x 3.64% = $2,366.00.

IRS won't say anything until at least 14 months after you turn in the return because that's how long it takes them to get around to looking at returns. So aggressiveness gets you a lower tax bill for at least two years.

Possible consequences of being aggressive

I just told you what's **certain** to happen if you're aggressive. Now let me tell you what else **may** happen.

What *might* happen if you're aggressive

I. **Nothing**. IRS only audited .80% of all individual returns in '90. When it comes to tax audits, "many are filed but few are chosen."
II. **Audit**. But being audited doesn't necessarily mean you'll owe more taxes. Audits can come out several different ways.
    A. IRS owes **you** money. That happened on 82,405 individual returns in 1990.
    B. **No change**. That happened 12% to 15% of the time in '90—depending on who did the audit.
        1. Revenue agents   12%
        2. Tax auditors   15%

    C. **Deficiency assessment**. About 78% of taxpayers audited in '90 were asked to pay more as a result. But that doesn't mean you **have** to pay. If you're assessed a deficiency, you have two choices:
        1. **Pay** or
        2. **Fight**. If you decide to fight, there are three possible outcomes:
            a. **Win**. No tax or interest.
            b. **Lose**. You pay tax and interest.
            c. **Draw**. The judge splits the difference between what **IRS** says you owe and what **you** say you owe. Not necessarily 50/50.

Of course, if you fight, you have to pay the **costs of fighting**—attorneys fees, court costs, etc. You pay those costs win, lose, or draw. I'll tell you how taxpayers fared fighting the IRS in the chapter on "Doing Battle With The IRS."

Decision tree

The diagram below is called a "decision tree." It's a useful technique for visualizing and computing the best alternative when you have a decision to make. There are two main symbols in a decision tree: a box and a circle. Boxes represent **decisions** which **you** make. Circles are **events** which occur after your decisions and which are beyond your control.

At each box, the "branches" of the decision tree represent your **alternatives**. At each circle, the branches represent possible **outcomes**. At each circle or event, you put the **probability** of each outcome on that branch. I know you don't know the probability for certain in most cases. Guess the best you can. You do **not** put probabilities on the box or decision branches because once you've chosen one, the probability of that one is 100%.

Example

You bought a property. The tax assessor improvement ratio is 65%. The insurance company ratio is 85%. 65% would be conservative; 85%, aggressive. Your first year tax savings from your depreciation deduction is $10,000 higher if you use the aggressive ratio. The diagram on the next page shows your choices.

Your choices in a judgmental area

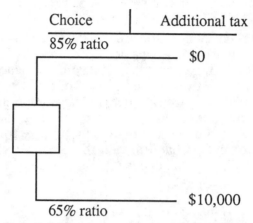

Your choices in a judgmental area

As I said, only .80% of all individual tax returns were audited in 1990. But some types of individuals had a **higher** chance of being audited. This table shows the breakdown for the various classes.

Your chances of *not* being audited

Income Class	% Not Audited
Short Form, TPI* less than $25,000	99.56
Long form, TPI less than $25,000	99.44
TPI of $25,000 to $50,000	99.26
TPI of $50,000 to $100,000	98.91
TPI over $100,000	95.29
Schedule C (Bus. or prof.) TGR** under $25,000	98.64
Schedule C with TGR of $25,000 to $100,000	98.14
Schedule C with TGR over $100,000	96.62

   * TPI stands for "Total Positive Income."
** TGR stands for "Total Gross Receipts."

Real estate investors file Schedule E (Rent and Royalty Income) rather than (or in addition to) Schedule C. Unfortunately, IRS does not include statistics on Schedule E audits in its *Annual Report*. I suspect they are quite similar to the Schedule C figures, because operating rental properties is considered a business.

The highest chance of audit is for businesses with receipts over $100,000. Followed by individuals with total positive incomes over $50,000. You'd have receipts over $100,000 if you owned about 20 apartments. Fewer single-family rental homes would put you over $100,000.

Actually, the table above only shows the **average** taxpayer's chance of not being audited. **Your** chances may be greater if you take an aggressive position which the classifier (people who decide which returns to audit) is looking for.

Adding the possibility of IRS challenge to the tree

Continuing the example, let's say you are in the income class **most likely** to be audited. In other words, your total gross receipts are greater than $100,000. Based on IRS statistics for 1990, there's a 3.38% chance you'll be audited and a 96.62% chance you won't. Let's add that event to the decision tree and add branches for the audit/no audit possibilities. We'll write the possibilities on audit or not on the branches.

IRS May Challenge

Possibility of IRS challenge

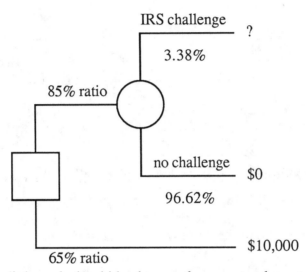

To be thorough, the audit branch should lead to another event—the outcome of the audit. There you would put branches for the three possible outcomes:

- IRS owes you
- no change
- you owe IRS.

To avoid the tree becoming unwieldy, I'm not going to do that. Instead, I'll assume that IRS claims 65% is the proper improvement ratio and therefore you owe them $10,000 in taxes plus interest.

Let's say you decide to fight all the way to a trial. You'll recall there are three possible outcomes:

- win
- lose
- draw.

I'll assume you choose to fight in Tax Court. More about the various courts later.

In 1990, the taxpayers and the IRS split the money in dispute in Tax Court 27/73. IRS got 27% of the money it sought. But the victory/loss breakdown is much more in favor of the government. IRS won 37% of the time in 1990. The taxpayer won 4% of the time. And the court decided partly for and partly against the taxpayer 59% of the time. I'll use those victory/loss percentages on the outcome of the trial branches of the decision tree.

Outcome of Tax Court trial

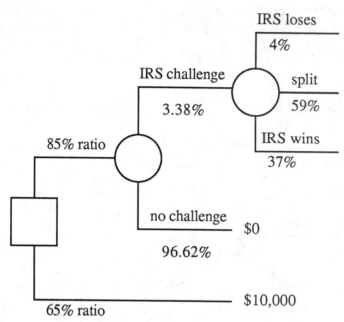

Note that all the probabilities at each event total 100%. 4% + 59% + 37% = 100.0% and 3.38% + 96.62% = 100.0%.

We know the cost of the conservative choice (the 65% improvement ratio) is $10,000 more in taxes. And we know that if we're aggressive (85% ratio) but don't get audited, we pay 0 additional taxes. Now let's figure the cost of the three win, lose, or draw outcomes.

The cost of fighting

Win, lose, or draw, you incur costs if you fight. If you act as your own attorney, which I recommend in many cases, your costs are your time and filing fees. The filing fee is $120. I'd guess the trial would kill a day or 8 hours. Preparation would take a two or three days, for a total of 32 hours.

If you make $50,000 a year, your time is worth about $25 an hour. ($25/hr x 40 hours = $1,000/week x 52 weeks = $52,000) So 32 hours x $25 an hour = $800. Adding the $120 filing fee and a couple or three hours advice from a tax attorney would bring the total cost to about $1,000. I'll use that figure for the cost of fighting in this example.

Taxes and interest

If you win, you pay only the $1,000 it cost you to fight.

If you lose, you pay the cost of fighting, the taxes in question ($10,000 in this case) and the interest. How much interest depends on how many years elapse between when the tax was due and when you paid it. The typical Tax Court decision comes about six years after the tax year in question.

Guessing the interest rate during those five years is harder. I'll use the IRS interest rate for January 1, 1990 to March 31, 1990, 11%, as the interest rate you'll have to pay. And don't forget that it's compounded daily. At 11%, the interest on $10,000 is $9,346 (compounded daily) in six years. So the bill if you lose in Tax Court is $1,000 + $10,000 + $9,346 = $20,346.

For the partial victory alternative, I'll assume the judge rejects both your 85% ratio and IRS's 65% ratio and says 75% is the correct one. In that case you'll owe $5,000 instead of $10,000 in back taxes. And, therefore, only $4,673 in interest. So the total if you split the difference is $1,000 + $5,000 + $4,673 = $10,673. Let's add those figures to the decision tree.

Cost of each outcome

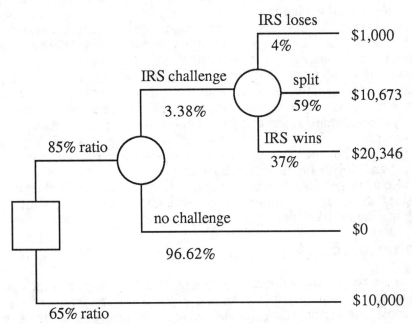

We're not finished yet. We still have to take into account the **time value of money**.

The time value of money

I said that the "lose" outcome will cost you $20,346. Choosing the conservative 65% ratio at the outset would have cost $10,000. So being conservative is $10,346 cheaper than being aggressive and losing, right? Wrong.

If you are conservative, you pay $10,000 in additional taxes **right now**. If you are aggressive and lose, you pay $20,346 in taxes, interest and costs **6 years from now**. There's a big difference between money paid now and money paid 6 years from now. And it's not just inflation. It's the **opportunity cost**.

If you get to use the money in question for 6 years, you can earn interest on it. Right now, money market funds are paying about 9%. $10,000 invested at 9% compound for 6 years would produce $17,125.53.

You ought to be able to earn at least a 20% return

Can you do better than 9%? Of course. If you were willing to tie your money up for 6 years, you could invest in second mortgages and get a sound return of about 13%.

That's not a second mortgage on a property **you're** selling. They only pay about 10% because the seller/lender is getting part of his return in the form of an inflated price. I mean investing in second mortgages on **someone else's** property.

By "sound" second mortgages I mean second mortgages that were properly created. That typically means the borrower has at least 25% equity in the property, he passed a thorough credit check, and the property value has been confirmed by an independent appraiser. The risk on such a mortgage is quite low. Second mortgages typically yield about 3% more than first mortgages. Right now, firsts are yielding about 10%. So you should be able to get about 10% + 3% or 13% on a second mortgage.

But the title of this book is *Aggressive Tax Avoidance for* **Real Estate** *Investors*—not **mortgage investors**. And which is riskier—real estate investing or mortgage investing? Real estate investing. If real estate is riskier, it ought to command a higher return than mortgage investing. Which it does. How high?

I think you ought to earn 20 to 40% per year minimum in real estate investing. And that's **after** taxes. The money market and mortgage yields were **before** taxes. Whenever I talk about 20 to 40% returns, people start thinking, "This guy's smoking pot." Nope.

If you can't do better than second mortgage yields, in other words 13%, then you ought not be investing in real estate. So that's the floor. And real estate investing can't yield just one or two percent more than mortgages because the risk of each is not that close. I figure you need to add at least 5% to justify the additional effort and risk of managing property versus endorsing checks.

That's another reason 20 to 40% returns are not outrageous. Money market funds and mortgages are pure investments. But real estate is **not a pure investment**. It's a **combination** of an investment and a **job** or business. So you need to be paid not only a return on your investment but also a "wage" for the time you spend. Looked at in that light, you'd be a fool to put up with the hassles of managing rental property for a return that's only slightly higher than you could earn lying in a hammock endorsing mortgage payment checks.

Present value calculations

Whenever you are comparing a future sum to a present sum, you must discount the future sum to its **present value**. It's impossible to make a valid comparison until you've done that. Unfortunately, most people, including the vast majority of college graduates, were never taught how to do present value calculations. I don't have the space here to teach you how to do those calculations. (It's explained in my book, *How to Use Leverage to Maximize Your Real Estate Investment Return.*) So you'll have to trust me if you're not familiar with the mathematics.

The $1,000 you'll spend if you fight will be spent over about 4 years—starting when you get audited. But for the sake of simplicity, I'll assume you pay it on the day of the Tax Court trial. The present value of $1,000 to be paid 6 years hence is $304.19 when discounted at 20%. Where did I get 20%? That's the opportunity cost: what you could have earned on the money if you had it instead of IRS. That's what all the discussion about rates of return up above was about.

The present value of $10,673 to be paid 6 years hence is $3,246.60 when discounted at 20%. And the present value of $20,346 to be paid 6 years hence is $6,189.01 when discounted at 20%. Adding these figures to the decision tree we get:

Present value of each outcome

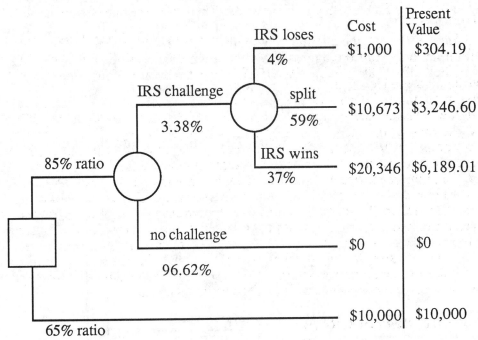

How to do the decision tree calculations

In this example, the best decision is obvious without doing any further calculations. If you're aggressive, the worst thing that can happen has a present value of $6,189.01. That's much better than what's **sure** to happen if you're conservative (pay $10,000). But I'll show you how to do the calculations anyway. Then you'll be able to use the decision tree for other problems where the outcomes are closer—and you'll be able to follow the other decision trees in the book.

Once you've put the outcome present values on the tree, you work backwards to see which decision is the best one. To do this, you calculate a weighted average at each event. Start with the latest one. Compute the weighted average by multiplying the probability of each outcome by its present value. Like this:

Probability	Present value
4% x 304.19 =	$12.17
59% x 3,246.60=	$1,915.49
37% x 6,189.01=	$2,289.93
Weighted average	$4,217.59

That weighted average is the value of getting to the **second** event. Then you calculate the value of getting to the **first** event. To do that, you use the answer you got in the first weighted average.

Probability	Present value
3.38% x $4,217.59=	$142.55
96.62% x $0 =	$000.00
Weighted average	$142.55

Zero is the present value of not being audited at all. So the weighted average value of getting to the first event (being challenged) is just $142.55. Once you've done all the events on the tree, you have the value of each branch of the **decision** box. Then the best one is the one with the lowest value. The lowest wins because we're talking about paying **out** taxes. If the outcome numbers on the tree were **income** figures, the alternative with the **highest** value would be best.

In this example, choosing the aggressive alternative has a value of $142.55. Choosing the conservative alternative has a value of $10,000. Which would you rather pay? $142.55 or $10,000. Obviously, $142.55—the aggressive choice, is better. Much better. These event values are added to the tree below:

Expected value of the aggressive choice

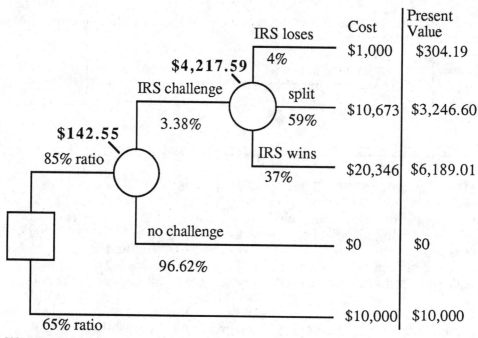

Probability of each outcome

I said that you have a 4% chance of winning **if** you go to trial. (Unless, of course, your case is different from the typical taxpayer on whom the percentage is based.) But I also said you only have a 3.38% chance of being audited. So what's the overall probability of being challenged and winning? Easy. Just multiply the probability of being challenged by the probability of winning. 4% x 3.38% = .14% Here are the rest.

Overall probabilities

Challenge			Outcome			Overall probability
Yes	3.38%	x	Win	4%	=	.14%
Yes	3.38%	x	Draw	59%	=	1.99%
Yes	3.38%	x	Lose	37%	=	1.25%
No	96.62%	x	Only one outcome		=	96.62%
Total						100.00%

Note that the overall probabilities have to add up to 100% just like the total probabilities at each event.

What the decision tree means

In this example, if you're conservative, you pay $10,000 more taxes the first year—guaranteed and immediate.

If you're aggressive:

1. The most probable (96.62%) outcome is no challenge—so no additional tax at all.
2. The worst outcome, being challenged and losing, has a present value of just $6,189.01. So an aggressive **loss** is better than a conservative "win!"

This example and the decision tree shows the two main reasons why the aggressive philosophy makes more sense than the conservative.

1. You probably won't be audited at all and
2. The time value of money is so high (at least 20% to a real estate investor), the interest rate on taxes so low, and the audit/judicial process so slow that an aggressive defeat is better than a conservative "victory."

Want to dispute some of the assumptions I used?

Maybe you disagree with some of the assumptions I made in this example. Fine. Change the number or numbers you disagree with and recompute. Matter of fact, I'll do a few for you right here.

I already used the highest probability of audit category. But let's push it a bit higher to see what happens. Let's say the chances of being audited are 10% instead of 3.38%.

If probability of audit is	cost of aggressiveness
3.38%	$142.55
10.00%	$421.76
75.00%	$3,163.19
100.00%	$4,217.59

For good measure, I checked 75% and 100% too. So if you were planning on arguing that an aggressive stance would **increase** the probability of audit—and thereby make conservatism make sense, forget it.

Still don't buy my claim that you can earn at least 20% in real estate? OK, skeptic. Let's try lower figures. And to give myself an even bigger handicap, I'll keep the probability of audit at 100%!

If the discount rate is	cost of aggressiveness
20%	$4,217.59
15%	$5,668.66
10%	$7,628.26

Want me to try below 10%? Forget it. That's what a lot of real estate articles do. They use 5% and 10%. They're nuts. You can beat 5% and 10% in government bonds. Discounting real estate investments at those rates is ridiculous. Besides, since the **worst** outcome if you're **aggressive** is better than the **sure** outcome if your conservative, even a **zero** percent discount rate won't make the conservative approach come out better.

How 'bout my $1,000 cost of fighting? Did I hear an attorney in the reading audience harrumph and say, "You can't fight a case in court for $1,000 in attorney fees."

If the cost of fighting is	expected value of aggressiveness is
$1,000	$142.55
$10,000	$244.96
$100,000	$1,170.30

Harrumph, yourself. By the way, if I pay you more, Mr. Attorney, I expect the probability of victory to increase. That would reduce the expected value of aggressiveness still further.

If you're still not satisfied, do this. Get hold of a computer and a spread sheet program for it. Tell the computer how to do the decision tree calculations. Then keep changing the variables until you find a set you feel reflects reality.

This is called "sensitivity analysis." That's a five dollar phrase for, "Let's see what the answer is if we change this number."

Aggressiveness pays

The point of all this is that aggressiveness pays. It makes economic sense. I'm not one of those rabid IRS haters who wants you to fight them for the sake of fighting. I'm a bottom line guy. I look at the:

• Time value of money,
• Delay in getting to trial, and
• Probabilities of audit, victory, loss, and draw.

and I conclude we ought to be aggressive.

4

How to Find—and Use—an
Aggressive Tax Adviser

When I wrote the first edition of this book, I thought tax advisers would be hostile to it. Because it often contradicts advice they've been giving—and charging for—for years.

I also thought that if you found a well-trained-in-real-estate, experienced-in-real-estate tax adviser, you'd be OK. I have since concluded that's not true.

Not a peep

In fact, I haven't heard a single hostile word from tax advisers since this book first came out in 1981. And lots of professional tax advisers have been buying it. One said it "changed my life." He said his peers now regard him as one who has come under the spell of a cult guru, namely me.

Maybe there are plenty of tax advisers who do not like the book. But they just don't bother to tell me so. But I would have expected to hear from a reader or two who said, "My accountant says you're wrong." On the few occasions when I have received such calls, I was able to cite chapter and verse as to why it was the **accountant, not me**, who was wrong.

The last such incident involved my telling a 1986 caller that you could deduct home office expenses even though your home office business (renting income properties) showed a loss. The accountant had overlooked the *Scott* decision (84 TC 683) and admitted that I was right after he checked it. (Note that the *Scott* decision was "repealed" by the Tax Reform Act of 1986.)

The real truth about tax advisers

The tax advisers like this book better than I thought they would. But I now respect them less than I did when I wrote the first edition of this book. Because lately I've learned that even the "best" real estate tax advisers put out a lot of drivel. In other words, you can go to a local general practitioner accountant and pay $75 an hour for "accounting old wives' tales." Or you can pay $150 an hour at a top real estate accounting firm and get "accounting old wives' tales" accompanied by a four-page computer analysis purporting to prove the "old wives' tales" correct.

What do I mean by "accounting old wives' tales?" Here's a list.

Some 'Old Wives' Tales' of tax accounting

- "Installment sales make more sense than selling for cash."
- "Exchanging can make sense sometimes."
- "You're eligible for the home office deduction. But don't claim it. It'll trigger an audit."

The above tales are generally bad advice.

Find the best and your troubles are over

I used to think that if I told you how to find a tax adviser in the top five percent or so as far as real estate and tax knowledge were concerned, you'd be home free. Wrong. Practically every tax adviser pushes some of the old wives' tales.

Some might wonder if my minority status makes me wonder if the others are right and I'm wrong.

Nah.

I've been giving pretty much the same advice since 1981 (modified by changes in the laws since then)—at seminars and speeches—and in my books and newsletters. I've heard just about every argument my opponents make. And whenever I see an article on one of the subjects where my position is in the minority, I eagerly read it. They invariably repeat the same old wives' tales.

I've wondered how so many professional tax advisers can put out so much garbage. And I've got a theory. In any group, most people follow a few leaders. So there are probably tax advisers who came to the same conclusion I did many years ago. But the leaders were saying the opposite. And the sheep did not have enough confidence in themselves to buck the leaders. So the advisers who agreed with me assumed that we must be incorrect and abandoned any opinions which conflicted with the majority view.

What about the leaders?

All right, so much for the sheep. But why are the leaders putting out incorrect information? Probably because they haven't thought things through. The analyses they publish are flawed.

As I said above, they often use discount rates which are too low—thereby leading to incorrect conclusions for real estate investors who have higher opportunity costs. Frequently, they simplify an example for the sake of explanation—but in doing so, they lose a crucial element. Many's the time I simplified an example at a seminar only to have a student ask that the numbers be redone using more real world figures. And almost invariably, the conclusion got reversed. So I long ago gave up doing simplified examples. Whenever possible, I try to use real world assumptions.

One common example of the simplification trap is in the debate over the wisdom of exchanging. The typical adviser "proves" that selling is better than exchanging with an example comparing the exchange of free-and-clear properties of equal value to the sale and purchase of the same properties. But that erases the main motive for exchanging—and its main benefit. You sell or exchange to move up to a larger property. And by exchanging, you save taxes, thereby allowing you to move up to a much larger property than if you sold, then reinvested.

Focus on taxes and court room victory rather than investment objectives

Another reason tax advisers give bad advice is that they focus on tax minimization and court room victory rather than the correct **investment** objective—namely, maximizing after-tax income.

I am not a tax adviser. I am a real estate investor. I did not go to accounting school or law school. I went to **business** school.

Accounting and law schools teach advisers not investors. So graduates of those schools have an **adviser, not** an investor, perspective. The paradoxical result is often they give bad advice.

Tax accountants are taught by school and experience to try to **reduce** their client's taxes. Lawyers are taught to **win** court cases. Those motivations are also mixed in with inevitable **conflicts of interest** like how can the tax adviser make his job easier and how can he **protect himself**, not his client, from trouble with the IRS.

Minimum taxes and victory in court are *not* the goal

As attractive as they sound, minimum taxes and court room victory are **not** your goals. You are a **real estate investor**, remember? Your goal is and should be:

> **maximum after-tax return on equity**

Since the goals of minimizing taxes and winning in court are so deeply ingrained in the typical adviser, you are not going to have much luck either talking them out of those goals or finding an adviser who takes the investor's return goal to heart. That's why **you** have to quarterback your tax team, not your adviser.

Often, the approach which minimizes taxes **hurts** investment performance. Overly high leverage is an example. Installment sales are another example.

In some few cases, they reduce the taxes you would pay compared to a cash sale. But they change you, at least in part, from a real estate investor to a mortgage investor. Mortgage investing pays **less** than real estate investing.

So while you're counting the money the installment sale saved you on your taxes, the **bigger** profits you could make if the installment note were in real estate equity slip silently, invisibly away.

What the installment sale advocates have never figured out is that you can only defer the **taxes** on the sale of your property by deferring the **income** from the sale. So installment sales reduce the present value of the taxes you pay, all right. But they do the exact same thing to the value of what you get from the sale of your property. There never was a better example of cutting off your nose to spite the IRS than the extremely popular installment sale.

Lawyer myopia

Lawyers tend to always be preparing for victory in court. That's proper when the choices are six of one and a half-dozen of the other from an **investment** standpoint. Preparing for victory in court is also the proper **negotiating** stance to take with the IRS.

My graduate training was at Harvard Business School (HBS). Where accounting schools tend to teach, "**how** to count," and law schools tend to teach, "victory is **all** that counts," HBS teaches, "**what** counts."

As I explained in the previous chapter, victory in court is often irrelevant. Furthermore, preparing for court room victory costs time and money. And it requires conservatism—which costs you even more money in the form of unnecessary taxes.

Since preparing for court room victory has a cost, you don't want to buy any more probability of victory than you need. How much do you need?

Not much.

Ever been to court? I didn't think so. I've been four times in my life. Probably spent a total of 60 hours in front of a judge. Something that takes up 60 hours of your life doesn't count for much.

And if you do have to go to court over a tax deficiency, does victory count? As the decision trees in the previous chapter showed, whether you win or lose your battle with IRS may not change the decision on whether to be aggressive or not. Too many tax attorneys spend too much time—at the investment decision and fill-out-the-tax-return point—preparing for trials that will never take place—in order to win victories that are too remote and small to affect the investment or tax return decision.

Give your adviser a copy of this book

You need to do two things once you've located a good tax adviser:

1. Give him a copy of this book and
2. Stay in control of your tax decisions.

That's not a ploy to sell books. Loan him your copy if you don't mind never seeing it again. If you do not get him familiar with this book's approach, he will probably waste your time with old wives' tales or overly conservative assumptions about your tax goals.

Plus, it's human nature that once he has committed himself to a particular line of advice, he will resist the loss of face involved in admitting he was wrong. That resistance also wastes your time. So when you find an adviser with potential, try a conversation something like this (Tom is adviser; Dan, taxpayer).

> Dan: "I'm a real estate investor and I recently read a book called *Aggressive Tax Avoidance for Real Estate Investors*. Have you read it?"
>
> *Tom: "No."*
>
> Dan: "Well, the book pretty much convinced me that it takes the right approach—the approach I'd like you to use with my taxes."
>
> *Tom: "Well, let me take a look at it to make sure it's not **too** aggressive to the point that it violates the law."*
>
> Dan: "Sure. I brought a copy along for that purpose."

Why use an adviser at all?

After reading that you're going to have to retrain your adviser, you may wonder why bother with an adviser at all? Here's why.

1. **Training**. A well-selected tax adviser has extensive training. Three years at a good law school in the case of a tax attorney. Perhaps a masters degree in taxation. Several years of undergraduate accounting in the case of an accountant. In addition, a competent real estate tax specialist will have attended or taught at "continuing education" seminars for tax attorneys and accountants.

Obviously, people who have completed all that training know more about tax law than laymen—even laymen who have read this book.

Laymen can understand tax law

I do not mean to suggest that accounting and law are subjects which are beyond the understanding of mere mortals. That mistaken belief is too widespread already.

You can research the law pretty much the same as a pro can. It's written in **English**, not Latin.

But just because a tax adviser knows a lot about tax doesn't mean he knows it all. The typical taxpayer is so awed by his adviser's knowledge of taxes that he adopts the attitude that, "whenever taxes are involved, I defer to my tax adviser's judgment."

DON'T YOU DO THAT!

Your relationship to your tax adviser should be like that between a quarterback and a running back in football. The quarterback (you) does **not** defer to the running back's judgment. He **respects** it. And if the running back says, "I've been in the clear the last two times I went into the flat, the quarterback **may** call an audible pass play accordingly."

You call the plays. A running back's job is to execute the audible play the quarterback calls. And a tax adviser's job is to execute the "play" you call (within the bounds of the law). If you say, "Exchange," he darn well better help you do an exchange—**not** try to talk you out of it.

2. **Authority**. I have acted as my own attorney in court several times. One of the things I learned is that in lawsuits, your opponents rarely take you seriously—no matter how good your legal work is—unless you're represented by an attorney. That also applies to your opponent in tax cases—the IRS. As a result, you may find it difficult to negotiate a favorable settlement without the "muscle" of a professional adviser. (In one of my cases, we settled out of court shortly after I brought in an attorney who was my cousin.)

3. **Knowledge of the unwritten rules**. There's more to law than you can find in even the most thorough research in law books. Judges and attorneys have **unwritten** rules. Rules that conflict with the **published** rules.

Generally, the unwritten rules are **far more lenient** than the published rules. For example, in one of my federal cases, I won a motion to force the other side to send me pertinent documents. And, at my explicit request, the judge set a **deadline**. My opponent's attorney totally **ignored** the deadline.

I got out my copy of the *Federal Rules of Civil Procedure* to see what one does when one's opponent ignores a judge's order. One answer, according to Rule 15(b)(2)(D), is to file another motion asking the court to hold your opponent in **contempt**.

In fact, the judges don't do that except in extreme circumstances. They just set another deadline. As a West Point graduate, I marvel at the fact that federal judges are infinitely more reluctant to use their authority than 20-year old cadets are to use theirs.

Bertrand Russell said that, "All professions are conspiracies against the laity." I believe it. I asked an attorney friend why the judge let an attorney friend get away with ignoring my deadline. He said, "Judges are extremely lenient so they can get the same treatment from the attorneys. For example, the judge may want the attorneys' cooperation to take a long weekend to attend his daughter's graduation. So he's not in a position to play hardball when the attorney wants a delay. Besides, attorneys are paid by the hour. And judges get paid the same no matter what."

The existence of these unwritten rules outrages me. The right to represent yourself in court is diminished by everyone else playing by rules you are not privy to. But the unwritten rules exist so it helps to have an insider on your side who knows them.

4. **Experience**. An experienced adviser also knows the personalities at the local IRS office. Human relations have a lot more to do with how tax disputes are decided than most people realize.

Taxes are too important to be left to accountants

Most real estate investors look to their accountant or attorney first on tax matters. I think that's a mistake. Not that you shouldn't consult a tax adviser at all. You should in many cases. But not **first**. **You** should research the question first. **Then** call your adviser if you have any doubt about the law.

The common attitude is, "I'm the **real estate** expert. I let my **accountant** handle the taxes." The implication is that you can't know **both** real estate investment and income tax laws pertinent to real estate investment.

Not true.

Tax saving advantages have always been one of the main sources of return from real estate. The Tax Reform Act of 1986 (TRA '86) reduced the importance of tax savings. But TRA '86 did not come anywhere near eliminating the tax advantages of real estate investment.

Georges Clemenceau said, "War is much too serious a matter to be entrusted to generals." And your taxes are much too important to be left to your accountant.

Why *you* must know the law

You don't need to become an accountant or an attorney. But you **do** need to know tax law. For a number of reasons.

1. **Day-to-day decisions**. Every day throughout the year you make decisions pertaining to your real estate investments. Many of these decisions have tax ramifications. If you are ignorant of the law, you won't recognize the ramifications—and you'll blunder.

In most cases, a year-end visit to your tax adviser is too late to correct these blunders.

There's an example of this in the famous *Starker* decision (602 F 2d 1341). T.J. Starker was doing a delayed exchange. He had an attorney, Charles Duffy. But Starker did not consult Duffy at one stage of the exchange. Starker was supposed to receive property from the Crown Zellerbach Corporation. But at one point, he told Crown to deed two properties directly to his daughter instead of to him.

When IRS tried to tax the whole transaction, they lost—except on the two properties Starker told Crown to deed to his daughter. Had he asked his attorney, the tax could have been avoided. But Starker did not know that switching the grantee had any tax ramifications.

In other words, April 15th isn't the only "tax day." **Every** day is tax day, potentially. You can't have a tax adviser looking over your shoulder every day. So, to an extent, you have to be your own tax adviser.

2. **More efficient use of adviser**. If you don't know tax law, your tax adviser will have to spend part of each session giving you a kindergarten class on the law. That would be worse than paying a computer repairman—at computer repairman rates—to read the owner's manual to you.

Investors who don't know the law tend to ask questions like,

Why can't I claim the historic tax credit? The building's more than 100 years old.

An investor who **does** know the law would be more likely to ask,

I'd like to get the historic credit on 153 Harvard Avenue. It's not in the National Register. But it is in a historic district. Do you think I have a chance of getting it declared 'significant' to the district?

3. **Evaluating your adviser**. This is the **most important reason** why you must know the

tax law. How can you tell if your accountant or attorney is worth a darn unless you know something about the tax law?

Most people pick their tax adviser on the basis of his "deskside manner." They can't choose according to competence level because they would not know a competent adviser from an incompetent one.

Frequently, people tell me that this book showed them that the family accountant had been giving them bad advice for years. But until they learned the law, they thought he was doing a great job.

John Zacarro, husband of 1984 Democratic vice-presidential nominee, Geraldine Ferraro, is a case in point. According to the Big Eight accounting firm of Arthur Young, Zacarro's family accountant of 40 years, Jack Selger, "did not take advantage of the many tax shelters that were readily available." (*Time*, September 3, 1984)

A famous real estate book author who shall remain nameless switched from having an accountant do his taxes to doing them himself the year he first read this book.

Reading this book will make you a well-informed consumer of tax advice. Then you'll be able to tell whether your tax adviser knows his stuff or not.

4. **Counteract adviser conservatism**. Most of us are more conservative when we handle other people's affairs. Tax advisers are often more conservative when they're giving **you** advice than they are on **their own** tax return.

If conservatism were free, that'd be fine. But it's not. If you follow conservative tax advice, you'll pay more than the law requires. You can **tell** the adviser not to be conservative. But suppressing his conservatism is easier said than done.

Most of your tax adviser's other clients **are** conservative. They tell him,

> *Just make sure I don't get audited.*

So tax advisers tend to assume that everybody who walks through their door has the same goal—avoiding audit—and he does your tax return accordingly.

Avoiding audit is a very dumb goal. For one thing, it's virtually impossible. You might still be audited no matter how conservative you are. And the conservatism which most people use to avoid audits is typically a self-inflicted "audit" which is far more severe, thorough, and costly than the vast majority of real audits.

IRS is trying to intimidate your tax adviser

Natural adviser conservatism is enough of a problem itself. But in recent years, the IRS has added an artificial reason for advisers to be conservative—a campaign to intimidate tax preparers.

There is nothing wrong with the rules *per se*. The problem is how IRS has used them. *Money* magazine did a good piece on this ("Whose Side Is Your Tax Preparer On?" February 1980).

Trick questions, 'abusive' shelters, a devastating letter

In that article, *Money* told how one IRS office gave its agents a list of errors to look for. Some of the errors were so obscure that even the best CPAs and IRS agents would make them. Commenting on the IRS's campaign to intimidate tax preparers, Virginia Beach accountant Louis Mirman said,

> *When it comes to a gray area in the tax law, most tax preparers are going to look out for themselves rather than the taxpayer.*

More recently, the IRS has been pushing a campaign against "abusive" tax shelters. At one point, they tried to prevent tax advisers from giving opinions to limited partnership organizers unless the adviser believed "the tax benefits will be upheld in court." That's analogous to the NCAA saying no college football games may take place in which one of the teams is an underdog.

The Tax Equity and Fiscal Responsibility Act of 1982 (TEFRA) includes a $5,000 penalty for using the Tax Court primarily for delay. That sounds scary in view of my point that delay is one of the main benefits of going to Tax Court. But you still have the right to dispute IRS's opinion of your tax bill. And as long as you have a "substantial authority" for doing so, nobody can penalize you. But I don't doubt that tax preparers will be intimidated by that new penalty and will try to get their clients to settle rather than fight in Tax Court.

TEFRA also added a new penalty for "aiding and abetting" an underpayment of tax. It's $1,000 for each return or document. Of course, aiding and abetting breaking the law is wrong. But in tax law there are so many judgmental areas. So stiffer penalties have the effect of turning tax advisers into client-paid IRS agents. The more penalties, the more conservative advisers become. And the more taxes you'll pay.

Your tax adviser has other clients to worry about

Your adviser has to deal with the local IRS people not only on **your** return. He also has to deal with them on the returns of his **other clients**. Like the shop steward who'll give in on Joe's grievance if management will give in on Fred's, your tax preparer tends to view your return as only **part** of his overall relationship with the local IRS.

If he goes to the mat with IRS on every single return, IRS is liable to get tough with **him**. So he'd better only go to the mat occasionally—if ever—from his perspective. But aggressive tax avoidance means you go to the mat **every time** there's a dispute over your return and the stakes are high enough—not just when your tax adviser thinks he's saved up enough "nice guy" points with the local IRS office.

You can only tell if your adviser is pulling his punches with IRS over your return if **you** know the law. Then you can either straighten him out or get rid of him.

My general impression is that the accounting profession is terrified of the IRS. Their terror translates into your paying more taxes than you should—to protect them. Unless you recognize when your adviser is acting out of fear rather than good sense, you cannot evaluate the job your adviser is doing.

Of course, many accountants and probably a higher percentage of tax attorneys are **not** terrified of IRS.

Lack of knowledge of the tax law

A tax adviser's aggressiveness is directly proportional to his knowledge of the law. The more he knows, the more confident he is. The more confident, the more aggressive.

The sad fact is that a lot of tax advisers know little more than their clients. During the Vietnamese war, a lot of Vietnamese civilians made a living selling to GIs. You could never have a **conversation** with these people in English. But they made darned sure they knew enough English to sell their products.

Many tax advisers are like that. They know just enough about tax law to attract a bunch of clients. Over the years, they've developed an **act**—a routine. It consists of a repertoire of jargon, accounting old wives' tales, and arguments for talking clients out of aggressiveness. If you ask about a particular aggressive technique, they'll trot out some old bromide to talk you out of it. If you point out that the bromide is inaccurate, the adviser will fire a blast of jargon and another bromide or two at you. That's his whole act.

If you persist in trying to take him where he has never gone before, he'll resist mightily. For example, he may never have done an exchange. That will make him afraid to do one with you. But instead of saying, "Gee, I'm not confident about exchanges. I'd have to refer you to another adviser or bring someone in to help," he tries to talk you out of it.

Here are the reasons why tax advisers are often conservative.

Why advisers are conservative

- Natural tendency when handling another's money
- Most clients **want** conservatism
- IRS campaign to intimidate advisers
- Fear of harassment by IRS
- Fear that IRS may hurt adviser's practice
- Desire to preserve god-like image of always being right
- Fear of preparer penalties
- Lack of thorough knowledge of tax law

How to find a top notch tax adviser

Get a **specialist**. That's the most important thing I can tell you about finding a tax adviser.

You know that doctors specialize. You'd never go to a dermatologist for heart surgery. But you may be less aware that tax advisers specialize too.

There are corporate tax advisers, small business tax advisers, estate tax advisers, "family practitioner" tax advisers, and so forth. The specialty **you** want is **federal income taxation of real estate**. Most of the advisers who specialize in real estate taxation cover both partnerships and individuals.

Most of you already have tax advisers. And most of you are **not** using the kind of specialist I recommend. Rather you probably have a garden variety, small business tax adviser. Most of his clients are small, closely-held, family corporations. A few are like you. In fact, you may own a non-real estate business in the form of a corporation. Your corporation's accountant may not do individual tax returns normally. But he does yours as "a favor." That's a favor you can do without.

When you finish reading this book, there's an excellent chance you'll know more about real estate taxation than this kind of adviser. If that's the case, **he** ought to be paying **you** rather than the other way around.

I told you earlier that even the best tax advisers put out a lot of incorrect information. But at least they have the raw material for correct decisions.

For example, I once used an attorney/CPA in a real estate deal. That's a pretty high-powered combination. But during the deal, he became concerned about whether the corporation I was buying (it owned an apartment building I wanted) had claimed any investment tax credits. Little old non-attorney, non-CPA me had to explain to him that you can't claim the investment tax credit on property used to "furnish lodging."

That's because he was **not** a real estate specialist. Even the guys who mistakenly advise against exchanges and so forth would know about the lodging exception to investment tax credits if they specialized in real estate. So although it's true that practically every adviser out there will have to be retrained to an extent by this book, let's at least find you a guy who knows the laws as they pertain to real estate.

There aren't very many such specialists

Real estate tax specialists aren't common. There are probably only a couple in each major metropolitan area. Some areas of the country are "richer" than others when it comes to availability of real estate tax specialists. California probably has the most per capita; rural and Northeastern states the least.

I often get calls and letters from readers who ask me to recommend a good tax adviser in their area. I usually recommend the guys listed at the end of this chapter. Frequently, the caller says, "I was looking for someone closer to where I live."

Why the fixation on someone in 'your area?'

Why?

Why does he have to be in your area? You're looking for advice on the **federal** income tax law aren't you? If it's a federal law it's the same nationwide, right? (Actually, it varies slightly due to differing Appeals Court decisions and pertinent state laws.)

If you live in a small metropolitan area, say less than 150,000 population, there's a good chance that there is **no** qualified real estate tax specialist there. In that case, if you insist on using someone in your area, it's sure to end up the blind leading the blind. So forget that "my area" stuff—unless you live in a major metropolitan area.

And once you get out of your area, you might as well get the best you can, rather than the closest. In other words, if you live in Casper, Wyoming, and can't find a real estate tax specialist in Casper, you might as well look in Dallas as Denver.

All things being equal, a tax adviser in your area is best. But things usually aren't equal. I have never had a tax adviser in my area. And if you can't find a top guy in your area, you shouldn't either. All a distant adviser means is that you use the phone and mails a little more—and you tend to waste less time.

Why not the best?

I think you ought to get the best tax adviser in the nation. That doesn't necessarily mean the most famous. The most famous guys usually give lousy service so they're not really the best. The best cost a little more—maybe $175 an hour versus $100 or $125 for a run-of-the-mill guy. But the difference in confidence, competence, and aggressiveness is enormous.

Most investors would be willing to spend the $175. Their problem is one of self-esteem. They don't think they're "good enough" to use the best in the nation. "Little old me use the best?" they think. Sure! Why not?

Your attitude ought to be, "I'm not going to **assume** I have to settle for a mediocre tax adviser. I'm going to call the best and ask him to represent me. If he says no, I'll call the second best. I'll only settle for Mr. Mediocre when all the better advisers have turned me down." In fact, the first or second guy you call, no matter how high-powered, will probably agree to help with the problem at hand.

Education and training

As a general rule, the more tax education and training your adviser has, the better. It can be self taught. Most of **my** tax knowledge is self taught. But some education is necessary.

As far as classroom instruction is concerned, specialist-type information is generally given only in masters degree programs and continuing education seminars.

The NYU masters degree in taxation

Bill Tappan wrote the books *Real Estate Exchange and Acquisition Techniques* and *Real Estate Acquisition Handbook*. He says he is particularly impressed with tax attorneys who have a masters degree in taxation. He finds that, as a group, they have more confidence and aggressiveness than other types of tax advisers.

The number one L.L.M. (masters degree in taxation) program is New York University's. NYU is the "West Point of Tax Law."

Roscoe Egger became Commissioner of IRS when Reagan took office. One of Egger's programs for improving IRS was to send IRS attorneys and tax law specialists to NYU for advanced training. The IRS press release said, "Because of its reputation as one of the nation's most respected tax law centers, the New York University School of Law was selected to provide the training."

I've heard that the Congressional committees which write tax laws are riddled with NYU LLMs. Which suggests they not only teach about tax laws—they write them to begin with.

I'm not promising that every attorney with an LLM from NYU is great. I imagine they've anointed some duds. Nor am I saying that non-NYU grads aren't worth a darn. But I will say that it's an impressive credential which provides "circumstantial evidence" of an adviser's competence.

By the way, **you** can go to NYU—or at least a small piece of it. Every year they have a Tax Institute (several day seminar), usually in New York and a western city. It covers far more than real estate, though. You can also buy cassettes of NYU's annual Tax Institute. NYU's address is in the back of this book.

Other masters programs

NYU's LLM program is generally considered the best. But it's not the **only** one. Georgetown University has a program. There are also masters tax programs given by non-law schools. Some CPAs and attorneys have an MST—Master of Science in Taxation. And some MBAs major in taxation.

Any graduate study focusing on tax laws would be strong evidence that a tax adviser is serious and likely to be aggressive. Attorneys with LLMs from NYU are particularly interesting. So graduate level study of tax laws is worth looking for when you seek an aggressive tax adviser.

What he reads

You can **become** knowledgeable about taxes by attending a tax school. But you won't **stay** knowledgeable unless you continue to up-date your knowledge. In order to do that, competent tax advisers must subscribe to pertinent tax loose leaf services and periodicals. I mentioned many of these in Chapter 2. Any tax adviser who claims to specialize in real estate ought to subscribe to some or all of the following:

- *Real Estate Investor's Monthly*
- *Real Estate Tax Digest*
- *Federal Income Taxation of Real Estate*
- *The Journal of Real Estate Taxation*
- *The Federal Tax Guide*
- *Tax Notes*

If you come across a tax adviser who claims to be qualified but doesn't subscribe to any of these, ask him how he stays up-to-date on the latest court decisions, laws, rulings, and regulations. If he's got a satisfactory answer, fine. When you're looking for a tax adviser, the question, "What periodicals do you subscribe to to stay up-to-date?" is a legitimate one.

Seminars

Aggressive real estate tax advisers attend pertinent seminars and/or teach at them. Tax advice trade associations sponsor continuing education seminars. Some focus on real estate tax topics. Independent companies, tax periodicals, and educational institutions also sponsor seminars on real estate tax topics. Here's a list of some of the organizations.

• Local, state, and national bar associations
• Local, state, and national chapters of the American Institute of CPAs
• The Practising Law Institute
• American Law Institute
• The Real Estate Institute, NYU
• Realtors National Marketing Institute
• The Wharton School, Executive Education
• Northwestern Center for Professional Education

Other companies, organizations, and institutions give seminars. To find them, you'll just have to keep your eyes and ears open. If you're on any real estate mailing lists, you'll probably receive announcements of seminars in your area. Make note of who's teaching even if you don't plan to go. And when interviewing a prospective adviser, ask which real estate tax seminars he's attended or taught at recently.

Experience and track record

There's more to tax avoidance than book-learning. Your adviser should also have experience. Experience as a real estate investor would be desirable. So would experience negotiating with IRS. In the case of attorneys, trial and appeals court experience could be useful. That's especially important if you're fighting IRS; less so for tax preparation and deal structuring.

Tax advisers who **once worked for IRS** are worth finding. As long as they only worked for IRS for 2 to 5 years. I'm told that people who worked for IRS longer than that tend to be "brainwashed." In 2 to 5 years, the theory goes, you learn how IRS works. But if you stay more than 5 years, you become one of them.

Rapport

The more rapport you have with your tax adviser, the better. Unfortunately, rapport is the **only** selection criteria used by most people. That's the "bedside manner" I talked about earlier. Rapport **is** important. But not so important that it should be your only criterion.

Compatible tax philosophy

If you're aggressive, you need a tax adviser who's also aggressive. If you get a conservative adviser, you'll waste a lot of time arguing with him. Since he charges by the hour, that's a double waste. Education, experience and the other characteristics I've mentioned are important. But it's conceivable you could find a guy with all of those who is nevertheless very conservative. He's **not** the guy you want.

Service

Your tax adviser ought to provide good service. That means he meets reasonable deadlines, returns phone calls promptly, doesn't reuse documents from other deals with inappropriate parts left in, doesn't hand you off to an unqualified junior associate, and so forth.

Some professionals—particularly some attorneys, give lousy service. Lousy service is lousy service—whether it's the corner gas station or your tax attorney. For reasons unknown to me, people who would never tolerate lousy service from the gas station will put up with it for years from their tax attorney. If your tax adviser gives lousy service, get rid of him.

Sometimes, the most renowned real estate tax advisers are **not** the ones you should use. That's because they are the ones most likely to treat clients like dirt. So if I left you with the impression that the most famous guy is the one to get, let me add a warning. Lousy service is often directly proportional to fame. The **second** tier—tax advisers who aren't yet big names, may offer the best combination of competence and service.

Integrity

Your tax adviser ought to be honest. For two reasons:

1. Everybody ought to be honest because it's the only moral course.
2. Dishonest tax advisers attract IRS problems.

IRS has a "problem preparers list." If your adviser's on it, **you're** probably going to be on the "problem preparers' clients-to-be-audited" list. You don't need that. Nor do you need the presumption of evasion which IRS agents bring to such audits.

Diligence

You use a tax adviser for:

• Return preparation,
• Deal structuring, and
• Fighting with IRS.

In each case, laziness can cost you money. So you want an adviser who does the necessary weekly homework to keep up-to-date. You want one who will dig for ways to structure deals to your advantage. And, when you fight, you want a tax adviser who will dig for the evidence and authority (court decisions, rulings, etc.) you need to win.

Interest in your problems

By "interest in your problems" I don't mean you should find a bleeding heart. Rather I mean watch out for an adviser who is bored with mundane tax matters. This, like bad service, is a characteristic common among big names. They've done mundane things a thousand times. Now they want to be "creative."

Beware of such advisers trying to get you to do "creative" deals which are unnecessary. There are times when "creativity" is exactly what you need. But all things being equal, mundane is far better than "creative" when it comes to disputes with IRS. So don't let any adviser talk you into "creativity" for "creativity's" sake. Make him explain why you can't do the deal the mundane way before you go "creative." And if he isn't persuasive, and you can't convince him to help you do it the mundane way, get rid of him.

Should you ask your friends?

The main way people find tax advisers is to ask their friends. Is that valid? Probably not.

Your friends probably are not real estate tax experts. So they aren't qualified to tell who is. But they're not likely to say so. Rather they **will** recommend someone. How do they decide on whom to recommend? Bedside manner.

Another thing you have to guard against is your **being used to return a favor** or earn points with an accountant or attorney.

Real estate agents ought to know the names of local real estate tax attorneys. Especially if the agent specializes in **commercial/investment** real estate. But real estate agents often get referrals and other favors from accountants and attorneys. As a result, they may send you to a guy they owe a favor to, or a guy who they want to owe them a favor, rather than to the best guy. Of course, real estate agents aren't the only ones who might use you to return a favor or earn points with some adviser.

Your friends can help, however, if they know real estate and you trust them to make a recommendation with **your** interest at heart rather than their own. The last two tax attorneys I've used were both recommended by my friend Bill Tappan (author of *Real Estate Exchange and Acquisition Techniques*).

Teachers and speakers

One of the best ways to spot a top real estate tax person is to see his name listed as a teacher of a course or seminar on the subject. I keep all direct mail brochures I receive on real estate seminars. One reason is they provide a file of the names of interesting real estate people. Among the brochures are many on tax topics. And in virtually every case, the name and other details about the instructor are listed.

Trade conventions, both state and national, typically have a number of seminars. Sometimes, at tax adviser and real estate conventions, they offer a seminar or talk on a real estate tax topic. There's one or two speakers or a panel of 3 to 6 people. The subject of the talk, and the names of the speakers/panelists are listed in the convention program. These are typically leaders in the field.

You can get information on such convention seminars and their speakers from the sponsoring trade association. There's a list of real estate and tax related trade associations in the back of the book.

Maxwell-MacMillan's *Federal Tax Guide's* weekly *Report Bulletins* list tax seminars all over the country and their sponsors.

Trade association committees

Trade associations also have standing committees. For example, the American Bar Association (ABA) has a "Section" devoted to "Taxation." Under that "Section" are "Divisions" devoted to

- Depreciation and Investment Tax Credit
- Partnerships
- Real Estate Tax Problems
- Sales, Exchanges, and Basis.

The members of these committees are listed in the ABA's *Directory*. In each "Division," a Chairman, Vice-Chairman, and Special Advisor are listed. Presumably, these are ABA members with particular interest and expertise in these subjects. The phone numbers and addresses of these individuals are listed in the back of the *Directory*. Most trade associations have similar committees and directories in one form or another. You can generally get the directory or the information from it from the trade association office.

Book authors

Top notch real estate tax advisers often write books on the subject. So it may be worth your while to contact real estate tax book authors.

I'm not in the advice business other than through my writing. And I've already told you the names of three tax advisers who have impressed me. See the Acknowledgments section in the front of the book. Most real estate tax book authors **are** in the tax advice business, however. Or they know someone who is.

Where do you find the names of real estate book authors? The "Recommended Books" section at the back of this book is a good place to start. You can also check the *Subject Guide to Books in Print*. It's published by R.R. Bowker and is available in most libraries. Bowker also publishes *Law Books in Print*. The Real Estate Publishing Company (PO Box 41177, Sacramento, CA 95841) publishes *Real Estate Books in Print*.

How do you track down the author after you've found his name? Usually, the information in the "about the author" section will tell you enough. If not, you can write to him in care of the publisher. Or you might be able to track him down through *Who's Who* or *Contemporary Authors*. Both are typically in libraries. You can usually get the information over the phone by calling the reference desk.

Before I leave books, don't overlook the "Acknowledgments" section in most real estate tax books. There the author thanks people who helped him write the book. One of the tax attorneys I've used was listed in the acknowledgment section of Tappan's book on exchanging. So, if not the author, then perhaps one of the people who helped him will help you.

Don't assume a "big author" would never talk to little ol' you. Take it from me, book authors are "real people." Writing books is a job like anything else. The typical book author is a one or two person operation (author and spouse or assistant). Unless he's frantically running around doing talk shows (not likely in real estate tax law) or making speeches (more likely), he'll probably be pretty accessible. If he's got sense, he'll realize it's good to talk to his readers—if only for market research purposes.

Article authors

Book authors aren't the only writers of interest. Article authors may be an even better source. Certainly there are more articles written each year than books. So you have more to choose from. Although a book is better evidence of tax expertise than an article.

Where do you find real estate tax articles? Try Warren, Gorham & Lamont's *Index to Federal Tax Articles*. It lists pertinent articles and their authors from hundreds of law and real estate periodicals. And there are other legal periodical indexes.

You can usually get the address of the author by getting a copy of the article. Typically, there's a little blurb saying, "The author is a partner in the Kansas City law firm of O'Malley, Weinstein, and Wong." From there, it's just a simple matter of calling the information operator in Kansas City. If that information's not in the article, call the periodical.

Taxpayer's attorney in prominent court cases

I've mentioned a number of court decisions. And I'll mention a lot more before the book is finished. In some, the taxpayer acted as his own attorney. But in most, he had an attorney. And his attorney's name is usually listed in the decision.

The attorney may not have been a top notch expert on the issue in the case **before** it started. But I'll bet he is now. In the process of preparing for a trial, any attorney worth his salt will study the law on the item in dispute. By the time he's done, he's an expert on it.

That's true win or lose. In the first two editions of this book, I cited "winners of landmark cases" as attorneys to contact. I now say winners or losers. Unless a reading of the case reveals that it was lost through poor preparation on the part of the attorney. But losing doesn't prove the attorney is bad. The client may have presented him with an impossible situation. And there's no reason to restrict the category to "landmark" cases. All you really need is an attorney who fought a case like yours recently.

The attorney's name is usually printed on the first page of the court decision. Sometimes, only the name is listed. Other times; the name, law firm, and city. When only the name is given, you can often figure out the rest from the location of the court. Or, with just his name, you can look him up in Martindale-Hubbell's directory of attorneys. Or you could simply call the court and ask.

They'll usually tell you. I've called the U.S. Supreme Court for similar information. A perfectly normal secretary comes on the line and tells you what you want—even there. There is not, as you might expect, a thundering, deep-voiced judge demanding to know, "How dare you call the United States Supreme Court!"

Editors of trade journals

Editors of trade journals rarely are practicing tax advisers. But they probably know someone who is.

I once needed an attorney to help me negotiate with a major book publisher. So I called the editor of *Writer's Digest* magazine. He gave me the number of one of the best writer's attorneys in the nation. I called her and she represented me in the contract negotiations.

This suggestion does not apply to trade journals published by tax adviser trade associations. They'll tell you that all their members are qualified. Baloney.

Trade journals which accept advertising will probably steer you toward their advertisers if they have any who are tax advisers. Newsletter editors, of which I am one, have neither advertisers nor members to please. So they can give you their best advice.

Beware of big firms

John Beck is a San Francisco attorney/real estate investor. He used to work for a big name accounting firm. He remembers a meeting held to see how they could discourage "little guys" from being clients. They only wanted corporations and large companies.

So before you trot off to a big name firm consider that they may be holding meetings on how to get rid of people like you. One of the ways they probably come up with is charging you more than they charge the clients they want.

Special certifications and designations

Some organizations give certifications and designations which are indicators of tax law competence.

Certified Specialist—Taxation Law: This is a certification given by the California Board of Legal Specialization. As you would expect, it applies primarily to California attorneys. Only a few non-California attorneys have been certified by the California Board.

But tax law is pretty much the same throughout the nation. So you may want to use a California attorney even though you live elsewhere. That's especially true if the need involves an **exchange**. Exchanging is much more prevalent in California than elsewhere. And California is generally a leader in real estate.

The California Board of Legal Specialization (555 Franklin Street, San Francisco, CA 94102, 415-561-8265) will send you a copy of their roster of taxation specialists for $1.00. In the request, you must say that you want the roster for personal, not commercial purposes. By commercial they mean uses like an insurance salesman who tries to sell policies to everyone on the roster.

Texas has a certification for taxation law also. I know of no other state which certifies attorneys as tax specialists.

Don't forget what I said earlier. You want a **real estate** tax specialist. Many, if not most, of the California Tax Specialists do **not** specialize in real estate.

Attorney—C.P.A.s: Some tax advisers have both a law degree and a C.P.A. Many of these are members of the American Association of Attorney--C.P.A.s (24196 Alicia Parkway, Suite K, Mission Viejo, CA 92691, 714-768-0336). Again, you need a **real estate** specialist. Most attorney-C.P.A.s are not.

Enrolled Agents: An enrolled agent is one of the three groups eligible to represent a taxpayer before the IRS. The other two are attorneys and C.P.A.s.

There are two ways to become an enrolled agent: 1. Pass an IRS test; and, 2. Have at least five years experience as an IRS auditor.

In a previous edition of this book, I said you could take the test yourself if you're into gathering "merit badges." San Jose tax adviser Tom Smith didn't dispute that. But he wrote to tell me it's one of the hardest exams he ever took. He also has a masters degree in business administration from Stanford University. So it's not the **only** exam he ever took.

You can get the names of enrolled agents near you from the National Association of Enrolled Agents, 1135 15th Street NW, Washington, DC 20005 800-424-4339. I suspect that the number of enrolled agents who specialize in real estate is small.

No credential is sufficient

Does the fact that someone teaches or writes about taxes, or holds a certification, guarantee that he's the right adviser?

No.

Does the fact that someone does **not** teach or write about taxes, or hold a certification, prove that he's **un**qualified?

No.

Then why seek someone with such credentials?

First, teaching, writing, and being listed in a directory of specialists makes an adviser visible to us on the outside. In other words, they are ways of separating real estate tax specialists from the mass of tax advisers.

Second, the fact that someone writes, teaches, or holds a certification is some evidence, albeit imperfect, of competence in the field.

Finally, separating the real estate tax specialists from the rest of tax advisers is not the entire selection process.

How to interview a prospective tax adviser

In the material above, I did not mean to say that as soon as you find someone who wrote a tax article you say, "Great! You're hired." At that stage, you've found a **candidate**, not an adviser. Don't make the hire-or-not decision until after you've asked him a few questions.

A quality tax adviser won't mind questions about his qualifications

When I first proposed these questions in my tax seminar, I was concerned that top professionals might be offended by them. So I advised my students to ask them tactfully. But all of my seminar audiences included some tax professionals. And they said they'd **like** prospective clients to ask these kinds of questions. The reason is that they've spent years becoming a specialist and they'd love a chance to brag about it. In his book, *How to Win Friends and Influence People*, Dale Carnegie pointed out that everyone likes to talk about themselves and their accomplishments. In asking these questions, you're giving the prospective tax adviser the chance to do just that.

There are two kinds of tax advisers who will balk at answering these questions. The first group is made up of advisers who are more embarrassed about the answers than they are angry at the questions. But they'll likely react belligerently to the questions to cover up their lack of qualifications.

The second group is made up of tax advisers who have become convinced that they are universally known. They believe they are so famous that **everyone already knows** their qualifications. I got news for them, and you. There is **no** real estate tax adviser in the country who is so well-known that there aren't many smart, successful real estate investors who have never heard of him. And you don't want to work with the guys who **think** they're universally known anyway. They're so full of themselves they give lousy service.

Competent real estate tax advisers who possess accurate self-images and human size egos will be glad to answer these questions. If the guy you're considering balks, find someone else.

Tax adviser interview questions

- What year did you start your tax career?
- Did you ever work for IRS? In what capacity? How long?
- Roughly, how many times have you represented taxpayers in disputes with the IRS? What's your batting average?
- (For attorneys) Roughly how many times have you fought tax cases in court? Batting average?
- What legal/accounting/tax degrees do you have? From what institutions?
- What other tax training do you have?
- Do you have any tax certifications or designations?
- Have you attended continuing education courses or seminars pertinent to my problem (whatever you're going to the adviser for)?
- Have you taught tax courses pertinent to my problem?
- What periodicals or tax services pertinent to real estate taxation do you subscribe to?
- What is your fee?
- References: Professionals like attorneys and accountants may not give out the names of their clients without the client's permission. Obtaining that permission is time-consuming and a bit embarrassing to the adviser and it's a bother to the client to answer questions from some stranger. So I wouldn't ask a tax adviser for references on a transaction in which his fee is likely to be less than $2,500. If you're unhappy with him, you can just get rid of him. But if his fee is likely to be **more** than $2,500, and the involvement is such that it would be difficult to change advisers, ask for the names of clients he has worked with on similar problems. Examples would include hiring a tax adviser to fight IRS on a matter involving tens of thousands of dollars and/or litigation or a long, drawn out real estate transaction in which it would be costly to have to train a new adviser midstream.
- How would you set up a delayed exchange?
- Ask about a recent real estate tax law development.

Ask about a recent real estate tax law development

A good tax adviser is up-to-date. Every couple of months, an important court decision, ruling, regulation, or new law pertaining to real estate comes out. Your adviser should be aware of it. To test him, look up recent developments in one of the periodicals I recommended to you earlier in the book. *Real Estate Investor's Monthly* and *Real Estate Tax Digest* would be the best places to look. Make mental note of the details of a couple such developments and ask the prospective adviser about them.

Be careful about this test, though. If you pick an unimportant, obscure development, it's not a meaningful test. And give the guy enough slack to miss an item occasionally due to vacation or whatever.

One tax adviser told me he thought this test was too tough. I disagree. **I** could pass it. And I'm not a tax adviser who gives advice on a daily basis. For example, one year there was a ruling which said that a home office could be converted back to residential use and the entire home would be eligible for the 24-month reinvestment rule. If you asked me about that, I'd remember its main points and that it was a ruling. If you wanted more details, I'd have to look it up.

Questions to ask other clients

If you do get references from the adviser in question, here are some questions to ask them.

- Do you recommend (name of adviser)?
- Did he return your phone calls reasonably promptly?
- Did he meet reasonable deadlines?
- Do you feel you were overcharged?
- Were documents carefully prepared (rather than copied from other deals with inappropriate parts left in)?
- Were you shunted off to a junior associate?
- Would you describe the adviser as aggressive or conservative? (If the guy you're talking to hasn't read this book, his idea of aggressive may be very different from yours.)
- Did he seem to know tax law well?
- Do you plan to use this adviser again? If not, why not?

The proof is in the pudding

After you've interviewed the prospective adviser, (and where necessary, one or two of his clients) you should have a pretty solid basis for hiring him or not. But the **final** proof is in the pudding. How do you like working with him? How competent does he seem to be? How aggressive? Is he earning his fee? If there was a dispute with IRS, did he argue your case effectively?

I only use tax advisers on an *ad hoc* basis. I do not have anyone on retainer. I recommend you do likewise—unless you do deals on a monthly or weekly basis. If you just use the adviser every now and then, he'll hardly notice if you "fire" him by not using him again. But a retainer requires an actual firing which is unpleasant and traumatic. As a result, many investors can't bear to do the necessary firing so they continue to use, and pay, an adviser they're unhappy with.

Your arrangement with the adviser about his fee

Quality tax advice is usually expensive. Top notch tax attorneys charge well over $100 an hour. The better accountants and non-certified people are also in that range. I knew of one tax adviser who is neither an accountant nor an attorney who charged $200 an hour. So if you're not careful, you'll end up spending more on your tax **adviser** than you are saving in taxes.

Many laymen are intimidated by accountants, attorneys, and other professionals. Often, they're reluctant to bring up fees because they think doing so will make them look "small time." "Big time" investors, they imagine, never discuss fees. As in, "If you need to ask 'how much,' you can't afford me."

The Bar Association Code says discuss fees up front

The American Bar Association has a Model Code of Professional Responsibility—a sort of code of ethics. Regarding fees, it says,

> *Ethical Consideration 2-19: As soon as feasible after a lawyer has been employed, it is desirable that he reach a clear agreement with his client as to the basis of the fee*

charges to be made. Such a course will not only prevent later misunderstanding but will also work for good client relations between the lawyer and the client. It is usually beneficial to reduce to writing the understanding of the parties regarding the fee, particularly when it is contingent. A lawyer should be mindful that many persons who desire to employ him may have had little or no experience with fee charges of lawyers, and for this reason he should explain fully to such persons the reasons for the particular fee arrangement he proposes.

That is terrible writing which I can't let pass without translating it into readable English. Here's what they are trying to say:

You should agree on the fee with your client as soon as possible. That will prevent misunderstandings and make for good relations. It's usually wise to put the fee agreement in writing, especially when it's contingent. And don't forget that many clients have little or no experience with lawyers. You should be especially careful to give those people a complete explanation of how the fee will be calculated.

Only a fool fails to discuss the fee

Regarding the notion that "big time" investors never discuss the fee, forget it. To borrow a line from the Midas Muffler commercial, "How do you think big time guys got to **be** big time guys?" Not by giving blank checks to their tax advisers.

A good businessman controls his costs. To not do so is to risk becoming a **former** businessman. Professional fees for tax advice are no exception. I have seen many tax advice clients get hit with much bigger bills than they expected. In almost every case, that surprise can be traced to the same source—failure to agree on the fee at the outset.

Bring it up at the beginning—and put it in writing

I've worked with a number of tax attorneys and accountants. Rarely have **they** mentioned the fee up front—as urged by the Code of Professional Responsibility. That being the case, **you** initiate the fee discussion.

Here's how the discussion between you and the adviser should go.

Investor: "Bob, I want to exchange out of my Springfield property. I'll need you to check the listing agreement and exchange agreement. And I might need you for other things that come up. What will you charge?"

Adviser: *"Well, a lot of things can come up, Jack, so I can't give a fixed price. If I did, I'd have to pad it to protect myself. My **hourly** rate is $150."*

Investor: "OK. For now, all I need you to do is look over the listing agreement to make sure there's nothing in it that would jeopardize the exchange. Think you can do that in less than an hour?"

Adviser: *"Probably."*

Investor: "Fine, here it is. I'd like to have it back Tuesday. Is that a problem?"

Adviser: *"No."*

Investor: "I figure it'll take an hour or less. If it looks like it's going to run over an hour, Bob, please call me before you continue. OK?"

Adviser: "Will do."

As soon as you get back to your office, send the adviser a note restating the agreement:

"$150 an hour. Call before going over an hour."

Time and materials

Most real estate investors know that you should not deal with subcontractors on a "time and materials" basis. But they **will** accept it when dealing with a tax adviser. That's probably necessary because most attorneys and accountants insist on doing business that way. But that doesn't mean you have to give the adviser a blank check. Set a **limit**.

Warning: Some tax advisers will agree to the limit, then ignore it. Don't pay the bill. Send them the agreed amount and a copy of the agreement. I had to do that with a publishing attorney once. She apologized and adjusted the bill down to the agreed amount.

> **NOTE**
> **Setting a limit on tax adviser fees is one of the most important points in this book.**

Insist on an itemized bill

Do not tolerate bills that say merely, "For services rendered: $604." Barry Gallagher's book *How to Hire a Lawyer* has an excellent chapter on what a legal bill should look like—including a sample of a properly detailed bill.

50 tax preparers get 50 different answers for 50 different fees

Money Magazine does an annual survey in which they ask 50 different tax preparers to do the same tax return. They usually get 50 different answers for 50 different fees. Of course, there's only supposed to be **one** right answer. One year, the tax due ranged from $7,202 to $11,881. The preparer who charged the lowest fee—$187—said the tax due was $9,224. The guy who charged the highest fee—$2,500—said the tax due was $8,123. The low fee was H&R Block; the high one, Deloitte Haskins & Sells.

Advisers who know exchanges

Bob Baldassari, CPA, MS—Taxation
Brown, Dakes, Wannall and Nobrega, PC
3025 Hamaker Ct. Suite 401
Fairfax, VA 22031
703-698-6260

Nicholas P. Brountas, LLB
Vafiades, Brountas & Kominsky
23 Water Street
Bangor, ME 04401
207-947-6915

Bruce H. Burkholder, JD
Wiles, Doucher, Van Buren & Boyle
115 West Main Street
Columbus, OH 43215
614-221-5216

Jack Campbell, JD, LLM (Taxation)
P.O. Box 352
Albuquerque, NM 87103
505-842-5351

David DeJong, JD, LLM, CPA,
Chair—County Bar Assn. Tax Section
Stein, Sperling, Bennett, DeJong
25 West Middle Lane
Rockville, MD 20850
301-340-2020

Brooke Gabrielson, JD, LLM
Howser, Gertner & Brown
4340 Campus Drive, Suite 100
Newport Beach, CA 92660
714-852-8500

Mike Garcia, JD
Law Offices of Manuel D. Garcia
Grosvenor Center, Suite 2550
733 Bishop Street
Honolulu, HI 96813
808-522-0755

Richard Goodman, JD
One Kaiser Plaza, Suite 701
Oakland, CA 94612
510-763-2300

Harold Justman, JD
Fimmel, Justman & Rible
3130 LaSelva Drive, Suite 307
San Mateo, CA 94403
415-573-0307

John G. Karones, JD
547 Williamsburgh Road
Glen Ellyn, IL 60137
708-858-2226

Roger Lageschulte, LLB
1155 North 130th, Suite 310
Seattle, WA 98133
206-368-8656

Mark Lee Levine, JD, LLM, CCIM,
MAI, PhD, SRS, CPM
2303 E. Dartmouth Avenue
Englewood, CO 80110
303-758-2221

Joseph Lipari, JD
Roberts & Holland
30 Rockefeller Plaza (20th floor)
New York, NY 10112
212-586-5200

Susan M. McLaurine, CPA
Johnston, Gremaux & Rossi
500 Lennon Lane
Walnut Creek, CA 94598
510-944-1881

Robert Mercurio, JD
Lane & Mittendorf,
99 Park Avenue
New York, NY 10016
212-972-3000

Bill Merritt, JD, MBA, LLM
Merritt & Tenney
200 Galeria Parkway, NW, Suite 500
Atlanta, GA 30339
404-952-6550

Tom Nitti, JD, Certified Specialist
Taxation Law
1255 Lincoln Blvd. (3rd Floor)
Santa Monica, CA 90401
310-393-1524

David Scatena
Polly, Scatena, Gekakis & Co.
Suite 304, 655 Mariners Island Boulevard
San Mateo, CA 94404
415-578-1200

Michael Smith, JD, CPA
Gambrell, Clarke, Anderson & Stolz
3600 First Atlanta Tower
Atlanta, GA 30383
404-577-6000

John Southerland, JD
2033 North Main Street, Suite 700
Walnut Creek, CA 94596
510-932-8500

John C. Suttle, JD, CPA, LLM, MBA
Certified Specialist Taxation Law
50 California Street, Suite 700
San Francisco, CA 94111
415-781-0250

Charles W. Thompson, JD, LLM
Lippenberger, Thompson & Welch
250 Montgomery St., Suite 500
San Francisco, CA 94104
415-421-5300

Christopher von Gal, JD, LLM
100 Colony Square, Suite 1800
1175 Peachtree Street, N.E.
Atlanta, GA 30361
404-892-8300

William Wasserman, JD
Loeb & Loeb
1000 Wilshire Blvd., Suite 1800
Los Angeles, CA 90017
213-688-3402

Louis S. Weller, JD
Weller, Drucker & Brooks
425 California Street (18th Floor)
San Francisco, CA 94104
415-434-0400

Allan J. Weiner, JD, CPA
Melrod, Redman & Gartlan
1801 K Street, N.W.
Washington, DC 20006
202-822-5300

Exchange Facilitators

(Not needed generally, but may help if you or your attorney is inexperienced at exchanges.)

Chicago Deferred Exchange Corp.
111 W. Washington, ML 0648
Chicago, IL 60602
312-630-2931

Bill Kramer
750 Hammond Drive
Atlanta, GA 30328
404-843-2500

Brandt Nicholson
San Francisco Bay Counties Exchange
Services
153 Bulkley Avenue
Sausalito, CA 94965
415-332-9116

NOTE: The above tax advisers do not necessarily endorse anything in this book. Nor do I know enough about them to guarantee their work.

NOTE ALSO: The above tax advisers are **not** in the free advice business. Please do not expect them to answer your questions without your paying for their time.

I'm looking for **additional** advisers to recommend. Especially in areas where I do not now list any like the Northeast, Midwest, Florida, and Texas. If you know of an adviser who is good and whose experience includes **exchanging**, please let me know his or her name and phone number.

The Best Lawyers in America

A book titled *The Best Lawyers in America* is published periodically. It is based on a survey of lawyers who rate their fellow lawyers. That won't tell you who gives lousy service. But it should be useful otherwise.

However, I consulted one of these attorneys, once. To my amazement, he misstated some of the most basic laws in his specialty.

It lists 7,200 lawyers by city and specialty. Real estate and tax are among the specialties listed. The book costs $95 which makes it a good one to ask your local **library** to order. The address is Woodward/White, 129 First Avenue, S.W., Aiken, SC 29801 (Telephone: 803-648-0300). If you can't find it in a library, better you should spend $95 for its recommendations than pay a mediocre lawyer hundreds of dollars.

5

Doing Battle with the IRS

What to do if you're audited

An audit starts with a form letter. For most people, it's a moment of terror. It shouldn't be. That terror usually reflects more ignorance than reality.

Ignorance is one reason people fear audits. Another is that they've cheated on their taxes. For example, they may have claimed a medical deduction for a personal expense which doesn't qualify as a medical deduction. According to a poll taken by *Psychology Today* magazine, 38% of their readers cheat on their income taxes.

People who cheat did not learn to do so in this book and I have little sympathy for them.

Aside from the moral, ethical, and legal reasons for not cheating, there are **practical** reasons. Most cheating is nickel and dime stuff. But as a result of their nickel-and-dime cheating, taxpayers are terrified of an audit.

In order to avoid an audit, they take conservative positions all over their tax return. I'll bet you dollars to doughnuts that the extra taxes they pay because of their efforts to avoid audit far exceed the nickel-and-dime savings they achieved by cheating.

Another practical reason for not cheating is that you may get caught. Getting caught cheating on your income taxes can cost you your reputation. Your reputation is far more important than your money. As someone once said,

A reputation is like fine china: easily cracked, and never really repaired.

Don't cheat

Don't cheat. Don't cheat because it's wrong. Don't cheat because the audit-avoidance that cheating requires costs you more than the cheating saves. Don't cheat because it could cost you your most valuable asset, your reputation.

Henceforth, I'll assume that you haven't cheated. In which case, the audit notice should be viewed the way you would view a challenge to play chess or tennis or some other game.

An audit is usually a limited investigation

An audit is an investigation, in part. The typical taxpayer envisions the auditor going over everything. There is a type of audit known as a Taxpayer Compliance Management Program audit (TCMP) which goes over everything...but that's a random-selection, government research project. TCMP "auditees" are selected according to social security numbers. You do not get selected for a TCMP because of a questionable item on your return. Besides, only about 40,000 TCMPs are done every two years. I was selected for a TCMP audit on my 1988 return.

The normal audit (over two million a year) does not go over everything. The IRS classifiers (the folks who decide which returns to audit) identify an average of **three items per return**. Both classifiers and auditors are supposed to identify "all significant items"—but they haven't got time.

They usually stick to the classified items

If an auditor spots a "significant item" during an audit of other items, he's supposed to pursue it. In reality, he's inclined to stick to the items identified by the classifier. A General Accounting Office (GAO) study (G G D-79-59 "IRS' Audits of Individual Taxpayers And Its Audit Quality Control System Need To Be Better") found that auditors examined an **un**classified item only about 16 to 18% of the time. And at the time of that study, expanding the audit had to be approved in advance by the auditor's supervisor.

So unless you antagonize the auditor, or force him to expand the audit by blurting something out, the audit will most likely be confined to the items specified in the initial letter. In most cases, you'll probably find that the items the IRS wants to audit are not the ones you feared.

Fight every item

"Charitable contributions! That's what they want to audit! I was afraid it was about my exchange."

Don't tell them about your exchange. Go to the audit and fight like heck over your charitable contributions. If you go in and say "I'll pay" with an obvious look of relief, the auditor's likely to get suspicious and dig further.

Preparing for the audit

If the item being audited is clear cut, just get the receipt or document which proves the deduction is legit. If the item is a judgmental one, you've got work to do.

These matters are supposed to be decided on the **quantity** and **quality** of evidence you can muster to support your position. And most of the time, they probably are decided on that basis. So gather as much of the best evidence you can.

You should think of yourself as a lawyer preparing to argue a case in court. Matter of fact, it could end up being exactly that. But at the outset, the "court" is the meeting with the auditor. The better job you do there, the less chance you'll have to spend additional valuable time on appeals within the IRS and the courts. In perhaps a majority of the cases, your time is more valuable than the money in dispute.

But never forget that the decisions as to how much tax you owe will be made by human beings—whether it's the auditor, or a tax court judge. Whether he likes you, whether he has a hangup about the type of deduction in question, pressures from his superiors, etc. can affect his decision.

Get help from a pro

If the audit involves significant amounts of money, or if there's even a hint of criminal charges, get a pro to help. I explained how to find and select a competent tax adviser in the previous chapter. If you don't have an adviser, notice of an upcoming audit is a good time to get one.

Who goes? You? Your adviser? Or both?

I recommend both—until you have a great deal of confidence in your adviser—the kind of confidence that comes only from observing him work over an extended period. You can make sure the adviser is representing you well and he can prevent you from being intimidated by the auditor.

In her book, *How to Survive a Tax Audit*, Mary L. Sprouse says, "I am sometimes appalled by the indifferent, perfunctory, negligent, and slovenly representation some taxpayers pay for. Often these taxpayers have given their representatives complete discretion to act on their behalf and are oblivious to their peril." She says that in some audits, it's apparent that the adviser **never looked at his client's tax return until the audit**. Ms. Sprouse was an attorney and IRS audit manager. I represented myself and my IRS auditor said that was quite unusual.

There's a similarly disquieting note in Holloran's "Strategy When Going to Conference and Appellate" in *Federal Tax Practice and Procedure*. He says approximately 60% of the tax advisers who represent clients before the IRS appeals conferees are unprepared at the initial conference. No doubt **100%** sent bills to their clients though.

Eleventh hour preparation

The week or so before the audit meeting, I strongly recommend that you read the audit preparation sections of several excellent books—most written by former or current IRS agents. This is to make sure you enter the audit with the proper attitude toward the auditor. It would be best, if you could get all of these books. They're all relatively brief and readable. Get as many as you can, in any event.

How to Survive a Tax Audit by Mary Sprouse
All You Need to Know About the IRS by Paul Strassels
The April Game by Diogenes
In This Corner, the IRS by J.R. Price
Pay Less Tax Legally by Barry Steiner

At some time during the audit process, you should also read:

Your Income Tax by J.K. Lasser (read Chapter 38 "What happens after you file your return")
Federal Tax Guide Prentice-Hall paragraphs 39,611 through 41,831 cover procedures relevant to fighting the IRS
The Taxpayer's Audit Survival Manual by Vernon K. Jacobs and Charles W. Schoeneman

There's an excellent section on preparing for an audit in Saltzman's *IRS Practice and Procedure* (paragraph 8.06[4]).

What you're up against

The average taxpayer believes the IRS and its auditors are all-knowing and all-powerful. Not true. Not even close.

As I said at the outset of this chapter, most people fear the IRS. That fear derives more from ignorance than reality. Let me try to eliminate or at least reduce the fear by reducing the ignorance.

An average of 115,360 people worked for IRS in 1989. They had to deal with 199,567,000 income tax returns.

Billions of things to check

I don't have statistics on it but let's assume that the average tax return includes five forms, each of which has 70 numerical entries. That's a total of 69,848,450,000 entries for those IRS employees to examine. They also had to process thousands of Freedom of Information Act requests, requests for miscellaneous public documents, Justice Department requests, and Privacy Act requests. And they have to process all those 1099s and W-2s and other forms. In all, IRS received about a billion information documents a year. So they have a bit more to do than harass little ol' you.

IRS has dozens of other duties on top of the data avalanche

They've got just one year to process all that stuff because come next April 15th, another 70 billion numbers and a billion information documents will cascade down upon them. And during that year, they've also got to have their Christmas party, attend continuing education sessions, take vacations, answer taxpayer questions, send refund checks and return forms, etc., etc., etc.

Auditing is not the IRS's main job

Add to that the fact that auditing is not the main job of the IRS. The main job is simply processing those 200 million returns. The IRS has more data processors than it has auditors. Finding understatements of taxes is a secondary role.

Sure, they've got computers, and computers can help with the mathematical computations. But the essence of aggressive tax avoidance is the position you take on **judgmental** questions. The computer can check your math, but it cannot second guess your judgment.

Furthermore, the numbers which appear on your tax return are in many cases only the tip of an iceberg of calculations which do not appear on your return. The computer can only check calculations for which all of the necessary numbers are on the return. It cannot, for example, analyze the improvement ratio you chose for your building, because it has no data for doing so. That has to be done by a human auditor.

Of the 115,360 people working for IRS in 1989, only 29,898 fell under the category of "Examinations" (auditing). So, it is we 200,000,000 taxpayers against 30,000 auditors. We have them outnumbered 6,667 to one. Starting to feel a little bit better about it?

Who are the auditors?

IRS has a **mystique**. The dictionary says that "mystique" refers to a "body of attitudes that become associated with a person or institution and give it a superhuman or mythical status." You can make rational judgments as to how to deal with IRS only if that mystique is stripped away. Too many tax decisions are being made on the basis of the mystique rather than the reality.

There is an excellent description of the personality, training, educational achievements (or lack of them) of the typical IRS employee in Paul Strassels' *All You Need to Know About the IRS*.

IRS pay is modest

The average member of the examinations part of IRS received pay **and benefits** of $41,033 in 1989. Private tax advisers generally make much more.

They do not admit to working for the IRS when asked in social situations because hatred of the IRS is so pervasive.

A significant percentage of IRS auditors, maybe the one you're talking to, do not want to work for the IRS. They want to work for people like you. They're only working for the IRS to improve their resume. Then they quit and become tax advisers.

The auditor is under time pressure

When he's at work in the field, the auditor is under constant time pressure. His bosses want him to close cases as soon as possible. The basic idea is to get some money out of the taxpayer, close the case, and move on to the next one. Doing the world's greatest audit on you is not encouraged. Audits are supposed to be completed within 26 months of when the return was filed.

So forget the notion that IRS auditors are superhuman—but don't underestimate them either. They **do** have some valuable experience and they do know how the IRS works—which puts you at somewhat of a disadvantage.

What IRS is really trying to do with their audits

Part of the reason for audits is to get the extra taxes they bring in. But the main reason is to intimidate the rest of us. The Commissioner of Internal Revenue admitted that. In response to a question at a Congressional hearing, IRS Commissioner Donald Alexander said, "Congressman, the truth is that we have such a limited budget, such limited manpower to enforce the income tax laws and collect the revenue that the only way we can keep people in line, the only way we can keep them honest and paying their taxes, is to keep them afraid."

We've all seen western movies where two or three "good guys" have the task of capturing a much larger group of "bad guys." It's night time and the bad guys are gathered around a campfire in the woods. The good guys are outnumbered, but the bad guys don't know that.

So the good guys hit upon a plan. They'll "surround" the bad guys. Then they'll come crashing through the trees making as much noise as they can. They'll yell and blow bugles and fire their weapons as fast as they can reload. They'll shake tree branches and throw rocks. And, of course the bad guys always fall for it and surrender.

The IRS is similarly outnumbered and outgunned. And they are using similar tactics. They use audits to make the maximum "noise." The purpose is to convince the public that, like Chicken Man in the radio series, "they're everywhere, they're everywhere!"

In his book, *All You Need to Know About the IRS*, Paul Strassels tells how he and his IRS colleagues, "joked about the best publicity the IRS could possibly receive. Put Johnny Carson through the wringer and have him tell a few, scary, funny stories on late-night TV."

If you'll watch the news media around the first three months of each year, you'll notice that IRS puts out an unusually high number of saber-rattling news releases. They also like to file cases against famous people about then.

What if you don't agree with the auditor's findings?

After you present the evidence to support your deductions, the auditor will decide how much additional tax, if any, you owe. He is under some pressure to bring home at least some of your bacon. So he's reluctant to let you off scot-free even if you've proved your case.

Tax advisers generally recommend throwing the auditor some sort of bone for appeasement. That approach galls me—but I can see that human nature may demand it. Being right isn't always enough. As someone's tombstone proclaimed,

He was right, dead right, as he sped along, but he's just as dead as if he were wrong.

An audit is a negotiation

Most people think of an audit as a sort of trial. To an extent, it is. But the auditor only has the power to compel you to go over his head. He does not have the power to make you pay the tax he thinks you owe. He does **not** have the power to penalize you.

An audit is more of a **negotiation** than a trial. You have the power to tell the auditor to stuff his assessment—and he knows it. You'll have to go over his head if you do that, but you can do it. The other side of the coin is that the auditor has the power to force you to go over his head or into Tax Court.

You don't **want** to go higher because it's time consuming, you might lose, and so forth. The auditor doesn't want you to go higher because it holds the case open, exposes his work to closer scrutiny by his superiors, etc. The IRS may be concerned that if you go to court and win, everybody will do what you did when thousands of tax advisers read about it in tax periodicals.

The auditor's ultimate objective is to get you to sign Form 870. Form 870 basically says, "I give up." The auditor writes on it how much tax and penalties, if any, he thinks you owe. Then he asks you to sign it. In a dispute with the IRS, this is the first moment of truth.

What Form 870 means

If you sign it, you must pay the tax in question—**now**.

If you sign it, you cannot haul the IRS into Tax Court. Remember Tax Court is the one where you don't pay until you **lose**.

The fact that you signed Form 870 does not prevent you from suing to get your tax payment, interest and penalties **back** in a District Court or the Claims Court.

The only good deal, if you can call it that, for signing the form and paying the tax is that the interest meter stops.

They may ask you to sign Form 872

IRS can't assess back taxes after the statute of limitations has run out. On most taxes, that's 3 years after you filed the return. If the amount in question was "in excess of 25% of the amount of gross income stated in the return," it's 6 years. If that deadline approaches during the audit, IRS will probably ask you to sign a Form 872 or 872a.

Form 872 is called a "Consent to Extend Time to Assess Tax." In it you agree to postpone their deadline for getting additional tax from you. Form 872 is often called a "Fixed-Date Waiver" because you set a **new** date after which they cannot assess back taxes. The alternative is called an "Open Ended Waiver" (officially it's a "Special Consent to Extend the Time to Assess Tax"). That's Form 872a. It gives the IRS **forever** to assess back taxes on the tax return in question.

You **do not have to sign** Form 872 or Form 872a if you don't want to. I see no reason why you would **ever** sign the open ended version. And the only reason to sign the other would be to accommodate an agent who's making a good faith effort to complete the audit promptly but just doesn't have enough time left. Other than that, feel free to refuse.

If you must, sign a *restricted* waiver

It's possible to **restrict** the waiver to one or two issues. To do so, you spell out in the agreement with IRS that you are extending the statute of limitations deadline **but only as it pertains to the specified items in dispute.** You have to be careful about the wording of this. IRS will try to word it in a way that's so broad that it's not really restricted.

If you sign a restricted waiver, the statute of limitations will take effect on the normal day for every aspect of your return **except** the specified items. I like that a lot better than the unrestricted fixed-date waiver. And I can think of no logical reason why IRS should object—although they probably will. Hang tough. They'll probably decide half a waiver is better than none.

Initial offers, target offers, final offers

When you negotiate over anything—purchase of real estate, foreign treaties, labor contracts—you ought to decide beforehand what your first, target, and final offers will be. This is true of an IRS audit as well.

Your first offer is what you put on your tax return. The IRS's first offer, is what the auditor seems to be asking for at the outset of the audit.

During the audit, you may give a little ground. Whether you should give ground, how much, and where, depends on how strong you think your position is versus the agent's position—as well as on how much is at stake.

If you and the auditor cannot resolve your differences

If you refuse to sign Form 870, the auditor bucks the case up to his superiors. Chapter 2 contains a diagram of the whole process from the audit to the Supreme Court. For more valuable information on this process, I strongly recommend that you read *IRS Practice and Procedure*. Here's a list of the various events in the protest chain and approximate times between the various events.

Protest schedule

File return	**14 to 18 months**
Audit letter	**two to four weeks,** possible to request postponement
Audit (typically takes one hour to several days)	**about one to seven days**
"Report of Individual Income Tax Changes" and opportunity for appeal within IRS	**thirty days**
(Notice of Deficiency)	**ninety days**

The 'window of invulnerability'

The statute of limitations stops the IRS from going after you. But it does not stop **you** from going after the **IRS.** You also have deadlines. But they are **different.** And the fact is that yours are **longer.** That creates a "window of invulnerability." During the window of invulnerability,

you can sue the government for a refund on a past year, but they can**not** assess you back taxes for that year. They can only defend themselves against your suit.

In order to take advantage of the "window of invulnerability," you must pay the tax then sue to get it back. You can**not** use the Tax Court. If you use the Tax Court, the IRS may, **at any time**, raise new issues regarding the year you are arguing about in Tax Court.

Example

Here's how the window of invulnerability works. After you are audited, you wait as long as possible to pay the tax—typically, that would be the 90th day after you received the notice of deficiency. That would mean you would be paying the tax about two years after the day you filed the return in question.

Let's say you file the return on April 15, 1983. You're audited and pay additional tax on April 15, 1985. After you pay the tax, you have **3 years** to file a refund request (Form 1040X). That means your deadline for filing for a refund is April 15, 1988.

But the IRS's deadline for raising new issues regarding the return you filed on April 15, 1983 is April 15, 1986—3 years after you filed the return.

Almost certainly your request for refund will be denied. And they have to do that within 6 months of receiving it. So if you waited 'til the last minute—April 14, 1988, and they take the full 6 months, you'll receive your denial on October 14, 1988.

Once you receive the denial, you have two years to file a lawsuit to get your money back. That means you have until October 14, 1990 to file your suit. That date is the tail end of the "window of invulnerability." The **beginning** of the "window of invulnerability" is April 15, 1989—the 6th anniversary of the filing of the return—the day the statute of limitations expires for all items except fraud. If you got an extension, the statute starts to run on your extended filing date.

So you have an 18-month "window of invulnerability" (in this example, the size of the window depends on how fast you are audited and how fast IRS responds to your 1040X) during which you can try to get back some of the taxes you paid for 1983—but during which IRS can**not** try to get additional taxes for that year from **you**.

Big disadvantage: no interest

As I told you earlier, IRS doesn't have to pay you interest until you tell them they owe you money. In this case, you don't tell them until April 15, 1988—so you lose 3 years of interest (you paid the tax on April 15, 1985).

I don't know how the interest works after you receive the denial. Maybe they wipe out the fact that you sent in the 1040X as far as interest is concerned. Or maybe the interest stops accruing from the day you get the denial until you file suit. Or maybe you get it for the whole time from 1040X filing until winning the suit. I don't know because the law is so new.

In any event, if the invulnerability is important to you (for example, you're scared of being declared a dealer), you should file your suit **the day after the 6 year statute of limitations runs out.** Then the interest meter will start running or resume running or whatever. Even though you may have a year or more after the 6 year statute expires, there's no point to any delay beyond that expiration.

A bigger disadvantage in my mind is the loss of the real estate return you could have earned on that money. Remember you have to **win** the law suit to get your money and interest. If you file over 6 years after the return was filed, by the time you win the trial, approximately **10** years will have elapsed. For 8 of those 10 years, IRS had your money. A lot of real estate investors have become millionaires in less time than that. That's why the Tax Court is generally better. And there's no "window of invulnerability" in Tax Court.

But always use the 'window of invulnerability' when not in tax court

If, however, you decide **not** to go into Tax Court, do not throw away the biggest benefit of the District Court and Claims Court—the "window of invulnerability." **Always** wait until the last minute to file your 1040X; i.e., just before the third anniversary of the return due date. Then, always wait until the "window of invulnerability" begins before you file your suit in District or Claims Court.

Your chances if you appeal within IRS

The IRS Annual Report does not give these figures anymore. But when they last did, tens of thousands of taxpayers appealed the auditor's tax bill within IRS. The taxpayer and the IRS agreed to settle about 76% of the cases at that stage. The average tax paid in those cases was only 26.58% of what the auditor said was owed. So appeal.

Don't miss the tax court deadline

Once you've received a Notice of Deficiency, you have a choice. You can fill out a form (called a "petition") and send it to the **Tax Court** or you can **pay the tax**.

In order to get into Tax Court, you **MUST** meet the ninety day deadline! There ain't no fooling around here. One day late and you're dead. NO EXCEPTIONS. No sad stories.

'Small' and 'large' Tax Court

If the amount in dispute is $10,000 or less, you have the option of using the "Small Tax Case Procedure"—a sort of small claims court for tax cases. The advantages of this are supposed to be "simplified procedure" and "early trial." The simplified procedure is good. We could do without the early trial, however.

The other difference between the small case procedure and the regular procedure is that neither party can appeal the decision if the small case procedure is used. You can get a free brochure called "Election of Small Tax Case Procedure & Preparation of Petitions" by writing to:

United States Tax Court
400 Second Street, N.W.
Washington, D.C. 20217

Small tax case schedule

File petition for small tax case	**about one year**
Trial calendar assignment	**sixty days**

Trial--no appeal of decision, pay tax upon receipt of decision

Regular tax case schedule

File petition	**about four years**
Trial calendar assignment	**ninety days**

Trial	**?**
Decision	**thirty days**
Motion to reconsider, vacate or revise	**ninety days** from decision
File notice of appeal	

You have to post a bond or collateral to appeal

At this time, you must either pay the tax or post collateral or an appeal bond. An appeal bond must be for twice the amount of tax, interest, and penalties owed. What does that mean? It means you turn over to the court government bonds or notes to hold as security or that you get a bonding company to agree to pay the government up to twice the amount owed if you lose your appeal.

What will the bonding company want? One that I spoke to said they'd charge about 3% per year for an amount of $100,000 and they'd demand full collateral in cash or the equivalent.

So you can earn interest on the assets held either by the court or the bonding company while you're waiting for a decision from the court of appeals. Of course, the government is also going to get its interest if you lose.

Appeals case schedule

File appeal	**about two years**
Hearing calendar assignment	**ninety days**
Hearing	**?**
Decision	**ninety days**

Notice of appeal--File application for Supreme Court hearing (called a writ of certiorari, "cert" for short) You have the right to appeal to the circuit court of appeals and they must hear the case if you do. The Supreme Court, however, can refuse to hear your case. If they do, the ballgame's over.

Supreme Court events

Decision on writ of certiorari
Hearing calendar assignment
Hearing
Decision

You probably will **not** get a chance to argue your case in front of the Supreme Court. They only take cases to resolve disputes between circuits or to handle very important matters.

So when you lose your application for cert, or your Supreme Court case, whichever comes first, it's all over. You must now pay your tax and any interest or penalties due. No more bonds or delays.

The time value of money again

Because of the time value of money, the relatively high returns available in real estate investing, and the relatively low interest rate on tax deficiencies, it pays to delay paying tax as long as possible.

I cannot imagine any reason to pay the tax IRS says you owe until the last day of the 90-day period following the Notice of Deficiency. If you don't plan to fight your case in the Tax Court, just wait until the last minute to pay the tax—that 90th day.

In the absence of other considerations (which I'll discuss shortly), the low interest rate and ability to postpone payment until you've lost the case makes fighting the case in the Tax Court worthwhile from a time value of money standpoint. There is, however, no time value of money advantage to fighting in District Court, Claims Court or the Appeals Courts.

Recent Tax Court decisions came down about six years after the tax year in dispute. So taking aggressive positions for which there is a reasonable basis will, at worst, get you 6 years use of the money at the current IRS interest rate.

And that assumes that you totally lose the case. Remember that you can win a complete or partial victory, too.

Should you fight?

The IRS auditor says you owe money. You explained why you think you're right...but he didn't buy it. Should you fight?

Fighting takes time. And time is money. If you use an attorney to represent you, or paid expert witnesses, fighting will require out-of-pocket payments. But **not** fighting costs money too—the tax you have to pay.

Setting "the principle of the thing" aside, the basic choice is which will cost you less—fight or flight.

There is also an important uncertainty—your chances of winning. The decision tree introduced in Chapter 3 is the proper way to make your decision. The difference is that the decision here is not whether to claim a particular deduction, but whether to fight. So you're starting at a different point on the tree.

Should you fight in Tax Court?

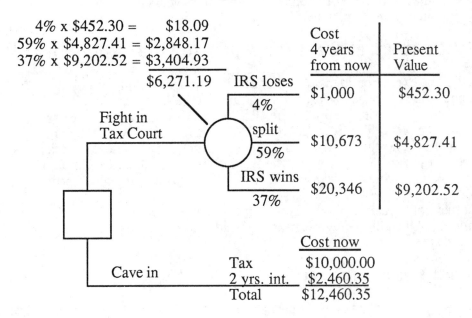

4% x $452.30 = $18.09
59% x $4,827.41 = $2,848.17
37% x $9,202.52 = $3,404.93
                  $6,271.19

	Cost 4 years from now	Present Value
IRS loses 4%	$1,000	$452.30
split 59%	$10,673	$4,827.41
IRS wins 37%	$20,346	$9,202.52

Fight in Tax Court

	Cost now
Tax	$10,000.00
2 yrs. int.	$2,460.35
Total	$12,460.35

Cave in

Note that the present value of the fight choice is greater than it was when looked at from the deduct or not position. That's because the outcome of fighting was 6 years off then—now it's only **4** years off.

But the cost of **not** fighting has gone up too—from $10,000 to $12,460.35 because of the 11% interest which has been accruing.

And even though the present value of the fight choice has gone up, it's still less than the pay option. And the worst thing that can happen if you fight—losing and paying $20,346, still has a smaller present value, $9,202.52 than giving up without a fight.

Again, I'll acknowledge that you and your tax adviser may question some of the probabilities or the cost of fighting. But even if the probability of your winning were **zero**, the **worst thing that can happen**, fighting would be the better choice. It would take a 100% probability of loss **and** a hefty increase in your attorney fee, to make giving up show a lower value than fighting.

The decision on fight or pay is closer than the decision on aggressiveness versus conservatism. But fighting still has a decisive edge.

Fight over large amounts, pay small ones

But no matter what assumptions you make, fighting in Tax Court **delays payment** of the tax and the value of that delay is significant. If you ran all sorts of scenarios through the tree, you'd find that the more money's at stake, the more it makes sense to fight.

Your probability of winning the case, which many advisers seem to regard as **paramount**, is really **almost irrelevant** at the Tax Court level (except that you cannot file the suit for purpose of delay). The reason is that you can earn more on the use of the money than the government charges you for using it while you're waiting for a decision.

The key variables in deciding whether to fight or not are the amount of tax the auditor wants and how much it will cost you to delay payment by filing a petition in Tax Court. The costs are primarily **your time** and any **fees charged by a tax adviser** for helping you with the fight.

The costs of fighting a $10,000 assessment are not that much different than the costs of fighting a $500 assessment. But the use of $10,000 for four more years is much more valuable than the use of $500. So you may want to pay the $500 rather than fight.

Take IRS to court at least once just for the experience

I will make one exception to that piece of advice, though. I think you ought to fight one just for the experience. Think of it as a sort of seminar and the value of the time you put into it as tuition. Seems to me everybody ought to take the IRS to Tax Court at least once (assuming you have a case). The "small claims" Tax Court is probably the place to do this "practice run."

I think you should do this because I suspect that you overestimate the difficulty of fighting the IRS. I suspect that you'll come out of the trial, even if you lose, exhilarated. That you'll have greatly increased confidence. That you'll say, "Hey, that wasn't anywhere near as bad as I thought it would be!"

I suspect that you'll learn from the experience of taking IRS to court. As a result, your post-trial attitude will be, "All right. You guys beat me once. But now I see how the game is played. Next time I won't make the same mistakes. Let's try that again."

Go watch a tax court trial

Another project you might want to undertake—either as preparation for a trial of your own or just for general purposes, is to visit the Tax Court to observe a trial. Call the Tax Court in Washington at 202-376-2754 and ask them when and where you can observe a Tax Court trial near your home. If you expect to use the Small Tax Case procedure, ask to observe a case being tried under that procedure.

Tax Court trials are usually held in federal buildings in major cities during business hours. They are free and open to the public. You just go in, sit down and watch. You can come when you want and leave when you want. If you work downtown, you can probably see such a trial by taking an early or late lunch one day.

Anything I can do to get you to lose your fear of the IRS and the courts will make you a more aggressive taxpayer. That, in turn will reduce your taxes. Neither the IRS nor the courts are as fearful as you probably think if you've never fought a deficiency assessment.

Traffic ticket trial

I once had an auto accident in a blizzard. A state trooper gave me a ticket for "driving too fast for conditions." He also suggested that I had a good chance of getting off because the electric speed limit signs on that road had been set too high at the time. So I checked "not guilty" on the form I received and went to the court on the appointed evening.

When I arrived, I found a court room full of other people who had received traffic tickets. They had also decided to plead not guilty.

Everyone was talking tough. They weren't going to let the cop get away with this, etc., etc. Then an officer barked "ALL RISE!" In marched a stern looking judge dressed in the traditional black robes and the bailiff started calling cases.

All the tough talk of a few minutes earlier notwithstanding, every single person who was called answered, "Guilty, your honor," when asked how they pleaded. Mind you, these were the same people who had sent in a form saying they intended to plead not guilty. If you wanted to plead guilty, you didn't have to go to court. You just sent your fine in by mail.

Why did they all plead guilty? Because they were totally intimidated by the judge and the setting.

When my name was called, I pleaded, "Not guilty." After all, I didn't drive all the way to the court for nothing. When I said those words, the crowd sucked in its breath as if I had just called a

Hell's Angel a sissy. The judge asked me two questions, said "Not guilty," and called for the next case.

After seeing that it was possible to plead not guilty and escape not only with your life but also with a victory, everyone who followed me also pleaded not guilty.

Don't be intimidated

I tell this story to illustrate how intimidated most people are when it comes to courts and judges. And to illustrate that you shouldn't be so intimidated. I suspect that one of the reasons the judge found me not guilty was that I was the first one who had given him a chance to be a judge. If everyone pleads guilty, he has nothing to do, you know.

By the same token, Tax Court judges don't want to find the taxpayer guilty every time either. So don't be so afraid. Don't be so sure that you'll lose. The judge is a human being just like you. He pays taxes too. He probably likes the IRS even less than you because he deals with them every day.

Your chances in Tax Court

54,076 taxpayers had the IRS in Tax Court in 1990. Of those, 9,326 chose the small tax case procedure. In all cases decided, IRS got only 27% of what it sought.

In **small** tax cases, IRS did better. But even there they only got 46% of what they wanted.

Your chances in District Court

In 1990, IRS won 65.2% of the cases; taxpayers, 23.2%. They split on 11.6%. In terms of dollars, taxpayers got back 18.2% of the refunds they wanted.

Your chances in the Claims Court

In 1990, IRS won 73.5%; taxpayers, 14.3%. They split on 12.2%. In terms of dollars, taxpayers got back 45.1% of the refunds they wanted.

Your chances in the Appeals Courts

Unless your case is better than most, you'll probably lose if you go to the Circuit Court of Appeals. In 1990, the IRS won 75.9% of the cases. In 5.9%, IRS won in part and the taxpayer won in part. Taxpayers only won 19% of the time.

The Supreme Court decided only four tax cases in 1990. IRS, 3; taxpayers, 1.

Actually, *your* chances may be different

The figures on how often taxpayers won in 1990 do not necessarily say how you'll do. That depends on the facts and how well you and/or your attorney present your case. It also depends on the mood of the judge and other factors.

The taxpayer often wins

You should know that the taxpayer's record in the courts is pretty good. Most people probably would flunk a quiz on how often the taxpayer wins. You are no longer in that group.

Next time an auditor tries to pressure you into signing Form 870, you should remember or refer to these figures.

What Happened to Taxpayers Who Refused to Cave In			
Level of Appeal	Taxpayer Total Victory	Taxpayer Partial Victory	Money to Taxpayer
Small Tax Court	5.0%	49.0%	54.0%
All Tax Court	4.0%	59.0%	73.0%
District Court	23.2%	11.6%	19.2%
Court of Claims	14.3%	12.2%	43.1%
Court of Appeals	19.0%	5.1%	?
Supreme Court	25.0%	0.0%	?

Summarizing your chances in court

In Tax Court, your chances of winning are barely relevant to deciding whether or not to fight there. You get the time value of money benefits if you fight whether you win or lose. So victory in Tax Court is a "bonus" which is not required to make fighting there worthwhile. Although you must have good grounds for filing the suit to avoid penalties for using the Tax Court for delay.

In the other trial courts (District Court and Claims Court), there is no time value of money advantage. This is because you must pay the tax first, then sue to get it back. As a result, you only fight in those courts when the probability that you'll win is good and the amount at stake is high. If you do the decision tree, you'll find that these two variables are decisive.

Should you fight in District Court?

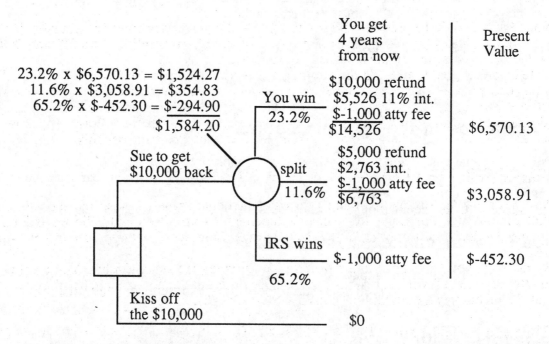

Note how this decision differs from fighting in Tax Court. In Tax Court, even the **worst** outcome was better than not fighting because the use of the money was worth more than the cost of fighting. But here, the worst outcome is **worse** than not fighting. It still makes sense to fight, however, given these assumptions, because the chances of a split or victory are relatively high.

In other words, District Court is a bit of a gamble.

Once you've lost in a trial court, the decision tree for the next step—appeal to the Circuit Court, changes again. Here's the decision tree on a $10,000 dispute.

Should you appeal?

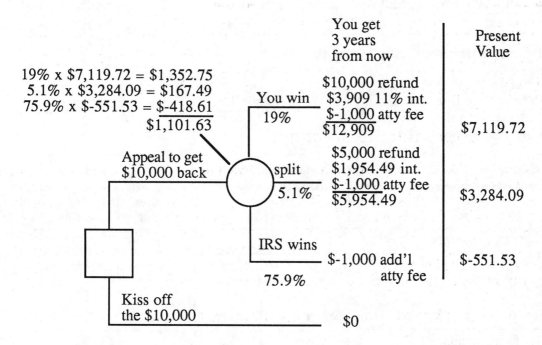

	You get 3 years from now	Present Value

19% x $7,119.72 = $1,352.75
5.1% x $3,284.09 = $167.49
75.9% x $-551.53 = $-418.61
           $1,101.63

Appeal to get $10,000 back

You win 19%
$10,000 refund
$3,909 11% int.
$-1,000 atty fee
$12,909 $7,119.72

split 5.1%
$5,000 refund
$1,954.49 int.
$-1,000 atty fee
$5,954.49 $3,284.09

IRS wins 75.9%
$-1,000 add'l atty fee $-551.53

Kiss off the $10,000 $0

Note that although the present values of the split and you win outcomes are relatively high, they are chewed to pieces by their probabilities. After applying probabilities of 9.5% and 2.0%, the weighted average of the appeal choice is only $253.95.

Note also that you do **not** add the attorney's fees for fighting at the District Court level to the fees for the Appeals Court level. This is because when you make the decision to go to the appeals court, the District fees are already spent. That's called a **"sunk cost"** and is utterly irrelevant to the decision to appeal further. That's a difficult concept for some people to grasp. The only factors which are relevant to deciding whether to continue are **future** costs and benefits.

Recalculate the attorney's fees if you wish

Attorneys may harrumph that there's no way you could argue a case at the appeals court for $1,000. Fine. Again, I urge you to recalculate the tree for **your** situation. I believe this **format** for analyzing the decision is correct. You'll have to make sure the **figures** you use in your situation are realistic.

By the way, you can calculate the **breakeven attorney fee** using algebra. You want to know what attorney fee "F" will make the appeal choice **equal** to the **not** appeal choice. Since the not appeal choice has a value of zero, the equation looks like this:

$$.759F + .5.1(\$3,284.09) + .19(\$7,119.72) = 0$$
$$.759F + \$167.49 + \$1,352.75 = 0$$
$$.759F = -\$1,502.24$$
$$F = -\$1,502.24/.759 = \$2,002.95$$

The $2,002.95 figure is the **present value** of the attorney fee. Using a 20% discount rate, we find that $2,002.95 is the present value of a $3,461 fee to be paid three years from now.

In other words, if your appeal will not cost you more than $3,461 if you lose, it makes sense to appeal given the other assumptions in this example. Again the bigger the amount in dispute, the more likely it makes sense to appeal because the attorney fee should be the same regardless of the amount.

Choosing which court is complex

I've given you a number of decision trees which purport to depict the decision on whether or not to fight. Although the trees provide a basic format which is valid, there are a number of other factors you should discuss with a tax attorney on cases involving large amounts.

Here are some of the factors:

Choice of Court Factors				
Factor	Small Tax Court	Tax Court	District Court	Court of Claims
Knowledge of your geographical area	No	No	Yes	No
CPA or enrolled agent can represent you	Yes*	Yes*	No	No
Jury trial	No	No	Yes	No
When pay tax	When lose	When lose	Before file	Before file
"Window of invulnerability"	No	No	Yes	Yes
Appeal?	No	Yes	Yes	Yes
"Common sense" oriented	Somewhat	No	Yes	No
Percentage of cases tax-related	100%	100%	Low	25%
IRS opportuniites to use discovery	Least	Least	Most	Medium
Leniency on admitting evidence	Most	Most	Least	?
History of court on pertinent cases	Research	Research	Research	Research
*If they pass the Tax Court's examination.				

There's a good section on choice of a court in Garbis and Schwait's *Tax Court Practice*.

Choice of court can be *very* important

The *Freeland*, *Morse*, and *Ginsburg* cases show how important choosing the right court can be. They were partners in an investment. They sold their property and claimed long-term capital gains treatment. IRS said no. IRS said they were **dealers** and wanted to tax their gain at **ordinary income rates**. (Ordinary income rates were much higher than long-term capital gains rates then.)

Freeland chose to fight in **Tax Court**. He lost. **Morse** chose to fight in the **Court of Claims**. He won. Both decisions came down **before** Ginsburg filed his suit. Not surprisingly, he filed in the Court of Claims. Also not surprisingly, he **won**. (*Freeland*, P-H TC Memo paragraph 66,283; *Morse v. U.S.*, 371 F 2d 474; *Ginsburg v. U.S.*, 396 F 2d 983) Freeland was ticked. So he appealed to the Ninth Circuit Court of Appeals. He lost again. (393 F 2d 573)

I must note, however, that Ginsburg would have been out of luck if it had gone the other way. That's because you lose your right to sue in Tax Court if you don't make the decision within 90 days of receiving your final audit determination from IRS. If the Court of Claims had decided **against** Morse, Ginsburg's only alternative would have been the District Court. The only thing in its favor at that point would be that it had not yet decided the case.

Getting creamed in Tax Court

I've said I generally favor Tax Court, because you don't pay until you lose there. The fact that Freeland lost there doesn't change my mind. But there's **another** important difference between Tax Court and the other courts. In District Court and Claims Court, you argue over **specified disputed items** on your return. In Tax Court, you ask the Court to **determine your tax for that year in question**. In other words, the court can agree with you, or agree with the IRS. Or even come up with a **higher figure than the IRS did**.

That's because of the law regarding the Tax Court and the "window of invulnerability" I described earlier. As soon as you file a Tax Court petition, the statute of limitations clock stops ticking on that tax year until the Court decides the case. If you pay the tax, then wait until after the statute of limitations has expired to file for a refund in one of the other two courts, you **can** limit the court to just deciding the issue you want to dispute.

Here are two horror stories you may hear from a tax attorney trying to talk you out of using the Tax Court. IRS wanted Ferguson to pay $1,200 more. He took them to Tax Court. Tax Court had good news and bad news for Ferguson.

The good news was, that he was right about the amount IRS claimed being incorrect. The bad news was that the **correct** tax for the year in question was $300,000! (*Ferguson*, 47 TC 11)

John J. Raskob would have liked to switch places with Ferguson. IRS said he owed $16,000. He took them to Tax Court. Tax Court said he owed $1,026,000! Ouch! (*Raskob*, 37 BTA 1283)

Don't overreact to these horror stories

Before you forever swear off the Tax Court, consider this. The Tax Court can't pull some huge figure out of the air. You have to have a huge amount of **income** in order for the Tax Court or anyone else to hit you with a huge tax bill. In most cases, you probably know what the worst figure the Tax Court could come up with is.

Dealer status is the prime danger for a real estate investor. Unfortunately, it's an almost ever-present danger.

The other side of the coin is that the Tax Court coming up with a higher figure than originally sought by IRS is unusual. The Ferguson and Raskob cases are pretty old.

If dealer status or some other possibility exists, you may want to put that into your decision tree. If the probability of such a new issue being brought up is significant, and the potential addition to your tax bill is great, you may want to skip the Tax Court so you can wait for the "window of invulnerability."

Decisions on whether to fight in court are business not legal decisions

When I tell you to discuss the choice of a court with a tax adviser, I'm not saying, "Do whatever your adviser says." **You** still make the decision. You simply take what the adviser tells you about the various factors and plug them into your decision tree.

For example, he may say the Court of Claims has been uniquely favorable to your position on the matter in dispute. So you would plug a higher probability of victory into the tree.

The main fault I find with attorneys on decisions of this kind is that they tend to think only in terms of victory or defeat. They tend to not think of the time value of money and generally don't know how to analyze combinations of probabilities and dollar outcomes.

Deciding whether to fight a tax matter in court is a business not a legal decision. Like any other business, fighting in court has risks, costs, and possible rewards. Decision trees and time value of money are what you learn in **business school**. As far as I know, lawyers are **not** taught such things. As a result, paradoxical as it may seem, they are ill-prepared to decide whether or not to fight court cases. They can, however, provide some relevant information for **your** decision.

Should you act as your own attorney?

A man who acts as his own attorney has a fool for a client.

Attorneys have been telling us that for years. I don't buy it—at least not completely.

Dermatologist 1, IRS attorney 0

Dr. Curphey didn't buy it either. He's the Honolulu dermatologist who deducted one bedroom of the condo he lived in as a home office. He claimed he used it exclusively to manage his six rental properties.

Although he had no legal training (I assume), Dr. Curphey took on Jerome Borison, Esq. Mr. Borison is one of the 900 attorneys employed by the IRS's Office of Chief Counsel.

Dr. Curphey won—without the aid of an attorney. **You** decide whether he had a fool for a client. Seems to me he'd have been a fool if he had paid an attorney to argue a case involving only $189. (*Curphey*, 73 TC 61)

Earlene Barker's $4,984 exchange

Earlene Barker's case involved much more money—$4,984—and a much more complex issue, a three-way exchange. But she also decided to do without an attorney—and she also beat the IRS.

Ms. Barker defeated IRS attorney Charles Cobb in Tax Court. (*Barker*, 74 TC 42)

Phil and Sue Long

Phil and Sue Long of Bellevue, Washington acted as their own attorneys. IRS said they owed $38,000 on some rental property they owned. By the time the dust had cleared, the IRS **owed the Longs $146.01**!

Factors to consider when deciding whether to use an attorney

1. **Criminal charges:** If you know or suspect that IRS may be considering criminal charges against you, get an attorney. Always ask to see the ID of the auditor. "Revenue Agents" conduct normal audits. If the auditor is a "Special Agent," cut the meeting off and get an attorney.

2. **Amount in dispute:** Dr. Curphey's case only involved $189. That would not even pay for two hours of most tax attorneys' time. The smaller the amount, the less sense it makes to hire an attorney.

3. **Complexity of the dispute:** The simpler the matter in dispute, the less the need for an attorney.

4. **Law versus fact:** Some disputes involve matters of fact; others, matters of law. An improvement ratio dispute is an example of a matter of fact. Legal knowledge helps less than expert testimony as to land values, building costs, etc. The more factual the case, the less the need for

legal knowledge. (If you're involved in a dispute of fact, and you really want to get into the Perry Mason role, peruse the books in your local law library for ideas.)

5. **The value of your time:** If your time is more valuable than what you must pay your attorney, use an attorney.

Basically, an attorney:

1. Increases your chance of winning
2. Gives you more "muscle" for negotiating with IRS
3. Saves your time.

Having an attorney does **not guarantee** you'll win the case. You probably already knew that. But acting as your own attorney **does not guarantee that you'll lose either**. And as I've pointed out many times, winning isn't everything. Delay can be more valuable than victory in Tax Court disputes.

So I urge you to reject the "fool for a client" bromide. Replace it with:

> *A man who acts as his own attorney had better be able to afford the increased chances of losing the case and the extra time that representing himself entails.*

In disputes involving small amounts of money and simple issues, most of us can afford to act as our own attorneys.

I have acted as my own attorney three times

I've been to court three times acting as my own attorney. I already described the traffic ticket case.

In one other case, I sued a company in U.S. District Court. I acted as my own attorney on the advice of my attorney. In that case, the law limited what I could win to $1,000. So my attorney said, "Why don't you try it yourself." I did—and had a ball. I cannot tell you the outcome because we settled out of court. As part of the settlement, I agreed not to disclose the terms.

My third case was also settled on terms I agreed not to disclose.

I will say, however, that I am glad I acted as my own attorney.

I do not want to leave you with the impression that you should never use an attorney. But I do want to rid you of the common notion that you are a fool to go into court without one.

As I said in the previous chapter, you ought to take the IRS to court once just for the experience (assuming you have good grounds). After doing that, you'll be in a much better position to decide whether you need an attorney the next time.

86

6

Reed's Rules for Understanding Income Taxes

Few subjects are as widely misunderstood as income taxes. To make sure you don't fall prey to those misconceptions, I offer these Rules.

Reed's Rule #1: Income is good.

I once heard a man win a substantial amount of cash on a radio contest. Upon winning, he told the announcer he did **not** want the money. The reason he gave was that it would move him into a **higher tax bracket**. I suspect that most of the people who heard him were impressed with his financial acumen. That would be inappropriate. He was dead wrong.

If the rate at which you pay taxes applied to every dollar you earn, turning down additional income would make sense in many cases. Here's an example:

Let's say your taxable income is $34,000 which puts you in the 15% bracket (married filing jointly in 1991). The next bracket is 28% and applies to income **over** $34,000 but not over 82,150. The bracket above $812,150 is 31%. If you win a $100 prize in a radio contest, your taxable income will be $34,100. That puts you into the 28% bracket.

15% of $34,000 is $5,100. 28% of $34,100 is $9,548. By accepting a $100 prize, you've raised your taxes by $9,548 - $5,100 = $4,448. So you turn down the prize, right? Yes, **if** the tax rate applied to every dollar of income. But it does **NOT**.

It's marginal tax brackets that matter

That is **not**, repeat **not** how taxes work. The tax rate, 15% or 28% or whatever, does not apply to **every** dollar you earn. It applies only to additional or "marginal" dollars. Here's the tax rate schedule (married filing jointly) for 1991.

1991 Tax Rates: Married Filing Jointly				
Taxable Income			Plus percent	Of the dollars
Over	But not over	Pay	on excess	over
$0	$34,000	$0	15%	$0
$34,000	$82,150	$5,100	28%	$34,000
$82,150		$18,582	31%	$82,150

As you can see, the tax payable if your taxable income is $34,000 is $5,128 [$5,100 + (28% x $100)]. That's not 28% of $34,100. The 28% rate is only applied to the amount **above** $34,000. Income **below** that rate is taxed at a rate of only 15%.

The tax payable on taxable income of $34,100 (your normal income plus the $100 radio prize) is $5,128—just $28 more than without the prize. So you are required to give 28% of the prize to Uncle Sam—but you get to keep the other $72 after taxes.

If you rejected the $100 of prize money in this case, you'd be throwing away 72 after-tax dollars. That's dumb.

You never turn down income

Is there ever a case where it would make sense to refuse income because of the taxes on it? No.

That could only occur where the tax on the additional income was **more than 100%**. There is no such tax anywhere in the world as far as I know. (Sweden had a 103% tax rate briefly. They reduced it when they discovered what they had done.)

There are also some cases involving welfare type payments where additional income puts you outside the eligibility range. The combination of taxes on the additional income and the loss of welfare benefits can exceed the amount of the income. This is, in effect, a marginal tax rate of more than 100%. In almost every case, the welfare recipient does what the radio prize winner did. He refuses the money.

But I assume that the excesses of both the Swedish and American welfare states are not relevant to your situation. The maximum marginal tax bracket in the United States is 49.5% (I'll explain below). So no matter how much money you make, you always get to keep at least 50.5% of it. If the radio winner made $125,000 a year, he'd still be $50.50 better off accepting that prize than refusing it.

So turning down income to avoid being in a higher tax bracket does not make sense. Most of us don't have the opportunity that radio contestant had. But we **do** have opportunities to make money. If you ever hear yourself turning down such an opportunity because it would increase your income tax, an alarm should go off in your mind and a deep voice should start repeating "Income is good." There is no tax bracket so high that it makes turning down income sensible.

The Tax Reform Act of 1986 made tax brackets much more complicated

According to the media, the Tax Reform Act of 1986 "simplified" the tax law—at least as far as the number of brackets is concerned.

I beg your pardon.

The Tax Reform Act of 1986 **complicated** the question of what your marginal tax rate is unbelievably. For starters, it used to be that the higher your taxable income, the higher your tax rate. That was the case in 1987. And in 1990, it still worked that way—**up to a point**. But then it **reversed direction**. And additional dollars of income were then taxed at **lower** rates than the previous dollars. No kidding.

The tax table for 1990 was simply 15% up to $32,450 and 28% from there to $78,400 (married filing jointly). Above $78,400, your rate was 33% up to a point. Then it dropped gradually back to 28% over a $100 span. That point depends on how many exemptions you claimed.

Your 1990 marginal tax rate dropped back to 28% when...

Number of exemptions	Taxable income exceeded
2	$185,730
3	$197,210
4	$208,590
5	$220,070
6	$231,550

Add another $11,480 to the taxable income amount for each exemption above six exemptions. In 1991 and thereafter, you lose 2% of your personal exemption for every $2,500 or fraction thereof by which your adjusted gross income exceeds $100,000. You also get penalized to the tune of 3% of certain itemized deductions if your adjusted gross exceeds $100,000 up to a maximum of 80% of your itemized deductions.

Then there's the $25,000 passive loss exemption

If:

- Your adjusted gross income, not counting real estate, is $100,001 to $149,999, **and**
- You "actively participate" (I'll explain later) in rental real estate activity, **and**
- You and your spouse own at least 10% of the rental property in question, **and**
- Your interest in the rental property is **not** a limited partnership interest,

then you may have been in the 57.75% marginal tax bracket in '87 and the 49.5% marginal tax bracket in '88. Here's why.

If your adjusted gross income (AGI), not counting real estate, is less than $150,000, you get at least part of the benefit of the $25,000 passive loss limit exemption. The passive loss limit rule says roughly that rental property cannot show a loss for tax purposes until you get rid of it.

The $25,000 **exemption** says, "All right, we'll let you little Mom and Pop landlords deduct up to $25,000 in losses—but only if your adjusted gross not counting real estate is $100,000 or less. Once your AGI goes **over** $100,000, we start to **not** feel sorry for you—and we take away 50¢ of that $25,000 exemption for every dollar your AGI goes over $100,000."

For example, if your AGI is $100,001, you can't deduct $25,000 in rental property losses. You can only deduct $24,999.50 of rental property losses. At AGI of $100,002, $24,999, and so on until your AGI hits $150,000 at which point the entire $25,000 exemption will be gone (50% x $50,000 = $25,000).

Your bracket without rental property was 38.5% in '87 if your AGI ws $100,000 to $150,000. But if each additional dollar of AGI causes you to lose 50¢ of rental property loss deductions—and your property shows a tax loss—there's a sort of "surcharge" added to your bracket. In '87, the "surcharge" was 50% x 38.5% = 19.25% which when added to your already 38.5% bracket made a total bracket of 38.5% + 19.25 = 57.75%.

In '91 and thereafter, the maximum bracket is 31%. So the max bracket for active rental property owners with rental property losses is 31% + (50% x 31%) = 31% + 15.5% = 46.5%.

Example of 57.75% bracket

Here's an example to prove it.

Joe's '87 AGI not counting real estate was $110,000. He owns rental property which showed a $24,000 loss for tax purposes. He lost $10,000 x 50% = $5,000 of his ability to deduct $24,000 in rental property losses because his AGI exceeded $100,000 by $10,000. $24,000 - $5,000 = $19,000.

So his taxable income was $110,000 - $19,000 (rental property losses) = $91,000. His tax payable in '87 was (from '87 table) $24,590 + (38.5% x $1,000) = $24,590 + $385 = $24,975.

If he earns one more dollar of non-rental property income, his AGI will be $110,001. And he will lose $10,001 x 50% = $5,000.50 of his ability to deduct his $24,000 in rental property losses. $24,000 - $5,000.50 = $18,999.50.

So his taxable income will be $110,001 - $18,999.50 = $91,001.50. And his tax payable in '87 was (from table) $24,590 + (38.5% x $1,001.50)= $24,590 + $385.58 = $24,975.58.

See? His income went up by **one dollar** from $110,000 to $110,001. And his tax went up by **58¢** from $24,975 to $24,975.58. So he was in the 58% marginal tax bracket. (57.75% actually—I rounded to the nearest penny.)

When his AGI clears $150,000, he **dropped back** to the 38.5% bracket in '87, 33% bracket in '88.

Reed's Rule #2: Some kinds of income are better than others.

I'm not done yet. The "bracket simplification" of the Tax Reform Act of 1986 gets even more complex.

You are in **more than one** bracket at any given time. That's because under the TRA '86, there's income and there's income. Your bracket if you get an additional dollar of **passive** income is much different than your bracket for an additional dollar of **non-passive** income.

Now passive income is the most privileged kind of taxable income—because you can deduct **any** kind of deductible expenditures or losses from it. But you can only deduct a **limited** number of things from non-passive income.

In the example above, let's say Joe got an additional dollar of **passive** income, not an additional dollar of adjusted gross income other than real estate. That would mean his rental property loss would be $24,000 - $1 = $23,999. Then his tax would have been:

AGI	$110,000
Rental property loss	$23,999
Allowable loss deduction	$18,999
Taxable income	$91,001
Tax (from '87 table)	$24,975.**39**

Note that by earning one more dollar of passive income, Joe's tax only went up 39¢ (38.5¢ actually). So he was in the 38.5% marginal bracket if he earned an additional dollar of **passive** income. But he was in the 57.75% bracket if he earned an additional dollar of **non-passive** income.

There's still a zero-percent bracket

Suppose Joe had **not** $24,000 of rental property losses—but **$34,000**. That means he was over the limit of $25,000. Then his tax would have been:

AGI	$110,000
Rental property loss	$34,000
Allowable loss deduction	$20,000 ($25,000 - $5,000)
Taxable income	$90,000
Tax (from '91 table)	$21,015.50

Now give him one additional dollar of **passive** income.

AGI	$110,000
Rental property loss	$33,999
Allowable loss deduction	$20,000
Taxable income	$90,000
Tax (from '91 table)	$21,015.50

So what is the marginal tax rate on an additional dollar of passive income when you're already deducting all the passive losses you can? **Zero** percent!

In other words, when you've got more passive losses than you can deduct currently, you are in the zero percent bracket as far as additional **passive** income is concerned. And you will **continue** to be in the zero percent bracket until you get so much passive income that you start using less than your allowable exemption ($20,000 in the case of Joe in the example above).

So henceforth, when someone asks you what bracket you're in, you must ask, "**For what kind of income?**" before you can answer. Also, you need to ask, "**How much additional income?**" In the last example above, you are in the zero percent bracket for additional passive income. But only for the first $34,000 - $20,000 = $14,000 of such income. After that, you are in the 31% marginal bracket on passive income.

Are you confused?

I'm sorry if you are confused. I can only make things as simple as the underlying facts. And the fact is that you now have **two** tax bracket scales: one for **passive** and one for **non-passive** income.

And your bracket now goes **down** when you hit a certain high point.

Actually, there's one more thing.

Your alternative minimum bracket

The tax table for 1991 shows only three brackets: 15%, 28%, and 31%. But there's a fourth bracket in the code—the alternative minimum bracket. It's 24%.

Generally, the 24% alternative minimum tax (AMT) does **not** affect you if you are in the 28% bracket (or its invisible companion, the 46.5% brackets.)

The purpose of the 24% bracket is to keep you out of the 15% bracket. The tax tables giveth (the 15% bracket) and the AMT taketh away.

And as with other exemptions, there is a phase-out "window" for alternative minimum taxable income ($150,000 to $310,000 for married filing jointly). As with the other phase-outs, this one has the effect of bumping up the marginal tax rate as you pass through that window. Since you lose 25¢ worth of the $40,000 AMT exemption for every dollar your AMT income goes over $150,000, the effective AMT rate in that window is 24% + (24% x 25%) = 24% + 6% = 30%.

Then there's the long-term capital gains rate

You may have heard that they got rid of the distinction between long-term capital gains and ordinary income. Well, not quite.

In '91 and thereafter, you can be taxed as high as 28% on long-term capital gains.

In 1989, the House of Representatives approved a bill to lower the maximum long-term capital gains rate to 19.6% for assets sold between 9/14/89 and 12/31/91 and to 28% with basis indexed for inflation occurring thereafter. But the Senate rejected the idea and it died.

You need a computer

In the past, you could figure the tax implications of various real estate decisions on the back of an envelope. "Lessee, I'm in the 50% bracket. Price is $1,000,000 so about $850,000 for improvements. First year depreciation is 9% of $850,000 = $76,500. And that'll save me 50% x $76,500 = $38,250 on my taxes."

It ain't that simple any more.

To understand the tax implications of a real estate decision, you now need to plug the alternatives into a computer and see what the difference in tax payable is.

I like the MacInTax™ program which works with the Apple MacIntosh™ computer. Unfortunately, it makes you **manually** combine the alternative minimum tax and the regular tax And each year's version doesn't come out until late in the year or early the following year. If the law would stabilize (fat chance), you could use **the most recent** MacInTax™ to test decision alternatives.

I have enough trouble keeping up with the tax law. I will not try to keep up with computer tax programs. Suffice it to say that various computer and tax periodicals publish reviews of the various tax programs around tax time. You can get recommendations from friends. And if you are into computer-hating, find an accountant who can run your decision alternatives through **his** computer.

Reed's Rule #3: Losing money is not good.

Accepting this rule will prevent you from falling prey to the most widespread misconception about income taxes—the idea that losing money is a good thing for people in high tax brackets.

Case in point. On the "WKRP In Cincinnati" episode aired on April 21, 1982, Johnny Fever was perplexed at actions taken by "The Big Guy's" mother—the owner of the station. She seemed to be trying to **prevent** the station from becoming profitable. Sure enough. In a climactic confrontation, Johnny gets "The Big Guy's" mother to admit she secretly wants the station to **lose** money—for tax purposes.

The show's writers either fell prey to or were pandering to the common belief that losing money is good for people in high tax brackets. THAT IS UTTER NONSENSE!!!

It **is** true that investors often seek "tax advantaged" investments. But a true tax shelter does not **really** lose money. It only **appears** to on paper.

And it **is** true that corporations sometimes buy corporations which have losses for tax reasons. But the buying corporation does not want losses. It only wants the right to **deduct** the losses the previous owners have already suffered. There's a big difference.

Doctor Quackenbush is in a high tax bracket. He makes a hundred fifty thousand a year taxable. Like many other Americans, at the end of the year, he goes into a frenzied search for LOSSES! He does this because he believes that losses will reduce his taxes.

He's right.

Losses **will** reduce his taxes. So why not buy stock in a company which you know is about to go bankrupt. You'll probably lose 95 cents on the dollar—all deductible.

A Bank of America pamphlet on the effects of the Economic Recovery Tax Act of 1981 had this to say. "Individuals with investment income, which would have been previously subject to tax at a 70% rate, will suffer the greatest reduction in tax savings benefits from tax shelter write-offs."

Now that convoluted sentence might be technically correct. I don't know because I can't follow it. But they **are** saying that high income individuals will "**suffer**" as a result of their tax rate being lowered from 70% to 50%. The Bank of America entered the income tax hall of mirrors and lost their sense of direction.

But Bank of America's pamphlet writers are not alone. Seems like **most** people make that kind of mistake when they're thinking about losses, deductions, and such. Here's another way you could get a loss to deduct. Loan your life savings to a skid row wino. Chances are the wino won't pay it back. Then you can deduct the amount of the loan as a bad debt loss.

I got into a conversation with the sound technician when I was setting up a tax seminar once. He told me about a building he had just sold. The terms caused me to remark, "The buyer must have some heavy negative cash flow." He replied, "Yeah, but he's a doctor. He needed the losses."

There are plenty of airline pilots, movie stars, and small businessmen who do the same thing.

Avoid losses no matter what your tax bracket

Folks, I don't care if you're Kenny Rogers; you don't want losses. Losses reduce your bank account or your net worth or both. The reduction in bank accounts or net worth always **exceeds** the reduction in your tax liability. If you're in the **highest** marginal tax bracket, 33%, losing $10,000 reduces your tax by $3,333. But you lost $10,000, so you're $6,667 worse off than if you did **not** have the loss. It does **not** make sense to pay $10,000 for $3,333 worth of benefit.

Reed's Rule #4: Depreciation is mostly good.

If you buy a capital asset for investment or trade or business, you may deduct depreciation. The difference between undesirable deductions and desirable deductions is whether or not there is a corresponding **expenditure**.

The money you pay for property taxes is an expense for tax purposes. It's also an expenditure. An **expenditure is a payment**—by check, or cash, or whatever. An expense is **not** the same thing as an expenditure. An expense is a cost incurred in the pursuit of income.

Property taxes are **both** an expense and an expenditure. Depreciation is an expense, but not an expenditure. You deduct the property tax payment from your income for tax purposes. But you also deduct it from your **bank account** when you write the check. Obviously, you would not try to reduce your income taxes by telling the local assessor to increase your assessment. Even though that would definitely reduce your income tax.

You deduct depreciation from your income for tax purposes. But you do **not** deduct it from your bank account. That's why it's good. But why do I say "mostly" good?

Things *do* depreciate

If you buy a car for business purposes, you may depreciate it. Is that a tax shelter? Most people would say no. Why? Because the car really **is** going down in value. You would not go out and buy cars for depreciation deductions because they go down in value—which is another way to say they depreciate.

But real estate goes **up**, not down in value, right? Actually, real estate behaves just like the car in many ways. Cars decline in value primarily because their parts wear out. The parts of buildings wear out too. Carpet, for example, seems to last maybe five years on average in an apartment building. You can depreciate it, but you'll also have to **replace** it after five years. Ditto the appliances, roof, asphalt, and so forth.

So **some** of the depreciation you deduct for tax purposes is **real**; in other words, over the long run, there **will** be a corresponding expenditure.

Reed's Rule #5: Deductible expenditures are bad.

A misconception as widespread as the notion that losses are good for high income individuals is the idea that, "If it's deductible, it's good." Not true.

You hear people say such things as, "What does he care? He can write it off on his taxes." They seem to think that if it's deductible, it's free.

A deduction is like a discount

You go to the hardware store and buy two identical cans of paint, each costing $10.00. One is for your **home**; the other for a **rental house** you own. You're in the 33% marginal tax bracket. The **before**-tax cost of each can of paint is $10.00. The **after**-tax cost of the can for your **home** is also $10.00. That's because repairs to your home are not deductible (unless they are fix-up costs within 90 days of sale). But the after-tax cost of the can for your rental house is just $6.67 because repairs to investment property are deductible.

So deductibility is like a discount. The true cost of the home paint was $10; of the rental paint, $6.67. But the rental paint was not free. You'd have been $6.67 better off after taxes if the rental property hadn't needed paint.

Tax credits are also like discounts

Another area of confusion is tax credits. At the end of every year I hear of investors who are "looking for tax credits." They equate tax credits with tax shelter. Tax credits are pretty much the same as deductions. Sure they're deducted from your **tax** rather than your **income**. If you're in the 33% marginal tax bracket, that means a tax credit is worth $1 \div .333 = 3$ times as much to you as an equal deduction. But it's still just a discount.

Let's say you rehab two buildings: one for business and one for personal use. Each costs $10,000. Because it's for business, one is eligible for the rehab investment tax credit which is 10% of the cost of the rehab. All that means is that one rehab, in effect, costs you $9,000 rather than $10,000. Are you better off tax-wise? No. You'd be better off if the building you're rehabbing didn't need to be rehabbed.

All of which leads me to the next Rules.

Reed's Rule #6: Don't buy something just because you can deduct it or claim a tax credit, and...

Reed's Rule #7: *Do* take deductibility and rehab tax credits into account in order to arrive at the after-tax cost when you're considering an acquisition, purchase, or rehab.

Many investors try to rehab property eligible for tax credits at year end to reduce their taxes. That's not sensible behavior.

It **would** be sensible to move up a rehab you were going to do anyway. Then the credit falls in **this** tax year rather than the next. But it's not sensible to rehab a building you weren't going to rehab anyway just to get a tax credit.

It would be sensible to **take the credit and depreciation deductions into account** when considering alternative courses of action. But it does not make sense to spend $10,000 (in the rehab example) just to get $1,000 worth of tax savings.

Reed's Rule # 8: Don't sell an investment property unless the tax due on the sale is $2,000 or less. Exchange instead.

This Rule will startle most investors. What I'm saying is that you virtually never sell investment real estate. You almost **always** exchange.

That's not the advice you typically get. The average investor considers exchanges to be just one of many options. The average investor thinks exchanging has advantages and disadvantages. Investors generally rank exchanging with installment sales as a tax saving device.

Exchanging is the only way to go in the vast majority of cases

I disagree with all of these notions. Exchanging is not one of many options; it's the **only** option which makes any sense at all in about 80% of the cases. The other 20% are investors with enough suspended losses to absorb the gain—or tiny gains. They shouldn't exchange because the tax payable is worth less than the minor effort of arranging an exchange.

There are also some investors with close to zero tax brackets because they have huge negative cash flow. They ought to correct the situation if they have negative cash flow. Once the situation is corrected, they'll need to exchange too. Even if they don't correct the situation, they'll probably need to exchange because the gain on a sale comes in a lump and tends to overcome even the losses from the negative cash flow.

As to the idea that exchanging has advantages and disadvantages—that's true, but you need a sense of proportion. Exchanging takes more effort than most straight sales. Not enormously more effort, just a bit more effort. The tax payable if you do **not** exchange, however, typically runs into thousands, even tens of thousands of dollars. I am appalled at the casual way in which real estate investors say, "Oh I'll go ahead and pay the tax. Exchanging is too much trouble."

The savings are enormous

How much tax? How much trouble? I'll explain why it's worth the trouble in the section of the book on exchanging.

Installment sales are a way to pay taxes...not save them

You shouldn't even mention installment sales in the same breath as exchanges. To suggest that they are both tax saving devices is to reveal that you haven't thought much about them.

There is one basic difference between installment sales and exchanges. In an installment sale, you **pay taxes**. In an exchange, you don't.

If you like paying taxes, sell property on an installment sale basis. If you **don't** like paying taxes, exchange. As a matter of fact, it makes far more sense to sell for cash and pay all your taxes in one year than it does to sell on an installment basis. The reasons are the time value of money and recent changes in installment sale law.

If you sell and pay all the taxes, at least you can invest what's left in real estate. If you sell on an installment sale basis, you're cutting off your investment program to spite the IRS. Sure IRS doesn't have the tax on the installment portion, but you don't have the cash either. You've gone from being a real estate investor, which is wise, to being a **mortgage investor**. By doing so, you hurt IRS a little and hurt yourself a lot.

Recent law changes

The law relevant to installment sales has changed dramatically in recent years. There was a flirtation with very high, mandatory interest rates. Congress traded that in for a longer depreciation period.

The Tax Reform Act of 1984 required that you pay all the recapture due on an installment sale the year you sell—even if the payments you receive in the year of sale are less than the tax payable—even if the payments in the year of sale are **zero**.

And if that was not enough, the Tax Reform Act of 1986 administered the *coup de grace*—at least on installment sales of trade or business or investment property where the sale price—not loan amount—of the property is more than $150,000. Fortunately, the Revenue Act of 1987 more or less repealed the onerous installment sale rules of the Tax Reform Act of 1986. More about that later.

Don't sell, exchange.

Reed's Rule #9: The only thing worse than a deductible expenditure is a non-deductible one.

Mortgage amortization, personal items, etc., are examples of nondeductible expenditures.

Reed's Rule #10: It is better to deduct than to depreciate.

"Deducting" here means that you write off the expense in question all in **one year.** Depreciating means that you write it off over a period of years. Deducting is better because of the time value of money.

Sometimes, whether to deduct or depreciate is a judgmental question. When it is, try to justify deducting.

Reed's Rule #11: When you can't deduct it, try to depreciate it. If you can't depreciate it, try to add it to basis.

If you **repair** the roof on an investment property, you may **deduct** it. If you **replace** the roof on an investment property, you must **depreciate** it. If you repair the roof on your personal **residence**, you may **not** deduct or depreciate it. But if you **replace** the roof on your personal residence, you may **add it to basis**. That will reduce your gains tax if you ever sell the house.

Expense Hierarchy

Real estate depreciation is mostly good.

Deductible expenditures are bad.

Expenditures which can only be depreciated are worse.

Expenditures which can only be added to basis are worse yet.

Expenditures which are nondeductible and cannot be added to basis are worst of all.

Summary of Reed's Rules

1. Income is good.

2. Some kinds of income are better than others.

3. Losing money is not good.

4. Depreciation is mostly good.

5. Deductible expenditures are bad.

6. Don't do something just because you can deduct it or claim a tax credit.

7. Do take deductibility and tax credits into account in order to arrive at the after-tax cost when you're considering an action.

8. Don't sell an investment property unless the tax due on the sale is $2,000 or less. Exchange instead.

9. The only thing worse than a deductible expenditure is a non-deductible one.

10. It is better to deduct than to depreciate.

11. When you can't deduct it, try to depreciate it. If you can't depreciate it, try to add it to basis.

PART TWO:
WHEN YOU ACQUIRE PROPERTY

7

How to Take Title

There are 8 main ways to take title to real estate:

- Sole proprietorship
- General partnership
- Limited partnership
- Corporation
- S corporation
- Tenants in common
- Joint tenants
- Trust

I favor sole proprietorship

I favor taking title as sole proprietor. That means you or you and your spouse are the owners. Why do I prefer that method? Simplicity mostly. Also, tax benefits are greatest and your tax status is clearest for sole proprietors.

Disadvantages of partnerships

Most investors think partnerships are equivalent to sole ownership for tax purposes. A partnership, the line goes, is not taxed. It is merely a "conduit."

That's true as far as it goes. Trouble is it doesn't go far enough to give the whole picture. Partnerships are a conduit all right. But they're also a **pain in the neck**. Here's why:

Must file partnership returns

A partnership may not have to pay taxes, but it **does** have to file returns. "So what?" you say. It's a time-consuming pain. Form 1065 (U.S. Partnership Return of Income) runs four pages and a 2-page Schedule K-1 (Partner's Share of Income, Credits, Deductions, Etc.) must be filled out for each partner. If you have a professional tax adviser prepare the returns, there will be an out-of-pocket cost. It may not be a tax *per se*. But if an IRS requirement causes you to lay out money, what's the difference?

Exposure to partnership penalties

Your partnership will never pay any tax. But it very well may pay penalties. I had a partnership with a newsletter I used to write for to put on seminars. I provided the program; they provided the audience. We split the profits 50/50. Simple, right?

So how come I got a notice from IRS that we owed $500 in penalties? Turns out that IRS couldn't find my return. So I sent them a copy of it. Then they said the last page was missing. That page contains details of assets and liabilities. I told them I didn't send the last page because it didn't have anything on it. As stated earlier in the return, our partnership had no assets or liabilities.

After many phone calls, photocopies, and letters, IRS agreed that not sending in a blank page did not warrant a $500 fine. But I spent at least that in the value of the time it took to straighten this out. That partnership is no more. Mainly because I was fed up with the paperwork and the fact that every partnership is a target in the IRS shooting gallery. Here are the penalties partnerships are heir to.

Penalties partnerships can be hit with

- False statements by promoter.......................20% of gross income
- Overvaluation of at least 200% ....10% of income
- Failure to supply taxpayer ID No..................$50 per failure
- Failure to make exchange statement...............$50 per failure
- Failure to register tax shelter.......................$500 to $10,000
- Failure to maintain list of investors................$50 per failure
- Failure to furnish partners with returns...........$50 per failure
- Failure to file partnership return ....$50/partner/month; $250/partner max.

Partnerships can be audited now

By participating in a partnership, you earn the dubious opportunity to be audited **twice** in one year—once as an individual and once as a member of a partnership which is being audited. This came in as part of the Tax Equity and Fiscal Responsibility Act of 1982. Partnerships with 10 or fewer partners can choose **not** to be auditable. But others may be audited. Before, only partners could be audited. An audit of the partnership will use up the time of at least one member of the partnership and/or the partnership's tax adviser. That's more money—money paid **because** of the IRS, if not **to** the IRS.

State tax returns too

Not only do you have to file **federal** partnership returns. Your **state** will want you to file similar returns with them. More time and money and exposure to penalties.

You cannot exchange into or out of a partnership

I'll explain exchanges later in the book. Suffice it to say here that they are the biggest tax break of all—one which you should take advantage of on almost every transaction. But you won't take advantage of your ability to exchange if there's a partnership on one end of the transaction.

"Interests in a partnership" are explicitly not exchangeable according to the Internal Revenue Code section 1031(a)(2)(D).

The inability to exchange into or out of a partnership is **enough reason all by itself** to keep me from ever getting involved in a partnership.

Uncertain tax status

One of the problems of **limited** partnerships is their uncertain tax status. The law says that if a partnership has too many of the characteristics of a corporation, it will be taxed as a corporation. That would be disastrous.

A corporation is the opposite of a conduit. It's more like a tax **dam**. Any income made by a property owned by a corporation causes the corporation to pay tax. Money left over after paying the corporation's taxes may be paid to the shareholders as dividends. At which time it will be **taxed again**. Furthermore, any losses or depreciation deductions the corporation's real estate has are bottled up inside the corporation and do not help the tax picture of the shareholders at all.

Read any limited partnership prospectus and you'll find a paragraph on this subject. It's written by an attorney and usually contains words to this effect. "Gee, guys, we **think** this group will not be taxed as a corporation. But you can never be sure, you know. We wish you luck."

Non-tax reasons for avoiding group ownership

- Far less liquid than sole owned property
- Must follow group's strategy
- Personality conflicts likely
- Complicates estate planning
- Must comply with state laws on the group in question
- Must comply with federal securities laws in some cases
- Attorneys fees for drawing partnership agreement
- Reduced financeability

Not a book on limited partnerships

I will not cover limited partnerships in this book, except very briefly. The reason is that they are a whole separate area of expertise—one which I long ago decided **not** to take up. Indeed, most of the people who **did** take the subject up have gone on to greener pastures in the wake of the Tax Reform Act of 1986.

Corporations are rarely used for real estate investing

I've already mentioned the main problems of corporations:

- Double taxation
- Tax shelter bottled up inside corporation.

Corporations also have these disadvantages:

- Attorneys fees to establish corporation
- Very complex state corporation laws
- Very complex state corporation tax laws
- Very complex federal securities laws
- Very complex federal tax laws
- Lack of liquidity if closely held
- Lenders usually insist on personal signature
- You cannot exchange into or out of a corporation (via section 1031. There **are** merger and liquidation sections which permit tax-free transactions under some circumstances.)
- Most of the non-tax disadvantages of partnerships also apply to corporations.

I get the impression that most of the "little people" who incorporate do so because they think "it's the thing to do when you go into business." Plus they're often scared of failure and/or liability for lawsuits. So they think of a corporation as a way to avoid liability. It is. But when real estate investing is the business's purpose, a corporation is a costly way to get protection from liability.

If you're a fraidy cat real estate investor, inve t via limited partnerships, not corporations. I don't recommend limited partnerships, but well-selected ones may be better than not investing in real estate at all.

If you take title as sole owner, which **is** what I recommend, you can protect yourself from lawsuit liability with appropriate insurance policies. And you should. On larger properties, you can protect yourself from debt liability by getting a sole security clause in the mortgage. Although that's easier said than done. And as far as failure is concerned: don't.

S corporations

An S corporation seems to combine the advantages of a corporation with the advantages of a limited partnership. Like a partnership, it is a conduit which is not taxed. So the tax shelter benefits of the business flow through to the owners and the income flows through untouched by corporate taxes. But S corporations have most of the liability limiting aspects of regular corporations.

As a result of the Subchapter S Revision Act of 1982 real estate investors can now make use of S corporations. That's because the **passive income restriction** was eliminated. Rent income is passive income in the eyes of the law. And the S law **used to** says if more than 20% of your income was from passive sources, you could not be an S corporation. Now you can be Sub S even if 100% of your income is passive.

At present an S corporation is better than a corporation for real estate investing—but not much. But the mere fact that you now **can** use S corporations doesn't mean that you **should**. I recommend against it.

The Tax Reform Act of 1986 caused a flurry of articles recommending S corporations for real estate. In an article I wrote in my newsletter, **Real Estate Investor's Monthly**, I said S corporations still have too many disadvantages. ("Are S Corporations the Answer to the New Tax Law?" October 1986)

Tenants in common

If you must invest as a group (meaning with someone other than your spouse), and the group is small and compatible, tenants in common is probably the way to go. The reason I say that is **you can exchange into or out of tenants in common.**

Tenants in common each own a percentage of the property in question. It may be 50/50, or 80/20 or 20/20/60 or whatever. The percentage each owns is specified in the deed. If you are a tenant in common, and you die, your share is passed to **your heirs**. That's different from the more common joint tenancy in which the surviving joint tenants get the share of those who die.

Tenants in common do **not** have to file a "tenants in common tax return." Although each has to report his share of income and losses on his individual tax return. Tenancy in common has no tax identity or tax problems whatever except one—the possibility that the law may decide that your tenancy in common is a partnership. In which case, you have all the tax problems of partnerships.

The difference between a partnership and tenants in common

Regulation Section 301.7701-3(a) says in part:

> *The term 'partnership' is broader in scope than the common law meaning of partnership and may include groups not commonly called partnerships...A group undertaking merely to share expenses is not a partnership...Mere co-ownership of property which is maintained, kept in repair, and rented or leased does not constitute a partnership. For example, if tenants in common of a farm property lease it to a farmer for a cash rental or a share of the crops, they do not necessarily create a partnership thereby. Tenants in common, however, may be partners if they actively carry on a trade, business, financial operation, or venture and divide the profits thereof. For example, a partnership exists if co-owners of an apartment building lease space and in addition provide services to the occupants either directly or through an agent.*

This reg seems to say that you cannot have tenants in common for tax purposes unless the investment property is very passive, like leasing of raw land. But a reg is not necessarily law, however. I'm not aware of any court cases which either uphold or conflict with this reg. But I suspect it is subject to challenge as exceeding the IRS's authority.

A tenant in common can deduct all taxes if he pays them, even though he's entitled to reimbursement from the other tenants in common under state law. (*Lulu Lung Powell*, 26 TCM 161)

Joint tenants

Joint tenancy is an **estate planning** rather than a tax planning method of taking title. It's normally used between husbands and wives or other close relatives. I think it would be rather strange to use it between unrelated parties unless they had become such close friends that they were "family."

Trusts

Trusts are also an **estate-planning** device primarily. Estate planning is beyond the scope of this book. And beyond the scope of my expertise. Like partnerships and corporations, they are cumbersome. And they must file tax returns. **Charitable remainder trusts** are an interesting way to turn your real estate into non-real estate, **tax free**. See "How to get out of real estate tax free" in the August, 1990 issue of *Real Estate Investor's Monthly*.

For more information on ways to take title

There's an excellent section on this subject in Alvin Arnold's *Real Estate Investor's Deskbook* (Warren, Gorham, & Lamont).

8

Tax Differences Between Property Types

Different property types are treated differently by the Internal Revenue Code. As a result, you may want to consider those differences when deciding which type of property to acquire. Although, anyone who makes tax aspects paramount is probably overestimating the value of the benefits.

Residential versus non-residential

There are three differences between residential and non-residential investment property:

• Depreciation period
• Eligibility for rehab investment tax credit
• First-year expensing.

A residential property which is also your residence comes under still other rules. Residential gets the better depreciation period—27.5 years instead of 31.5.

Rehabilitation investment tax credit

Non-residential buildings which were first placed in service before 1936 are eligible for a 10% rehab investment tax credit. According to prior law and the Senate Finance Committee Report preceding the Tax Reform Act of 1986, residential buildings are not eligible for the rehab investment tax credit. But the Act itself does **not** say only non-residential buildings qualify. I suspect this will be corrected in a technical corrections bill in the near future. But until it is, you can claim the rehab investment tax credit on residential property.

Once the expected correction is made, residential buildings will **only** be eligible for a rehab investment tax credit if they are **historic**. All other things being equal (which they never are), this tax law difference would make non-residential, non-historic buildings first placed in service before 1936 and in need of rehabilitation **more valuable** than similar residential buildings.

We're talking gut rehab unless you've owned the building a long time

Any old rehab won't do. It's gotta be a **gut** rehab. That means the property you buy is more or less a **shell**. **Reconstruction** investment tax credit would be a more accurate name for it. So don't think, "I'll buy non-residential properties because any money I spend on rehab will be eligible for the tax credit." You pretty much have to go into the construction business to qualify for the rehab investment tax credit.

The word in the law which requires gut rehab is "substantial." In order to get the rehab investment tax credit, the rehab must be "substantial." And the law defines "substantial" to mean you have to spend more than the adjusted basis of the property—or $5,000—whichever is greater.

If you **bought** it, that means you have to spend more on the rehab than the purchase price. For example, you'd have to spend more than $100,000 to rehab a building you just paid $100,000 for in order to get the credit. However, if you paid $100,000 ten years ago—and now have a basis of $60,000, you could qualify by only spending $60,001.

Historic means *certified* historic

You don't qualify for the historic property rehab tax credit (20%) just because you think your building is historic. It ain't historic until the **Secretary of the Interior** says it's historic.

"How," you may wonder, "do I get the Secretary of the Interior to drop by my property?"

Not to worry. He has delegated his authority to your State Historical Officer. Every state has one. He probably wears a bow tie and elbow patches.

To find out whether your building is **already** certified historic, contact your State Historical Officer. If it's not certified historic, but you wish it were, do the same thing. Your State Historical Officer will tell you how to go about nominating your building for historical status and what his requirements are to succeed. For further information, get the book, *Tax Incentives for Historic Preservation* (address in the back of this book).

The *rehab* has to be certified, too

Once the Secretary of the Interior has certified your building as historic, you can't just do any old rehab work you want. Noooo, sir. Once you get cozy with the government, you **stay** cozy with the government. The Secretary of the Interior has to approve the work you do, too.

Or at least your State Historical Officer has to tell the Secretary of the Interior to approve it. He's supposed to do that if the work you do is "consistent with the historic character of such property or the district in which such property is located."

I'm not part of the wine and cheese crowd that gets off on this nonsense. Rather I want to know what it means to the bottom line. What it means is red tape and extra rehab expense. Getting your building and your work certified historic means red tape, i.e. paperwork and delay. Having to please some historic bureaucrat means you'll have to spend more than you wanted on the rehab. The bureaucrat will probably insist on some changes to your plan to justify his existence. And you'll have to put **your** money where the local preservation crowd's mouths are—"clothing " your building in what **they** have decreed is the "uniform of the day."

Most tax authors are all excited about the historic tax credit. I'm not. I'm not a contractor so the prospect of gut rehabs doesn't appeal to me—even if the government promises to foot 20% of the bill. (The paperwork, delay, and do-it-as-the-preservationists-say requirements run the bill up above what it would have been. In effect, that reduces or wipes out the benefit of the credit.)

More importantly, I do not work for the government—not even temporarily. I have zero patience for red tape and bureaucratic interference so I would not do well in my dealings with those folks. If gut rehabs and dealing with the government are your things, you may want to take advantage of the historic tax credit. But if you're just a guy who wants to pay less tax, forget it. It's probably not worth the trouble.

Lodging versus non-lodging

I've just been talking about the **rehab** investment tax credit. Now I want to talk about the plain old **investment tax credit**. The investment tax credit (ITC) was repealed by the Tax Reform Act of 1986 effective January 1, 1986. But the **definition** of property eligible lives on as the criterion for first-year expensing.

First-year expensing applies to **personal** property, not **real** property. So you may think it doesn't apply to us real estate investors. Not true.

In most cases, the real estate you buy **includes** some personal property. For example, buy a duplex and you usually get two ranges and two refrigerators.

If the property is used predominantly to furnish lodging or in connection with the furnishing of lodging," it's **not** eligible for the old investment tax credit and therefore not eligible for first-year expensing. So says § 48(a)(3) of the Internal Revenue Code.

What's the tax definition of 'lodging'?

In the business world, "lodging" usually refers to hotels and motels. In tax law, it's just the opposite. "Lodging" means apartments and **not** hotels and motels. Section 48(a)(3)(B) says lodging property is eligible for the investment tax credit as long as "the predominant portion of the accommodation is used by **transients**…" In other words, if people stay in your building on a transient basis, personal property contained therein is eligible for the old ITC and therefore first-year expensing.

Who's a 'transient'?

According to Regulation Section 1.48-1(h)(1)(i) and (2)(ii), a transient hotel or motel is one in which the occupants stay is "Normally less than 30 days." Therefore:

Stay is normally…	Personal property is…
Less than 30 days	Eligible for first-year expensing
30 days or more	**Not** eligible for first-year expensing

Or to put it another way:

If property type is...	Personal property is...
Hotel, motel, short-term resort rental or non-residential	Eligible for first-year expensing
Apartment, rental house, etc.	**Not** eligible for first-year expensing

Useful for year-end tax panic

First-year expensing is useful if you go into an end-of-year tax panic. First-year expensing is not prorated. Real estate depreciation is prorated. That means if you buy real estate at the end of December, it won't help much on your taxes because you only get one half of one twelfth of a year's deduction. But you get the whore year's first-year expensing even though you only owned the property one day during the year.

So if you're in a year-end tax panic, you may find it useful to buy non-residential and/or hotel or motel property. Apartments won't help as much because the only thing eligible for first-year expensing in an apartment building is coin-operated vending machines (washers and dryers typically). Of course, a real estate investment is a pretty big deal so you ought not run out and buy properties just to get first-year expensing. First-year expensing eligibility is just one of the things you should consider.

More about investment tax credits and timing considerations later.

Dealer property

Dealer property is a subject I'll cover in detail later. Suffice it to say now that it's far less desirable than investment property. Dealer property is not eligible for two big real estate tax breaks:

• Depreciation
• Exchanging.

Although the property type does not decide *per se* whether a property is dealer property or not, it's a factor. The following property types are **generally** considered dealer property:

• Subdivided land
• Condominium conversions
• New construction which is sold by the builder soon after completion.

Again, property type is **not** decisive when you're in a dealer versus investment dispute. But it's a factor.

9

Timing the Acquisition

Real property, end of the month; personal, December 31

As I told you in the previous chapter, real property depreciation is prorated. By the month. So if you buy in December, you only get one month's worth of depreciation. There is no proration **within** the month, however. So the most advantageous time to close on a property you're buying from a depreciation standpoint is the last day of the month. Last day of December, one half of one month's depreciation; last day of November, one and a half month's depreciation; and so forth.

You're not going to get rich on the tax benefits of buying on the last day of the month so don't let that interfere with some other important consideration which makes an earlier part of the month better.

Personal property depreciation is **not** prorated. It goes by the "half-year convention." The half-year convention says that no matter when in the year you buy a property, you get half a year's depreciation. And if the property's is eligible for first-year expensing, you get the **whole** first-year expensing deduction no matter when during the year you buy. So you might as well buy on December 31st.

There is an exception to the half-year convention. If more than 40% of your personal property acquisitions in a given year fall into the last quarter, you have to use the mid-**quarter** convention for all the personal property you acquired that year. That means each purchase is treated as if you bought it in the middle of the quarter in which you bought it.

Unfortunately, most of the personal property you buy will be as part of real property. Since the real property depreciation deductions are much bigger than personal property deductions, you probably will not want to wait until the end of the year to get them. In other words, where both personal and real property are part of a "package," the real property is dominant.

Buy real property as soon as possible. But, where otherwise convenient, you may want to postpone purchase of personal property like computers, cars, office furniture, etc. until year end.

Watch out for tax deadlines

The tax law is full of deadlines. One is December 31st. In the process of postponing a purchase **until** then, make sure you don't end up **after** December 31st. Then you have to wait a whole year for your deductions—both real and personal.

When it comes to buying a new home, you need to do so within 24 months of selling the old one. That's pretty well known. What may not be so well known is that the courts are sticklers for accuracy. "Almost" doesn't count. You have to close on the new home within two years of closing on the sale of the old one.

New laws

Every year, it seems, Congress passes a new tax law. Often, the benefits of the law only apply to property acquired after a certain date. The Accelerated Cost Recovery System, for example, only applies to property acquired after December 31st 1980. When the law is to take effect in the future (ACRS took effect in the past. It became law on August 13, 1981.), you may want to wait until then before acquiring the property. At present, I know of no laws that you should wait for.

Some dollar limits have timing implications

There are a few dollar limits in the tax law. First-year expensing is one.

First-year expensing

You can deduct up to $10,000 of the cost of property eligible for first-year expensing in one year. That's **instead of** claiming depreciation. But it's a better deal than depreciation so you should take advantage of it.

Since the first-year expensing limit is relatively low, many investors will hit it. Again, you may want to postpone eligible purchases until next year to avoid losing any of your ability to do first-year expensing. This might be important enough to postpone a purchase like a car or computer. But probably not important enough to warrant postponing a building purchase.

Your tax bracket this year and next

As a general rule, you want to acquire property as soon as you are financially able to. But it's conceivable that your tax bracket is so **low** is year, and will be so **high** next year, that you would be better off postponing the purchase until then. You'll have to do the numbers for your situation to see if that makes sense for you.

If you don't need it, don't buy it

I don't like "year-end tax strategies." I think people who implement year-end tax strategies are usually doing something stupid. Remember that paying lower taxes is not the be all and end all of life. As a real estate investor, your goal is **maximum after-tax return on equity**, not minimum taxes.

The tax timing considerations I described above are only that—**considerations**. They are **rarely decisive**.

While it's true that buying property eligible for first-year expensing at year end will save you taxes the following April, that doesn't necessarily mean you should do it. The rule is, if you need it, buy it. If you don't need it, don't buy it. And if you plan to buy it anyway, think about when is the **best time** to buy it from a tax standpoint. But don't run out and buy something just for tax reasons. Owning a herd of first-year-expensing-eligible white elephants is **not** better than paying taxes.

Pay state income taxes early

You can deduct state income taxes this year if you pay them this year, even if they are not due until next year.

10

Tax Information You Should Gather
at Acquisition Time

Evidence to back up your judgment calls

The main thrust of the aggressive tax avoidance philosophy is that you call judgmental questions in your favor. **Because** they are judgmental, it's possible that IRS may subsequently challenge you on them. If so, you'll need **evidence** to defend yourself.

An audit typically comes 14 to 18 months after you file the tax return in question. And you don't file the tax return until April 15th of the year after the events in question. So the auditor is asking you about a deal which was closed about **two years ago**. If you begin to look for evidence **then**, you're following a pretty cold trail.

The evidence you need is easiest to get **when you acquire the property**.

Evidence of values

Most of the evidence you need is to support values. The **total** value is clear cut. But the values of the land, personal property, and building components (applies to some exchanges) are judgmental. Appraisals have to be made. That doesn't mean you have to hire an appraiser. You usually make the appraisal **yourself**.

Evidence of useful life (still applies in some exchanges and in many state tax returns)

At acquisition time, you may also need to gather evidence to support useful lives. Useful lives were eliminated for future acquisitions by the Economic Recovery Tax Act of 1981. The Accelerated Cost Recovery System (ACRS) simply allows a 27.5-year recovery period on residential real property, 31.5 years on non-residential, and 5 or 7 years on most personal property. Under the **old** law, you had to select each building component's "useful life."

But the old law lives. If you **exchange** a property you owned before 1981, the basis of that property must be carried forward into the new property. Furthermore, **that** portion of the new property's basis **must be depreciated under the old rules**. So you have to select useful lives—and therefore you must be able to defend those lives.

Also, many **states** didn't like the Economic Recovery Tax Act of 1981. As a result, they chose to "uncouple" their tax law from it. Typically, they chose to stay with the old depreciation rules instead of the Accelerated Cost Recovery System. One list of such states included:

States still using useful lives

Alaska
Arkansas
California
Florida
Georgia
Idaho
Indiana
Iowa
Kentucky
Maine
North Dakota
Ohio
Oregon
South Carolina
West Virginia

I won't certify this list as complete. New York, for example, was debating whether to jump off the federal bandwagon. You'll have to check on whether **your** state does or does not use ACRS.

Receipts and settlement statement

Of course, you'll need to preserve your settlement statement. It contains a list of the various amounts you paid at closing. Many of these are supposed to be included in your basis. I'll explain that in greater detail later. For now, just make sure you get a receipt for every expenditure you make in conjunction with this acquisition.

The settlement sheet is usually **almost** a complete list. But not quite. You often pay other amounts **outside** of closing. For example, you may have paid your attorney an advance. Or he may bill you **after** settlement. You may have paid up-front fees to the mortgage lender a month or more before closing. Here's a list of the various costs you may incur when acquiring a property. You ought to have documentation of each—either on the settlement statement or on a separate receipt.

Make sure you get receipts for these:

Escrow fee
Disbursement or closing or settlement fee
Attorney fee
Title insurance premium
Recording fees
Survey
Preparation of transfer documents fees
Purchase commission (unusual but possible)
Option cost (if your purchase is the exercise of an option)
Termite inspector fee
Transfer taxes (if any)
Payment of any taxes, interest, etc. owed by seller
Loan appraisal fee
Credit application fee
Lender attorney fee
Lender's title insurance premium
Mortgage broker fee or commission
Points

Summary of evidence to gather

• Value of **land**
• Value of each item of **personal property**
• Value of **building components** (if exchange out of property you owned before '81)
• Condition of each component (for useful lives if applicable)
• Receipts

Where to get evidence of land value

The following can usually provide indication of the value of the land under the property you're acquiring:

• Tax assessor's land/improvements breakdown on tax bill
• Local MLS book (prices of lots for sale)
• Local real estate agents
• Your property insurance agent
• Local builders
• Building cost services (I'll explain shortly).

Tax Assessor

In the philosophy section, I made a big deal out of not falling over dead for the tax assessor's land improvements breakdown. Does the fact that I include it as a source on the land value mean I've changed my mind? No.

The reason you check the tax assessor's breakdown is that it might be favorable. If so, it's a useful piece of evidence. If it's **not** favorable, you have to dig up **other** evidence to refute it.

The tax assessor's breakdown is the one most people use. That's a mistake. They use it because it's easy. It appears to be the favorite, if not the **only** source most tax advisers and IRS auditors use. Tax advisers like it because they want a piece of paper, **any** piece of paper which takes them off the hook in case of a dispute with IRS. Too often, the tax adviser couldn't care less how much tax you pay—when it comes to the improvement ratio. He just wants to protect **himself**.

By using the tax assessor's breakdown, he can do like Flip Wilson's character "Geraldine." "She" says, "The devil made me buy this dress." Tax advisers say, "The assessor made me use that improvement ratio." It's a means of avoiding responsibility—and the effort required to support a better ratio.

The Tax Court wasn't impressed with the assessor's valuation in this case

In *Meirs*, TC Memo 1982-51, a taxpayer beat the IRS on an improvement ratio case. IRS wanted to use the assessor's 55% and 49% improvement ratios on Meirs' two condos. Meirs wanted to use **replacement cost**, which backed up his 80% improvement ratios. Meirs won. The Tax Court noted that the assessor's **total** value was way off. So they didn't have much confidence in his breakdown.

As I said a minute ago, zillions of people use the assessor's ratio. Thousands of tax advisers have never even **thought** of using anything else. Folks, that is one of the old wives tales of tax advice. If your tax adviser said to use the assessor's breakdown and made no mention of the possibility of using a higher ratio, you have reason to wonder if he should **continue** as your adviser.

Local multiple listing book

The local MLS book probably shows some land for sale. Many MLS books have a section showing listings which sold and expired. All three: for sale, sold, and expired, offer evidence as to land values. Ask a real estate agent, maybe the one who sold you the property, if you can look for such data in the MLS book.

Most MLS books say, "For MLS members only" on the cover. But few agents will turn down a layman who wants to see it. Make notes and/or photocopies of pertinent properties. Remember your goal is to find evidence to support the highest possible improvement ratio.

Local real estate agents

An experienced real estate agent can tell you what the land under your property is worth off the top of his head. If you know a local, experienced agent, ask him. **Write down** what he said and the date and time he said it. Even better, get him to put it in writing on his firm's letterhead. If necessary, **you** type what he said onto his firm's stationery and get him to sign it. Then preserve that letter for possible use in a dispute with IRS.

Insurance agent

Prior to closing, you have to arrange for insurance on the property. Insurance agents typically know the current local replacement cost for buildings like yours. It's usually expressed in dollars per square foot. Just ask your agent when you're arranging for the hazard insurance coverage.

You measure the property area, then multiply by the replacement cost per square foot. That gives you the improvement value. The land value is the total value minus the improvement value.

Appraisal theory requires that depreciation be deducted to reflect the fact that replacement cost is the cost of a **brand new** building. But the building you acquired is rarely brand new. In *Meeker v. Comm.*, TC Memo 1981-215 a taxpayer who used replacement cost lost because he failed to adjust for physical deterioration of the property.

To fight the adjust-for-depreciation argument, you want to gather evidence that the building you acquired was **like new**. Photographs of the property and statements from the seller as to when he replaced various components are the kinds of evidence you can use to refute or minimize the adjust-for-depreciation argument. Generalized statements about how well the building has been maintained and its condition can be helpful. Keep any sales brochure or ad copy on the property that contains such statements.

Local builders

Local builders know replacement (construction) costs better than anyone. Call one or two and ask about the property you're acquiring. It's best to call them around 7:30 am. They're often out at the construction site by 8 am. Again, **write down** who you talked to, what he said, and the date and time he said it. If possible, get it on his stationery.

Building cost services

There are three main companies which produce building cost services. A building cost service is a loose leaf binder which is updated quarterly. It shows what it currently costs to build various types of structures. Since building costs vary regionally, these services give regional figures. The services are called:

The Boeckh Manual
Marshall Valuation Service
The Dodge Manual

The publishers' names and addresses are listed in the back of this book. I called my county library to see if they have any of the three services. They have the *National Construction Estimator,* *The Building Cost Manual, The Vest Pocket Estimator,* and *The Building Estimator's Reference Book.* The county library called around for me and found that the Business and Government Branch of the Oakland Library gets the Marshall Valuation Service as well as two others. I have also seen two of the main services in the Business Branch of the San Francisco Library. Anyway, you get the idea of how easy it is to find these services.

Marshall and Swift offer two very cheap publications which may be all you need. They are the *Commercial Cost Estimator* and the *Residential Cost Estimator.*

A Sears catalog

For personal property, a Sears Roebuck or similar catalog is a pretty good appraisal tool. It contains the prices of refrigerators, ranges, furniture, etc. If you use it as a basis for part of your depreciation schedule, write down the prices and the year of the catalog. Better yet, photocopy the appropriate pages. You can get a Sears catalog from your nearest Sears store or catalog center. These days, they charge a small fee, which you get back if you buy anything through the catalog.

Component breakdown

If you are exchanging out of a building you owned prior to '81, or a building with pre-'81 basis carried forward in an exchange, you can and should use the component depreciation method on the old basis which is carried forward. In the component method, you break the building down into its building components. The reason is that they typically have shorter useful lives than the building as a whole. As a result, the component method gives significantly higher depreciation deductions in the early years.

The building cost services contain component breakdowns. By taking the percentage for each component and multiplying it by the total value of the building your acquiring, you get a rough estimate of the value of that component.

How accurate do you have to be on values of personal property and building components?

It seems to me that tax advisers and taxpayers get overly concerned about achieving pinpoint accuracy whenever they break down the value of a building into personal and real portions and/or building components. That's not necessary. "Close enough for government work" is the proper standard of accuracy.

There are no penalties for inaccurate appraisals until they reach at least 200% of the "correct" value. Even then, if you had a "reasonable basis" for the value you used—and chose that value in good faith, there's no penalty. Furthermore, even if you're more than 200% over, there's no penalty unless the resulting tax underpayment is at least $5,000.

A person in the highest tax bracket, 49.5%, would have to overstate a value by about $10,000 to underpay his taxes by at least $5,000. And the correct valuation would have to be $10,000 in order for $10,000 extra to be a 200% overvaluation. So no property or component which you value at less than about $20,000 would be likely to get you into trouble for inaccurate appraisal. That's why there's no use working yourself into a lather over whether the correct value of something should be $300 or $400.

Should you hire an appraiser?

Tax advisers often recommend—and sometimes insist—that you hire an appraiser, especially when you want to do a component breakdown. In part, that's due the the adviser's generalized "protect myself" mentality. In part it's due to Revenue Ruling 73-410.

Revenue Ruling 73-410 is the one which said it's OK to use the component method on **used** buildings. Prior to that revenue ruling, IRS said you could only use the component method on **new** buildings. That was because you had the contractors' bills on new buildings. The bills made it easy to come up with an accurate component breakdown. IRS said it was too hard to be accurate many years after the building had been built.

The reason they changed their minds is that they kept losing in court. The court agreed that it was more difficult to do a component breakdown on a used building, but they said it wasn't impossible—and there was nothing in the law to prevent taxpayers from doing it that way.

An IRS raised eyebrow

In Revenue Ruling 73-410, IRS approved a component breakdown for a used building. But the revenue ruling contained these words

> ...the taxpayer retained a firm of qualified appraisers which properly allocated his costs between nondepreciable land and depreciable building components as of the date of purchase.

I call that an IRS raised eyebrow. IRS did **not** say, "You must hire a firm of qualified appraisers to use the component method on a used building." They didn't say that because they have no authority to do so. But by saying that **this** taxpayer had done so, they strongly **implied** that you have to hire an appraiser.

Every tax adviser and writer of tax articles glommed onto that phrase and told his clients or readers that you **have** to hire "a firm of qualified appraisers." Fact is, there are thousands of accountants and attorneys who click their heels and say, "How high, sir?" when IRS raises an eyebrow. (The question "Did you deduct expenses for an office in your home?" on Schedule C is another IRS raised eyebrow. When they started putting that on Schedule C, fifty million tax advisers told their clients, "Don't claim a home office." Turkeys!)

Let me state my position unequivocally. **There is NOTHING in the tax law which says you have to hire an appraiser**. All the law says is that the allocation has to be **accurate**. You can make the allocation using **a dart board** as long as you're accurate. (Although, if the dart board gave the **wrong** answer, you'd be liable for penalties for not having a "good faith, reasonable basis" for your valuation.)

Revenue Ruling 73-410 is an IRS pout

The IRS frequently behaves like a spoiled child who must occasionally submit to parental (read "court") discipline. If the courts contradict IRS, it often complies only the most minimal, foot-dragging, grudging, bitter way.

In Revenue Ruling 73-410, IRS approves the component method on used buildings. But they do their darnedest to give the reader the impression he'd better not. IRS's purpose is to discourage the use of component depreciation. Since appraisals are expensive, people who believe they need one to use component depreciation are likely to say, "To heck with it. I'll use composite (the opposite of component—building is depreciated as one lump sum)."

Don't get an appraisal

I say don't get an appraisal. Here's why. What's the advantage of an appraisal you pay for over one you do yourself? Seems to me there are two advantages.

1. Saves your time.
2. Increases the chances of winning if IRS challenges you.

If I ever **did** get an appraisal to support an improvement ratio or personal property or component breakdown, it would probably be for reason number 1—to save my time. If the amount the appraiser will charge is less than the value of the time it would take **you** to do it yourself, hire an appraiser.

But that's not likely because one should make quick work of the appraisal. Remember pinpoint accuracy is inappropriate. And professional appraisers are prevented by habit and professional rules from doing quick work. They're going to make a big production out of it—and that'll cost you money.

What appraisers cost

An M.A.I. appraisal (M.A.I. stands for Member of the Appraisal Institute) on a house will cost you about $300. That's not a component breakdown, just an appraisal—which would probably show the land and improvement values. An M.A.I. appraisal on an income property would start at about $1,000 to $2,000.

Real estate agents and others will charge less. But you get what you pay for. In a dispute with IRS, the qualifications of your appraiser are often brought up. And on big disputes, you often ask the appraiser to testify (at your expense) in court. The less qualified your appraiser, the greater the chances you'll lose in court.

What's the value of increased chances of winning?

The main reason tax advisers tell you to get an appraisal, aside from protecting themselves, is to increase your chances of winning a dispute with IRS. But just what is that increased chance worth? For the answer, we return to the decision tree.

In Chapter 3, I said the 1990 probability of winning in Tax Court was 4%. Let's see how the decision tree changes if we **double** the probability of winning by hiring a professional appraiser to do the improvement ratio. I just picked the idea that hiring an appraiser would double the chances out of thin air. I'll test some other probabilities before we're done.

Doubling your chances of winning is worth $7.95

The weighted average value of the aggressive course of action (high improvement ratio) was $142.55 with a victory in Tax Court probability of 4%. When you double the probability, and reduce the loss probability accordingly, the value of the aggressive course drops to $134.60. So you are $142.55 - $134.60 = $7.95 better off for having gotten a professional appraisal.

If you use an appraiser

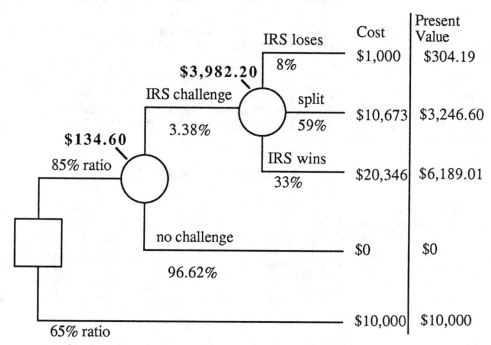

Can you get a professional appraisal for $7.95? No. Not even on a house.

And consider what the property value of the property in the decision tree must be. The conservative course of action costs $10,000 more in taxes. At a tax rate of 28%, that would require a $10,000/28% = $35,714.29 smaller loss. You deduct 3.64% of a property's improvement value per year on a residential property. So the $35,714.29 smaller loss must represent $35,714.29/3.64% = $981,161.81 less improvement value. Since the difference in improvement ratios that produces $981,161.81 less in property value is 85% - 65% = 20%, the total property value must be $981,161.81/20% = $4,905,809.07. If a professional appraisal is only worth $84.63 on a five-million-dollar property, how could you ever justify getting one on **any** property?

I also recalculated the decision tree to see what would happen if the probability of winning were raised to 100% through the use of a professional appraiser. The weighted average value of aggressiveness then dropped to $10.28. That's $142.55 - $10.28 = $132.27 better than without the appraisal. But still far less than you'd have to pay to get an appraisal on a five million dollar property.

Wait until you're challenged

You **do** have to make a good faith effort to use correct values when you fill out your tax return. You do **not** have to hire an appraiser. The main reason it doesn't make sense to hire an appraiser for tax reasons at the time of acquisition is that the **probability of audit is so low**. So why not wait until your challenged to hire an appraiser?

Do it **yourself** at acquisition time. Then, two years later, if you're challenged, hire an appraiser to go over the figures. If he comes up with different valuations than you did, tell IRS you'll agree to the appraiser's figures and pay the indicated amount of tax.

If IRS doesn't like your figures **or** your appraiser's, fight them. Enter your appraiser's report into evidence. If a large amount of money is in dispute, you may want to have him testify.

'But can he do an appraisal two years after the fact?'

One of my readers called to say IRS had told him he couldn't make an appraisal two years after the closing. He had to have made it back then or forget it. That's baloney.

For starters, what is the **IRS** auditor doing when he challenges your valuation two years after the closing? IRS certainly didn't have an appraiser check the values two years ago when you bought the property. So if **they** can hire an appraiser years after the fact, so can you.

Besides, appraisers are called on to appraise property as of some past date frequently. They'll tell you it's **harder** than a current appraisal. But it's not impossible. They just have to look up data from back when.

The value of an appraisal is higher at audit time

It's one thing to conclude that you ought not get an appraiser the year you buy the property. It's quite another to make the same decision when you're in a dispute with IRS over a valuation. There are two different decision trees. The first is dominated by the low probability of audit.

But the decision tree you face once the challenge has been made has a 100% "probability of audit." Recalculate the tree with that factored in. You also have to reduce the number of years until court decision from six to four since the two years wait until audit is now past. And you now have to pay more if you cave in. Not $10,000 as before. That's because two years worth of interest has built up since you filed the return.

Another problem: appraiser may side with IRS

There's another problem. The appraiser doesn't just come in and buttress **your** allocation of values. He makes his own. Or at least he's supposed to.

Cynics will say that an appraiser usually comes up with the value he thinks his client wants. And there's evidence to indicate that many do just that. But there's a good chance that the appraiser will decide that a value **between** yours and IRS's is correct. If you then switch to his value, you increase your chances of winning on the one hand, but you lose tax deductions on the other.

Do-it-yourself appraisals aren't free

All this talk of professional appraisals and their cost is liable to lull you into thinking that do-it-yourself appraisals are **free**. They aren't. **Your** time has value just like an appraiser's. If you can't spend more than $8.25 on an appraiser, you can't spend more than $8.25 of **your own** time appraising the property either. That's at the time of acquisition.

One-hour, do-it-yourself appraisal at acquisition; dig deeper if challenged

My conclusion is that you ought to spend a hour or so coming up with the improvement ratio, value of personal property, and, if applicable, values of building components **at the time you acquire the property**. Do **not** hire an appraiser. Sending a conscientious, intelligent secretary or assistant to the library to get hold of some cost studies makes more sense than paying some high falutin' guy for a pound of paper you don't really need.

That's at time of acquisition, when the chances of being challenged are quite low. If, however, you end up as one of the few, the proud, the audited, the economics change. At this stage, it makes sense to spend more to defend your valuations. But, in most situations, I **still** would not recommend hiring a professional appraiser, even when you're looking down the barrel of an IRS challenge.

As I mentioned, the appraiser may choose a less advantageous value than the one you used. Plus his fee is relatively high. If he only doubles or triples your chances of victory, hiring him is marginal—cost and benefit are about equal. And it's hard to believe that an appraiser could do better than triple your chances.

So instead of hiring an appraiser at the audit challenge stage, do-it-yourself again. Only **dig deeper**. Find additional information to strengthen the case you made back at acquisition time. Just as you can afford to spend more on an appraiser at audit time, so can you afford to spend more of your **own** time then.

A taxpayer who won on a do-it-yourself appraisal case

I know of one court case where a taxpayer did a do-it-yourself appraisal and won. *Offshore Operations Trust*, TC Memo 1973-212. It's not a real estate case, but it involved the accuracy of valuations which affected the tax due. I mention that only because some tax advisers seem so hooked on the belief that you have to hire an appraiser that they'd be amazed to know a do-it-yourselfer won.

Evidence of your non-dealer intent

Dealers cannot claim depreciation or exchange. Those are two good reasons to want to avoid being a dealer. The legal question of who is and who is not a dealer has never been clearly answered. But we **do** know that one of the factors the courts consider is your intent at the time you acquired the property. So you should preserve whatever evidence there is of your intent to **hold the property for investment**.

'Should I put a clause about my non-dealer intent in the purchase agreement?'

A lot of investors put a clause in their purchase agreements saying that they are purchasing the property for investment purposes. Should you? Can't hurt. But it probably won't help much either.

I attended a seminar at a national real estate convention a couple of years ago. In that seminar, a well-known real estate author was asked how he avoided dealer status. "Just write into your purchasing agreements that you are acquiring the property for **investment purposes**," he said.

Thousands of real estate investors think he's right. In fact, he doesn't know what he's talking about. There hasn't been a single court case in which the wording of a purchase agreement or any other document was taken into account in determining whether the taxpayer was a dealer. The judges know that talk is cheap.

Evidence that may help in dealer disputes

Not being a full-time in real estate can help show you're not a dealer. If you're not, preserve some evidence to prove it.

If you're acquiring the property to be your **prime residence**, preserve evidence of that. Write it into the purchase agreement. Mortgage loan applications often ask if you plan to occupy the property as your prime residence. If so, keep a copy of the application.

If you have other property which **is** dealer property, keep **this** property in totally separate accounts from the start. A taxpayer won a dealer case on that (*Pritchett*, 63 TC 149).

If you **inherited** the property, preserve evidence of it. Taxpayers have won using that too. (*Hopkins*, 15 TC 160) Ditto if you received the property as a **gift**.

Summary check list of information to gather at acquisition time

- Receipts for all expenditures in connection with the acquisition
- Settlement sheet
- Tax assessor's breakdown at time of closing (usually on property tax bill)
- Photocopies of lots for sale, sold, and expired from MLS book
- Real estate agent's opinion of land value
- Insurance agent's opinion f replacement cost of building
- Local builder's opinion of land value and replacement cost
- Photocopies of building cost service pages for your type of building
- Sears or other retail catalog for values of personal property
- Seller's statement (Ask for this **before** closing. Afterward, he may not bother to respond.) as to when he last replaced the following:

> Roof
> Carpet
> Refrigerators
> Ranges
> Drapes
> Pavement
> Heating plant
> Air-conditioner
> Hot water heater
> Gutters and downspouts
> Elevator
> Dishwashers
> Washers
> Dryers
> Other replaceables

- Purchase agreement wording to show non-dealer intent
- Evidence that you're not full-time in real estate

- Evidence that you plan to use the property as your prime residence
- Evidence that you inherited the property or received it as a gift
- Evidence that you keep the accounts of **this** property separate from your other, dealer property
- Affidavit stating that seller is not a foreign person and his U.S. taxpayer ID #.

PART THREE:
DEPRECIATION AND THE REHAB TAX CREDIT

11

How to Calculate Your Basis

Before you can begin filling out your actual tax forms, you need to calculate your "basis" in depreciable property. Depreciation is one of the most important tax savings devices for real estate investors.

These three items decide the size of your depreciation deduction:

1. Your **basis** in the property
2. Your **improvement** ratio (real property only)
3. **When** you acquired the property

I will explain all of these terms later in the book.

Your basis in the property

"Basis" is a tax word. If you bought the property, your basis is essentially what you paid for it. So don't let the word "basis" intimidate you into thinking there's something mysterious here. There's not.

Buying a property is only **one** way to acquire it. How you calculate basis depends on **how** you acquired the property. Let's take some of the less common ways first.

Gift

If you receive the property as a gift, your basis is the same as the basis of the person who gave it to you. The donee's basis is the same as the donor's basis, in lawyerese. (IRC § 1015)

Let's say your father bought a building lot for $3,000 many years ago. Now it's worth $20,000. He gives it to you. What is **your** basis? $3,000. Same as your father's.

If your father gave you a duplex he had bought for $50,000 and depreciated down to $42,000, your basis in that duplex would be $42,000—even if the duplex had appreciated to $80,000.

Inheritance

If you inherit the property, you get a **much better deal**. Your basis in inherited property is the fair market value at the time of death. (IRC § 1014)

In the duplex example above, your basis would be $80,000, not $42,000. If you received it as a **gift** and immediately sold it for market value ($80,000), you'd have a $80,000 - $42,000 = $38,000 gain.

But if you **inherited** the same property and immediately sold it, you'd have a $80,000 - $80,000 (basis) = $0 gain.

Gift taxes and inheritance taxes are beyond the scope of this book.

Exchange

Exchange is another way to acquire depreciable property. Before you can calculate basis after an exchange, you must calculate the tax payable, if any, on the deal.

Fill in the blanks in the following worksheet to calculate your tax payable ("recognized") on a partially taxed exchange.

Worksheet for Calculating Taxable Gain on Partially Taxed Exchange

PART ONE: Actual Gain

1. Fair market value of property received ...._____

2. Plus boot received (beginning equity less ending
   equity---zero or positive number only)............................_____

3. Plus liabilities on property gotten rid of ...._____

4. Less adjusted basis of property gotten rid of *..................._____

5. Less "sale" costs of property gotten rid of ...._____

6. Less liabilities on property received..............................._____

7. Less boot conveyed (ending equity less beginning
   equity---zero or positive number only)............................_____

8. Actual gain or (loss) (sum of lines 1 through 7)..................._____

PART TWO: Net Mortgage Relief

9. Liabilities on property gotten rid of ...._____

10. Less liabilities on property received.............................._____

11. Net relief from liabilities (zero or positive number only).........._____

PART THREE: Taxable gain

12. Net relief from liabilities (line 11)................................_____

13. Less boot conveyed (line 7).._____

14. Less "sale" costs of property gotten rid of (line 5)..............._____

15. Plus boot received (line 2) ...._____

16. Indicated gain (total of lines 12 through 15) ...._____

17. Taxable gain (smaller of line 8 or line 16)........................_____

Put this figure (line 17) on either IRS Schedule D or Form 4797.
* Don't forget the original cost of the **land** in the property gotten rid of. If you get the adjusted basis off a tax return, you're only getting the value of the **improvements**.

Form 8824

IRS has issued Form 8824 for "like-kind" exchanges. Here's the scoop.

Form 8824 Comparison With Worksheet

Question

5   asks for the date you identified the property to be received. That's to see if you met the **45-day deadline** in a delayed exchange.

6   asks the date you actually received the property. That's to see if you met the **180-day closing deadline.**

8-11   ask if the party with whom you exchanged was **related** and if so, whether they later disposed of the property. That's because the Omnibus Budget Reconciliation Act of 1989 **disallows** exchanges if they are with a related party and any of the parties disposes of the property within two years.

Lines

12-20   are IRS's version of the worksheet above.

12   [fair market value of other (not-like-kind) property given up] corresponds to line 7 (boot conveyed) on my worksheet.

13   [adjusted basis of (non-like-kind) property given up]. I have no line which corresponds. In most cases, the only non-like-kind property or boot given up is **cash** which doesn't need any gain calculation.

15   is labelled "Cash and FMV of other property you gave up, exchange expenses (if any), plus net liabilities assumed by other party." Relating it to this book, that is the sum of my lines 2 (boot received), 14 (sales costs), and 11 (net relief from liabilities). Furthermore, my line 11 is the result of an additional two-step calculation which my worksheet asks you to perform. By combining so many calculations in one line, IRS increases the probability that taxpayers will fail to include all of them and thereby **pay far more tax than they should.** In fact, the first time I read Form 8824, I missed the word "net" before "liabilities assumed by other party." Liabilities assumed by other party matches my line 3. But the word "net" means you subtract the liabilities on the property you received. Many other taxpayers and tax advisers will miss the extremely important meaning of the word "net" on Form 8824's line 15.

16   is my line 1 (market value of property received).

17   is an unnecessary subtotal which matches no line of my worksheet.

18   matches my lines 4 (adjusted basis of property gotten rid of), 5 ("sale" costs of property gotten rid of), and 7 (boot conveyed). My line 5 has a helpful asterisk which is not on the IRS form. It reminds you to put the **land value** of the property gotten rid of back into its basis.

19   (realized gain or loss) matches my line 8 (actual gain).

20   (recognized gain) matches my line 17 (taxable gain).

21   (deferred gain or loss) is the amount of tax you saved because you did the exchange. There is no such line on my worksheet. There is **no tax reason** for IRS to have you calculate that. Maybe the bigger the deferred gain, the more likely they'll audit the exchange documents to see if they can disallow it.

22   (basis of like-kind property received) matches line i (new adjusted basis) of the worksheet on page 127 of this book.

Example

You exchanged an apartment building in which the following applied:

market value of property gotten rid of	$500,000
existing loans on that building	$260,000
adjusted basis of that building	$250,000
"sale" costs	$5,000
equity in your old building	$240,000
market value of property being acquired	$1,000,000
loans on property being acquired	$770,000
equity in property being acquired	$230,000

Since you start this exchange with $240,000 in equity and end it with $230,000 in equity, the other party must give you $10,000 in cash to balance the equities.

Here's the worksheet filled in to calculate the taxable gain.

Worksheet for Calculating Taxable Gain on Partially Taxed Exchange

PART ONE: Actual Gain

1. Fair market value of property received $1,000,000

2. Plus boot received (beginning equity less ending equity---zero or positive number only)..................................$10,000

3. Plus liabilities on property gotten rid of...............................$260,000

4. Less adjusted basis of property gotten rid of * $250,000

5. Less "sale" costs of property gotten rid of................................$5,000

6. Less liabilities on property received....................................$770,000

7. Less boot conveyed (ending equity less beginning equity---zero or positive number only)..$0

8. Actual gain or (loss) (sum of lines 1 through 7).........................$245,000

PART TWO: Net Mortgage Relief

9. Liabilities on property gotten rid of.....................................$260,000

10. Less liabilities on property received....................................$770,000

11. Net relief from liabilities (zero or positive number only)......................$0

PART THREE: Taxable gain

12. Net relief from liabilities (line 11)..$0

13. Less boot conveyed (line 7)...$0

14. Less "sale" costs of property gotten rid of (line 5).........................$5,000

15. Plus boot received (line 2) $10,000

16. Indicated gain (total of lines 12 through 15) $5,000

17. Taxable gain (smaller of line 8 or line 16).................................$5,000

* Don't forget the original cost of the **land** in the property gotten rid of. If you get the adjusted basis off a tax return, you're only getting the value of the **improvements**.

How to calculate your new basis in an exchange

Fill in the blanks on this worksheet to get your new adjusted basis in an exchange.

Worksheet for Calculating New Basis After Exchange

a. Adjusted basis of property gotten rid of (line 4)...................._____

b. Plus "sale" costs (line 5) ...._____

c. Plus costs of acquisition on property received * ...._____

d. Plus liabilities on property received (line 6) ...._____

e. Plus boot conveyed (line 7)..._____

f. Plus taxable gain (line 17).._____

g. Less liabilities on property gotten rid of (line 3) ...._____

h. Less boot received (line 2).._____

i. New adjusted basis (sum of lines a through h) ...._____

* Don't overlook items paid outside of closing like attorney's fees or loan application fees.

Example

Add one fact to the previous example: you spend $4,000 acquiring the exchange property.

Worksheet for Calculating New Basis After Exchange

a. Adjusted basis of property gotten rid of (line 4)........................$250,000

b. Plus "sale" costs (line 5) $5,000

c. Plus costs of acquisition on property received * $4,000

d. Plus liabilities on property received (line 6) $770,000

e. Plus boot conveyed (line 7)...$0

f. Plus taxable gain (line 17)..$5,000

g. Less liabilities on property gotten rid of (line 3) $260,000

h. Less boot received (line 2)..$10,000

i. New adjusted basis (sum of lines a through h) $764,000

Purchase

If you **bought** the property, your basis is your **cost**. Not just the price, but also any other amounts you spent to become the owner. In real estate, most closing costs are part of your basis. Here's a list of items other than price which are included in your basis in a real estate purchase.

Expenditures which you include in basis

- Escrow fee
- Disbursement, settlement, or closing fee
- Attorney fee (acquisition portion only; not loan portion)
- Title insurance (if paid by you rather than seller)
- Recording fees
- Survey (if any)
- Preparation of title transfer documents
- Purchase commission (unusual but possible)
- Option cost (even if paid years earlier)
- Termite inspector's fee
- Transfer taxes (if any)
- Payment of taxes, interest, etc. owed by seller
- Legal fee for reducing assessment levied against the property to pay local benefits (Oddball situation)
- Any other capital expenditures connected to the acquisition

Loan items

In most cases, you also get a loan when you acquire property. Either a new loan or an existing loan. And there are usually costs associated with getting the loan.

On your principal residence, you can deduct points in the year you pay them if the points are:

> *incurred in connection with the purchase or improvement of, and secured by, the principal residence of the taxpayer...*

You **cannot** deduct points all in the year you paid them if you **refinance**—unless the refinancing was "in connection with" **improvement** of your principal residence. VA points paid by the borrower are **not deductible** because they are considered service fees, not interest. [J.K. Lasser's *Your Income Tax* ¶15.13]

All other loan charges are either have no tax consequences (your principal residence) or must be amortized over the term of the loan (investment property, business property, home office). Amortized means you divide the total charges by the term of the loan and deduct the result each year. For example, if you paid $15,000 to get a 30-year mortgage on an apartment building, you would amortize or deduct $15,000 ÷ 30 = $500 per year.

Loan expenditures which you must amortize on investment property

- Appraisal fee
- Credit application fee
- Attorney fee (portion attributable to loan)
- Title insurance for lender's policy
- Mortgage broker fee or commission

• Survey cost attributable to loan
• Points

Expenditures at acquisition time fall into three categories

• Basis items.
• Loan items.
• Operating expenses.

Basis items are depreciated (except for raw land). Loan items must be amortized (residence points being the only exception). You deduct operating expenses in the year to which they apply. The typical closing statement on the next two pages shows examples of the three kinds of acquisition-time expenditures. The basis items are labelled "B," the loan items, "L," and the operating expenses, "E." The charges which are not labelled are either seller charges or have no tax effect.

Form Approved
OMB No. 63-R1501

A. U.S. DEPARTMENT OF HOUSING & URBAN DEVELOPMENT	B. TYPE OF LOAN:

DISCLOSURE/SETTLEMENT STATEMENT

B. TYPE OF LOAN:
1. ☐ FHA   2. ☐ FMHA   3. ☐ CONV. UNINS.
4. ☐ VA   5. ☐ CONV. INS.

6. FILE NUMBER

7. LOAN NUMBER

OFFICE   NO.

If the Truth-in-Lending Act applies to this transaction, a Truth-in-Lending statement is attached as page 3 of this form.

8. MORTG. INS. CASE NO.

C. **NOTE:** This form is furnished to you prior to settlement to give you information about your settlement costs, and again after settlement to show the actual costs you have paid. The present copy of the form is:

☐ ADVANCE DISCLOSURE OF COSTS. Some items are estimated, and are marked "(e)". Some amounts may change if the settlement is held on a date other than the date estimated below. The preparer of this form is not responsible for errors or changes in amounts furnished by others. Advance disclosure of prorations of taxes and assessments is based upon the assumption that taxes and assessments are not delinquent.

☐ STATEMENT OF ACTUAL COSTS. Amounts paid to and by the settlement agent are shown. Items marked "(p.o.c.)" were paid outside the closing; they are shown here for informational purposes and are not included in totals.

D. NAME OF BORROWER	E. SELLER	F. LENDER

G. PROPERTY LOCATION	H. SETTLEMENT AGENT	I. DATES
		LOAN COMMITMENT	ADVANCE DISCLOSURE
	PLACE OF SETTLEMENT	SETTLEMENT 7/1/82	DATE OF PRORATIONS IF DIFFERENT FROM SETTLEMENT

J. SUMMARY OF BORROWER'S TRANSACTION		K. SUMMARY OF SELLER'S TRANSACTION	
100. GROSS AMOUNT DUE FROM BORROWER:		400. GROSS AMOUNT DUE TO SELLER:	
		401. Contract sales price	100,000
101. Contract sales price Ⓑ	100,000	402. Personal property	0
102. Personal property	0	403.	
103. Settlement charges to borrower *(from line 1400, Section L)*	2,596	404.	
104.		Adjustments for items paid by seller in advance:	
105.		405. City/town taxes to	
		406. County taxes 4/15/82 to 7/1/82	157.60
Adjustments for items paid by seller in advance:		407. Assessments to	
106. City/town taxes to		408. to	
107. County taxes 4/15/82 to 7/1/82 Ⓑ	157.60	409. to	
108. Assessments to		410. to	
109. to		411. to	
110. to		420. GROSS AMOUNT DUE TO SELLER	100157.60
111. to			
112. to		*NOTE: The following 500 and 600 series sections are not required to be completed when this form is used for advance disclosure of settlement costs prior to settlement.*	
120. GROSS AMOUNT DUE FROM BORROWER:	102753.60		
200. AMOUNTS PAID BY OR IN BEHALF OF BORROWER:		500. REDUCTIONS IN AMOUNT DUE TO SELLER:	
		501. Payoff of first mortgage loan	35,167
201. Deposit or earnest money	5,000	502. Payoff of second mortgage loan	
202. Principal amount of new loan(s)	80,000	503. Settlement charges to seller *(from line 1400, Section L)*	6,196
203. Existing loan(s) taken subject to			
204.		504. Existing loan(s) taken subject to	
205.		505.	
		506.	
Credits to borrower for items unpaid by seller:		507.	
206. City/town taxes to		508.	
207. County taxes to		509.	
208. Assessments to		Credits to borrower for items unpaid by seller:	
209. to			
210. to		510. City/town taxes to	
211. to		511. County taxes to	
212. to		512. Assessments to	
220. TOTAL AMOUNTS PAID BY OR IN BEHALF OF BORROWER	85,000	513. to	
		514. to	
300. CASH AT SETTLEMENT REQUIRED FROM OR PAYABLE TO BORROWER		515. to	
301. Gross amount due from borrower *(from line 120)*	102753.60	520. TOTAL REDUCTIONS IN AMOUNT DUE TO SELLER:	41363
		600. CASH TO SELLER FROM SETTLEMENT:	
302. Less amounts paid by or in behalf of borrower *(from line 220)*	(85000)	601. Gross amount due to seller *(from line 420)*	100157.60
		602. Less total reductions in amount due to seller *(from line 520)*	(41363)
303. CASH (☒ REQUIRED FROM) OR ☐ PAYABLE TO) BORROWER	17753.60	603. CASH TO SELLER FROM SETTLEMENT	58,794.60

ORIGINAL — BANK COPY

HUD-1 (5-75)

Page 2

L. SETTLEMENT CHARGES		PAID FROM BORROWER'S FUNDS	PAID FROM SELLER'S FUNDS
700. SALES BROKER'S COMMISSION based on price $100,000 @ 6%			
701. Total commission paid by seller			6,000.00
Division of commission as follows:			
702. $ to			
703. $ to			
704.			
800. ITEMS PAYABLE IN CONNECTION WITH LOAN.	Ⓛ	425.00	
801. Loan Origination fee %			
802. Loan Discount %			
803. Appraisal Fee to	Ⓛ	22.80	
804. Credit Report to			
805. Lender's inspection fee			
806. Mortgage Insurance application fee to			
807. Assumption/refinancing fee			
808.			
809.			
810.			
811.			
900. ITEMS REQUIRED BY LENDER TO BE PAID IN ADVANCE.	Ⓔ	451.40	
901. Interest from to @ $ /day			
902. Mortgage insurance premium for mo. to	Ⓔ	400.00	
903. Hazard insurance premium for yrs. to			
904. yrs. to			
905.			
1000. RESERVES DEPOSITED WITH LENDER FOR:		38.08	
1001. Hazard insurance mo. @ $ / mo.			
1002. Mortgage insurance mo. @ $ / mo.			
1003. City property taxes mo. @ $ / mo.		414.12	
1004. County property taxes mo. @ $ / mo.			
1005. Annual assessments mo. @ $ / mo.			
1006. mo. @ $ / mo.			
1007. mo. @ $ / mo.			
1008. mo. @ $ / mo.			
1100. TITLE CHARGES.	Ⓑ	35.00	
1101. Settlement or closing fee to			
1102. Abstract or title search to			
1103. Title examination to			
1104. Title insurance binder to	Ⓑ	50.00	
1105. Document preparation to			
1106. Notary fees to			
1107. Attorney's Fees to	Ⓑ+Ⓛ	300.00	
(includes above items No.:)			
1108. Title insurance to	Ⓑ	301.60	
(includes above items No.:)			
1109. Lender's coverage $			
1110. Owner's coverage $			
1111. Reconveyance fee			40.00
1112.			
1113.			
1200. GOVERNMENT RECORDING AND TRANSFER CHARGES	Ⓑ Ⓛ		
1201. Recording fees: Deed $3.00 ; Mortgage $5.00 Releases $6.00		8.00	6.00
1202. City/county tax/stamps; Deed $; Mortgage $			
1203. State tax/stamps: Deed $ 100.00 ; Mortgage $			100.00
1204.			
1300. ADDITIONAL SETTLEMENT CHARGES	Ⓑ	150.00	
1301. Survey to			
1302. Pest inspection to			50.00
1303.			
1304.			
1305.			
1400. TOTAL SETTLEMENT CHARGES (entered on lines 103 and 503, Sections J and K)		2,596.00	6,196.00

NOTE: Under certain circumstances the borrower and seller may be permitted to waive the 12-day period which must normally occur between advance disclosure and settlement. In the event such a waiver is made, copies of the statements of waiver, executed as provided in the regulations of the Department of Housing and Urban Development, shall be attached to and made a part of this form when the form is used as a settlement statement.

Warning: There are probably other expenditures which are includable in basis or otherwise deductible which are **not** on the closing statement. Go over the expenditures in your check book starting when you first made an offer on the property. Look for checks payable to the:

- Real estate agent
- Lender
- Seller
- Your attorney
- Subcontractors like surveyors and termite inspectors
- Title companies
- Escrow companies
- Local government
- Existing lender.

After you buy the property

As you claim depreciation deductions each year, your basis goes down. But it can go **up**, too. Additions to your basis occur in several ways:

- Improvements
- Legal fees to defend title
- Legal fees to reduce tax assessment
- Demolition costs (added to basis of land).

You should have a loose leaf notebook for capital (depreciable assets and land) assets which you own—with dividers for each asset.

12

Break Out Personal Property and Land Improvements

Six classes of property

As far as real estate investors are concerned, there are six main classes of property:

1. Five-year property
2. Seven-year property
3. Mobilehomes
4. Land improvements
5. Residential real property
6. Non-residential real property.

Property eligible for first-year expensing is a subcategory of the first two categories.

Each class must be depreciated differently. The higher the property is in the hierarchy listed above, the higher the present value of the deductions—which is good for you.

Here are the percentages of original basis you can deduct each year for each class:

Annual deductions as percentage of original basis*

Year	5-year	7-year	10-year	15-year	residential	non-residential
1	20	14.28	10	5	3.64	3.17
2	32	24.49	18	9.5	3.64	3.17
3	19.20	17.49	14.40	8.55	3.64	3.17
4	11.52	12.49	11.52	7.695	3.64	3.17
5	11.52	8.93	9.22	6.926	3.64	3.17
6	5.76	8.93	7.37	6.233	3.64	3.17
7		8.93	6.55	5.905	3.64	3.17
8		4.46	6.55	5.905	3.64	3.17
9			6.55	5.905	3.64	3.17
10			6.55	5.905	3.64	3.17
11			3.29	5.905	3.64	3.17
12-15				5.905	3.64	3.17
16				2.951	3.64	3.17
17-27					3.64	3.17
28					1.82	3.17
29-31						3.17
32						1.59

* Assumes January purchase

When it comes to deductions, sooner is better than later. So the shorter the recovery period, the greater the present value of the deductions. Also, the depreciation methods for the 5- through 15-year categories are **accelerated**. That's better than the **straight line** method required for residential and non-residential.

Did you only buy real property?

When you buy a building, do you only buy real property? Or do you get some real property and some personal property? A refrigerator, for example, is personal property. So is an electric range, tacked-down carpet, a dishwasher, lobby furniture, a clothes washer, a dryer.

Personal property gets a much better deal on depreciation than real property. So it's a big mistake to lump real and personal property together and depreciate both as real property. That would mean you are depreciating over 27.5 years carpet that you had to replace four years after you bought the property.

Get the *sequence* right, too

Step one: Break the purchase price into real and personal property
Step two: Break the real property into land and improvements.
Step three: Break the improvements into land improvements and structure.

Here's an example. You buy a rental house for $100,000. The typical schmuck would figure 30% is land and 70% improvements (based on his property tax assessment). He would then depreciate the 70% or $70,000 over 27.5 years giving him a first-year deduction (assuming January purchase date) of 3.49% x $70,000 = $2,443.

Here's the right way.

Personal property

Item	Cost	First-year depreciation
Used refrigerator	$200	$28.56
Used dishwasher	$150	$21.42
Used washer	$150	$21.42
Used dryer	$200	$28.56
Used carpet	$750	$107.10
Used range	$150	$21.42
Total	$1,600	$228.48

Real property

If the total cost was $100,000—and $1,600 of that price represents personal property—then $100,000 - $1,600 = $98,400 must be real property. **That** $98,400 figure needs to be broken down into land and improvements—**not** the $100,000 total which includes personal property.

The $98,400 consists of three categories:

1. Land
2. Land improvements
3. Structure.

I'll use the 70% improvement ratio to be consistent. But as I'll explain in the next chapter, you can probably do better than that.

Item	Cost
Land (30% x $98,400)	$29,520
Improvements	$68,880

Let's say the land improvements (paving, landscaping, etc.) are worth $5,000. That leaves $68,880 - $5,000 = $63,880 for the structure. The first-year depreciation deductions on those two items would be:

5% (from table)	x	$5,000	=	$250.00
3.49% (from table)	x	$63,880	=	$2,229.41

Total first-year depreciation deductions the right way

Personal property	$228.48
Land improvements	250.00
Real property	$2,229.41
Total	$2,707.89

Note that this total is $2,707.89 - $2,443 = $264.89 more than the typical schmuck would deduct. And if the property in question were worth $1,000,000 instead of $100,000, the disparity would be $27,078.90 - $24,430 = $2,648.90.

And don't forget the sequence: break out personal—then break **what's left** into land and improvements. If you get the sequence **backwards**, you'll get this:

What happens when you get the sequence backwards

Item	Cost	First-year depreciation
Personal property	$1,600	$228.48
Land (30% x $100,000)	$30,000	$0.00
Land improvements	$5,000	$250.00
Improvements	$63,400	$2,212.66
Total	$100,000	$2,691.14

Note that you do not increase your depreciation deductions by following this advice. You just bunch them closer to the beginning of your acquisition date. That increases the present value of the deductions. After the first six to eight years, the personal property deductions will drop to zero because they'll be fully depreciated. And after the first sixteen years, the land improvements deductions will drop to zero. Then you'll only have the 3.64% x $63,880 = $2,325.23 annual real property deduction—which is less than the typical schmuck's $2,443. When all is said and done, both you and the typical schmuck will have depreciated your property. But you'll claim your deductions **sooner** and you'll depreciate a **little more** because you got the sequence correct and therefore had a slightly allocation to land value.

First-year expensing property

Coin-operated washers and dryers are eligible for first-year expensing and they are the only things so eligible in apartments and rental houses. But in **non**-residential and hotel/motel, virtually everything that is not glued down is eligible for first-year expensing.

First-year expensing is an even better deal than regular personal property depreciation. So you want as high a percentage of your acquisition cost to be allocated to personal property as you can justify. And you want as high a percentage of that personal property to be allocated to property eligible for first-year expensing—at least up to the $10,000 per year limit on first-year expensing.

The legal definition of personal property

As a general rule, property is considered personal rather than real if it is not attached to real property—or, if it is attached, the attachment is not permanent. Most of the legal authority on the subject comes from disputes over what property was eligible for the pre-'86 investment tax credit.

From those disputes, here's a list of property which was held to be personal property and which many people might have thought was real property.

Signs—"Neon and other signs" says regulation § 1.48-1(c) Not "pole signs permanently embedded in concrete." *Southland Corporation v U.S.*, 42 AFTR 2d 78-6269 Movable signs are personal property. And identifying symbols in buildings (*Senate Finance Committee Report*)

Wall-to-wall carpet—If it's tacked down, rather than glued down. Revenue Ruling 67-349

Display racks and shelves—Regulation § 1.48-1(c)

Fire extinguishers—Rev. Rul. 67-417

Movable partitions—Office building stuff. Rev. Rul. 75-178 and *King Radio Corp. v. U.S.*, 486 F2d 1091

Telephone poles—Reg. § 1.48-1(c)

Truck bay doors—*Consolidated Freightways, Inc.,* 74 TC 768

Ornamental fixtures and pictures—But not art work. Senate Report PL 95-600 11/6/78 page 117

Special lighting for the exterior of a building—*Ibid.*

Generally, if it ain't glued down, call it personal property. And if it ain't connected to the building, call it land improvements.

What are land improvements?

- Landscaping
- Pavement (roads, parking lots, and sidewalks)
- Underground pipes and drains not serving the building
- Curbs
- Fences
- Bridges and tunnels
- Landscape sprinkler system and drains
- Site lighting
- Finish grading under the above but not under the building
- Canals (Rev. Ruling 75-137)
- Excavation for lagoon (less value of fill kept on site, *Tunnell v. U.S.,* 512 F 2d 1192)

The authority for depreciating land improvements over 15 years is:

- IRC 168(b)2 and (e)1
- General Explanation of the Tax Reform Act of 1986, Staff of the Joint Committee on Taxation, 1987 at 99, 102
- Revenue Procedure 87-56

See also "Performing a Cost Segregation Analysis to Maximize Property Depreciation," 2 *Real Estate Acct. & Tax'n* 22 (Spring 1987). Also, *Federal Income Taxation of Real Estate* ¶6.04[5] and ¶15.02[6].

Life estates

If a remainder estate is owned by a party unrelated to the life estate owner, the life estate owner may amortize his interest over the expected life of the life tenant. The taxpayer may simultaneously depreciate the improvements on the property. (See "Amortizing Life Estates and Term Interests After the Revenue Reconciliation Act of 1989" 68 Taxes 459)

13

How to Justify a High Improvement Ratio

Raw land is not depreciable. Most real estate includes both land and improvements.

> *If God put it there, it's undepreciable land. If Man put it there, it's a depreciable improvement.*

Another way to put it is that in order to depreciate something, you have to prove it has a limited life. Land and works of art are not depreciable because they last forever.

But you probably do not know that some things that **look** like land are actually depreciable improvements. **Paving**, for example.

Also, land preparation costs like **excavation** and **grading** are depreciable. (Revenue Rulings 72-96, 65-265, 68-193, and 74-265)

Landscaping is depreciable. As are buried pipes and wires.

Common house improvement ratios

According to the newsletter, *U.S. Housing Markets*, the following are common improvement ratios for single-family homes:

Typical U.S. home	75% to 80%
Duplex or townhouse	80% to 85%
Boston, Milwaukee, NY, Portland	70%
Riverside, Sacramento, San Francisco area	70%
Los Angeles, San Diego	60%
Water and view lots in Orange County, CA	25%

What the law says about your improvement ratio

You have to allocate part of your basis to land and part to improvements in the first tax return you file after you acquire a property. According to Regulation § 1.167(a)-5, you make that allocation by the **respective values of the land and improvements at the time of the acquisition**.

The actual wording is less clear:

> basis...cannot exceed an amount which bears the same proportion to the lump sum as the value of the depreciable property at the time of acquisition bears to the value of the entire property at that time.

The **over valuation penalties** are pertinent to the choice of an improvement ratio (value of improvements ÷ value of both land and improvements). But as I said earlier, an aggressive improvement ratio probably would not trigger an over valuation penalty because you have to be 200% too high. If 65% were the correct ratio, you'd have to use a ratio of 200% x 65% = 130% to trigger the penalty. Aggressive taxpayers rarely go above 90% to 95%.

How to calculate your improvement ratio

Nearly all real estate investors use the improvement ratio from their property tax assessment. That's usually nutso. Those ratios are generally low and inaccurate.

Professional appraisers cost too much to hire them just to come up with an improvement ratio.

Do-it-yourself is the only sensible way.

Remember to multiply the improvement ratio by **what's left** after you subtract the total value of the personal property that came with the building. Do **not** divide the total cost of the property into land and improvements **then** divide the improvements into real and personal property.

Remember also that grading, paving, landscaping, pipes, etc. raise the value of improved land over that of unimproved land. So in making your land appraisal, do not use comparable land sales in which the land in question had underground utilities, sidewalks, etc.

Agreement with seller

A lot of semi-sophisticated investors try to allocate the purchase price to land, real property improvements, and personal property in the purchase agreement. They think that settles it.

Wrong.

Courts are not impressed by agreement allocations

The seller couldn't care less what land, improvement, personal property allocation you make in the purchase agreement. All he cares about is the **total**. The courts know that.

The courts are only interested in what the agreement says about the allocation if the buyer and seller had "**substantial and opposite interests**." The total price you pay is the prime example of substantial and opposite interests.

In the case of *Commissioner v. Gazette Telegraph Co.*, 209 F2d 926, the court accepted an allocation made in the agreement because that buyer and seller had substantial and opposite interests. But in *Particelli v. Commissioner*, 212 F2d 498, the court said the allocation was just "window dressing" put there for the buyer's tax benefit—and the court ignored Particelli's agreement allocation.

Does that mean you shouldn't put a favorable-to-you allocation in the purchase agreement?

No. Go ahead and put it in. It can't hurt. And it might even convince a not-very-well-trained IRS agent to accept your allocation. But do not try to use it in a court proceeding unless you've got some evidence of substantial and opposite interests; i.e., some evidence that it is important for the seller to show the **lowest** possible improvement ratio.

High improvement ratios do not increase chances of audit

Your improvement ratio does **not** appear on your tax return. All you put on the IRS form is your "Cost or other basis." By that, they mean the cost or other basis of the depreciable **improvements**.

Not only is there no place on the form for your improvement ratio—there is no place for the **total** (land plus improvements) cost of the property either. So IRS cannot program its computers to **calculate** your improvement ratio from data on the return. The only way they can find out your improvement ratio is to **ask** you.

Therefore, choosing a high improvement ratio cannot increase the probability you will be audited. Because the classifier (guy who decides who to audit) cannot tell from the returns which taxpayers used high improvement ratios and which used low improvement ratios.

For example, you may put $450,000 as your **depreciable** cost on your IRS form. If your **total** cost was $500,000, that's a rather high $450,000/$500,000 = 90% improvement ratio. But for all IRS knows, that $450,000 depreciable cost may represent a conservative **50%** improvement ratio on a $900,000 purchase price.

The next page shows the depreciation and amortization form.

Form **4562**	**Depreciation and Amortization**	OMB No. 1545-0172
Department of the Treasury Internal Revenue Service	▶ See separate instructions. ▶ Attach this form to your return.	**19 89** Attachment Sequence No. **67**
Name(s) as shown on return		Identifying number

Business or activity to which this form relates

Part I Depreciation (Use Part III for automobiles, certain other vehicles, computers, and property used for entertainment, recreation, or amusement.)

Section A.—Election To Expense Depreciable Assets (Section 179)

1 Maximum dollar limitation	1	$10,000
2 Total cost of section 179 property placed in service during the tax year (see instructions)	2	
3 Threshold cost of section 179 property before reduction in limitation	3	$200,000
4 Reduction in limitation (Subtract line 3 from line 2, but do not enter less than -0-.)	4	
5 Dollar limitation for tax year (Subtract line 4 from line 1, but do not enter less than -0-.)	5	

(a) Description of property	(b) Date placed in service	(c) Cost	(d) Elected cost
6			

7 Listed property—Enter amount from line 28	7	
8 Tentative deduction (Enter the lesser of: (a) line 6 plus line 7; or (b) line 5.)	8	
9 Taxable income limitation (Enter the lesser of :(a) Taxable income; or (b) line 5) (see instructions)	9	
10 Carryover of disallowed deduction from 1988 (see instructions)	10	
11 Section 179 expense deduction (Enter the lesser of: (a) line 8 plus line 10; or (b) line 9.)	11	
12 Carryover of disallowed deduction to 1990 (Add lines 8 and 10, less line 11.) ▶ 12		

Section B.—MACRS Depreciation

(a) Classification of property	(b) Date placed in service	(c) Basis for depreciation (Business use only—see instructions)	(d) Recovery period	(e) Convention	(f) Method	(g) Depreciation deduction
13 General Depreciation System (GDS) (see instructions): *For assets placed in service ONLY during tax year beginning in 1989*						
a 3-year property						
b 5-year property						
c 7-year property						
d 10-year property						
e 15-year property						
f 20-year property						
g Residential rental property			27.5 yrs.	MM	S/L	
			27.5 yrs.	MM	S/L	
h Nonresidential real property			31.5 yrs.	MM	S/L	
			31.5 yrs.	MM	S/L	
14 Alternative Depreciation System (ADS) (see instructions): *For assets placed in service ONLY during tax year beginning in 1989*						
a Class life					S/L	
b 12-year			12 yrs.		S/L	
c 40-year			40 yrs.	MM	S/L	

15 Listed property—Enter amount from line 27	15	
16 GDS and ADS deductions for assets placed in service before 1989 (see instructions)	16	

Section C.—ACRS and/or Other Depreciation

17 Property subject to section 168(f)(1) election (see instructions)	17	
18 ACRS and/or other depreciation (see instructions)	18	

Section D.—Summary

19 Total (Add deductions on line 11 and lines 13 through 18.) Enter here and on the appropriate line of your return (Partnerships and S corporations—see instructions.)	19	
20 For assets shown above and placed in service during the current year, enter the portion of the basis attributable to section 263A costs (see instructions).	20	

For Paperwork Reduction Act Notice, see page 1 of the separate instructions.

Form **4562** (1989)

What you put on your tax return is your first offer in a possible negotiation with IRS

Remember that an audit is a negotiation, not a trial where you have to prove your innocence. He has the power to send you a deficiency letter. You have the power to take IRS to the Tax Court.

As in any other negotiation, your first offer should be as favorable to you as possible—within the bounds of the law. The bounds of the law are the definitions of negligence and so forth which I explained earlier. In a negotiation to buy real estate, you can be as ridiculous as you want with your first offer. But in your potential negotiation with IRS, you must make your "first offer" (tax return) fall inside the range of reasonableness and good faith required by the various provisions of the Internal Revenue Code. But you **do** have the legal right to make your "first offer" as favorable to you as possible **within that reasonable, good faith range**.

Remember that there is a more than 90% probability that IRS will accept your "first offer" (tax return) because they only audit a small percentage of returns. And if you are one of the few that are audited, the chances that the IRS guy will inquire about your improvement ratio are quite slim.

I'm not saying violate the law because you'll probably get away with it. Rather I'm saying that you should choose the most favorable improvement ratio which you can within the legal range because the probability that you will get to keep the ratio you pick is almost 100%.

14

The Rehabilitation Tax Credit

Credits are different from deductions

You deduct a **deduction** from your income. A credits is a much better deal. Because you deduct a credit from your tax payable—not from your income.

To put it another way, A $1,000 deduction will save you $385 if you are in the 38.5% bracket. But a $1,000 credit will save you $1,000—no matter what your bracket.

No more investment tax credit

Effective January 1, 1986, there was no more investment tax credit. The investment tax credit was important for owners of non-residential and hotel/motel property. Residential property owners could only use it for coin-operated washers and dryers and new elevators and escalators.

But the rehab tax credit lives on—in modified form—after the Tax Reform Act of 1986.

The rehab tax credit

The rehab tax credit amount is:

Property type	% credit
Non-residential* built before 1936	10% of rehab cost
Historic	20% of rehab cost

* The pre-TRA '86 law limited the credit to **non**-residential property unless the property was historic. And the Senate Finance Committee report which led to TRA '86 limited the credit to **non**-residential property unless the property was historic. But guess what? Congress forgot to limit the non-historic rehab credit to non-residential property **in the actual law**. See IRC § 48(g)(2)(A)(i)(II).

Congress will probably correct that in the future Technical Corrections Act to the TRA '86. But they might not make the correction retroactive.

The current law says you can claim the rehab tax credit on both residential and non-residential property built before 1936. If you make a qualified expenditure on a residential property, **claim** the credit. But **do not count** on being able to keep the credit in deciding whether to rehab a non-historic, residential building.

What you have to do to qualify

Your non-historic rehab must pass the following three tests to qualify:

1. 50% or more of the existing external walls must be retained in place as external walls and
2. 75% or more of the existing external walls must be retained in place as either internal or external walls and
3. 75% or more of the existing internal structural framework of the building must be retained in place.

These walls and framework tests do **not** apply to historic buildings.

Basis reduced by amount of the credit

If you spend $100,000 rehabbing a building, your basis in that rehab is normally $100,000. But if you claim a 10% or $10,000 credit on that rehab, your basis in the rehab would be $100,000 - $10,000 = $90,000.

Passive loss limits and the rehab credit

Your ability to claim rehab tax credits is limited by the passive loss limits. If your adjusted gross income is $200,000 or less, you can claim the **credit equivalent** of a $25,000 loss deduction. Note that I said "credit equivalent," **not** that you could claim a **credit** of up to $25,000.

If you are in the 38.5% bracket, a $25,000 loss would save you 38.5% x $25,000 = $9,625. So, in this example, your credit limit would be $9,625.

The $25,000 credit equivalent phases out at a rate of 50¢ for every dollar by which your adjusted gross exceeds $200,000. If your adjusted gross were $212,000, your limit would be $25,000 - ($12,000 x .50 = $6,000) = $19,000. At an adjusted gross of $250,000, the limit is completely phased out. In other words, taxpayers with adjusted gross incomes (not counting rental property losses or income) of $250,000 or more are **ineligible** for the rehab tax credit.

Qualified rehab is automatically 'active participation'

Limited partners and other who do not "actively participate" in the management of rental property generally cannot deduct rental property losses until they completely dispose of the property in question. But that requirement does **not** apply to the rehab tax credit. Investors who are not "actively participating" in management—even limited partners—can claim the rehab tax credit if a qualified rehab is done on a property they own.

The historic property rehab tax credit

I explained the historic credit in the chapter on tax differences between property types so I won't go into it again here.

15

Depreciation

Here are the depreciation deduction tables for each property type:

Depreciation deductions as percent of original basis

Year	5-year	7-year	10-year	15-year
1	20.00	14.28	10.00	5.000
2	32.00	24.49	18.00	9.500
3	19.20	17.49	14.40	8.550
4	11.52	12.49	11.52	7.695
5	11.52	8.93	9.22	6.926
6	5.76	8.93	7.37	6.233
7		8.93	6.55	5.905
8		4.46	6.55	5.905
9			6.55	5.905
10			6.55	5.905
11			3.29	5.905
12-15				5.905
16				2.951

For example, if you bought a computer (five-year property) for $2,000 in 1987, you'd deduct:

Year	% from table above		Original basis		Deduction
1987	20.00	x	$2,000	=	$400.00
1988	32.00	x	$2,000	=	$640.00
1989	19.20	x	$2,000	=	$384.00
1990	11.52	x	$2,000	=	$230.40
1991	11.52	x	$2,000	=	$230.40
1992	5.76	x	$2,000	=	$115.20
Total	100.00		n/a		$2,000.00

Residential real property placed in service after December 31, 1986

Year	Jan	Feb	Mar	Apr	May	Jun	Jul	Aug	Sep	Oct	Nov	Dec
1	3.49	3.19	2.88	2.58	2.28	1.97	1.67	1.37	1.06	0.76	0.46	0.15
2-27	3.64	3.64	3.64	3.64	3.64	3.64	3.64	3.64	3.64	3.64	3.64	3.64
28	1.87	2.17	2.48	2.78	3.08	3.39	3.64	3.64	3.64	3.64	3.64	3.64
29	0.00	0.00	0.00	0.00	0.00	0.00	0.05	0.35	0.66	0.96	1.26	1.57

Non-Residential real property placed in service after December 31, 1986

Year	Jan	Feb	Mar	Apr	May	Jun	Jul	Aug	Sep	Oct	Nov	Dec
1	3.04	2.77	2.51	2.25	1.98	1.72	1.45	1.19	0.92	0.66	0.40	0.13
2-31	3.17	3.17	3.17	3.17	3.17	3.17	3.17	3.17	3.17	3.17	3.17	3.17
32	1.86	2.13	2.39	2.65	2.92	3.17	3.17	3.17	3.17	3.17	3.17	3.17
33	0.00	0.00	0.00	0.00	0.00	0.01	0.28	0.54	0.81	1.07	1.33	1.60

The months across the top are for the month you bought the property.

If you wish, you can depreciate real property over **40 years** straight-line instead of 27.5 and 31.5 years. That would only make sense if using the minimum recovery period would result in losses which you could neither deduct currently nor carry forward to deduct in future years—or if using the minimum recovery period would trigger the **alternative minimum tax** and your tax rate is otherwise lower than the alternative minimum tax rate (21%).

A property is residential if 80% or more of its gross income comes from residential rentals. Hotel/motel space is **not** residential. Mobilehomes **are** residential.

If you move out of your house and turn it into rental property after 1986, it's treated as if you bought it when you convert it to rental. That is, the 27.5-year recovery period applies.

The definition of five- and seven-year property

Cars and light duty trucks are five-year property. So are computers, typewriters, and copiers. Seven-year property includes office furniture, fixtures, refrigerators, and equipment.

You want five-year rather than seven- whenever possible because the shorter recovery period increases the present value of the deductions.

Five- and seven-year property is depreciated using the **200% declining balance method** and the **half-year convention**. But you don't need to worry about either because those two facts are contained in the depreciation tables above. That would only make sense if using accelerated would result in losses which you could neither deduct currently nor carry forward to deduct in future years—or if using accelerated would trigger the **alternative minimum tax** and your tax rate is otherwise lower than the alternative minimum tax rate (24%).

You get a half-year's worth of depreciation in the year you dispose of five- or seven-year property. There's no table for that. Just take the percentage you **would** have gotten that year if you had **not** disposed of the property and divide it in half.

Special rules for cars

There's a special table for cars:

Car depreciation, 50% or more business use placed in service in 1989

Year	% business use	Lesser of
1	___% x	$2,660 or 20.00%
2	___% x	$4,200 or 32.00%
3	___% x	$2,550 or 19.20%
4	___% x	$1,475 or 11.52%
5	___% x	$1,475 or 11.52%
6	___% x	$1,475 or 11.52%
7 and later	___% x	$1,475 maximum

Congress got agitated about wealthy people writing off expensive cars. You can still write them off. But with the maximums in the table above, it'll take you a long time.

Reduce the caps on car deduction if you use the car less than 100% for business. For example, if you use the car 60% for business, your first year limit would be 60% x $2,660 = $1,596.

If you use the car less than 50% for business, you must use the **straight line** method with the half-year convention. Here's that table:

Car depreciation, less than 50% business use

Year	% business use	Lesser of
1	___% x	$1,330 or 10%
2	___% x	$2,660 or 20%
3	___% x	$2,660 or 20%
4	___% x	$2,660 or 20%
5	___% x	$2,660 or 20%
6	___% x	$1,330 or 10%
7 or later	___% x	$1,475 maximum

If you **start out** using the car or other personal property 50% or more for business—then use it **less than** 50% in future years—you must immediately switch to **straight-line** depreciation for the remainder of the recovery period. The extra deductions you got by using accelerated are **recaptured**. That is, you must pay the tax you avoided in the previous years.

Improvements

An improvement is depreciated as if it were a separate building. For example, if you put a $5,000 roof on an apartment building in August, 1987, you'd deduct the following for depreciation:

Year	% from table above		Original basis		Deduction
1987	1.36	x	$5,000	=	$68.00
1988-2014	3.64	x	$5,000	=	$182.00
2015	3.64	x	$5,000	=	$182.00
2016	.36	x	$5,000	=	$18.00

Real property placed in service before 1987

Here are the tables for real property placed in service from 1/1/81 to 12/31/86:

Property placed in service from January 1, 1981 to March 15, 1984

Year	Jan	Feb	Mar	Apr	May	Jun	Jul	Aug	Sep	Oct	Nov	Dec
1	12	11	10	9	8	7	6	5	4	3	2	1
2	10	10	11	11	11	11	11	11	11	11	11	12
3	9	9	9	9	10	10	10	10	10	10	10	10
4	8	8	8	8	8	8	9	9	9	9	9	9
5	7	7	7	7	7	7	8	8	8	8	8	8
6	6	6	6	6	7	7	7	7	7	7	7	7
7	6	6	6	6	6	6	6	6	6	6	6	6
8	6	6	6	6	6	6	5	6	6	6	6	6
9	6	6	6	6	5	6	5	5	5	6	6	6
10	5	6	5	6	5	5	5	5	5	5	6	5
11-15	5	5	5	5	5	5	5	5	5	5	5	5
16	0	0	1	1	2	2	3	3	4	4	4	5

Property placed in service from March 16, 1984 to June 22, 1984

Year	Jan	Feb	Mar	Apr	May	Jun	Jul	Aug	Sep	Oct	Nov	Dec
1	10	9	8	7	6	6	5	4	3	2	2	1
2	9	9	9	9	9	9	9	9	9	10	10	10
3	8	8	8	8	8	8	8	8	9	9	9	9
4	7	7	7	7	7	7	8	8	8	8	8	8
5	6	7	7	7	7	7	7	7	7	7	7	7
6	6	6	6	6	6	6	6	6	6	6	6	6
7	5	5	5	5	6	6	6	6	6	6	6	6
8-12	5	5	5	5	5	5	5	5	5	5	5	5
13	4	4	4	5	5	4	4	5	4	4	4	4
14-18	4	4	4	4	4	4	4	4	4	4	4	4
19	0	0	1	1	1	2	2	2	3	3	3	4

Property placed in service from June 23, 1984 to May 5, 1985

Year	Jan	Feb	Mar	Apr	May	Jun	Jul	Aug	Sep	Oct	Nov	Dec
1	9	9	8	7	6	5	4	4	3	2	1	.4
2	9	9	9	9	9	9	9	9	9	10	10	10
3	8	8	8	8	8	8	8	8	9	9	9	9
4	7	7	7	7	7	7	8	8	8	8	8	8
5	6	7	7	7	7	7	7	7	7	7	7	7
6	6	6	6	6	6	6	6	6	6	6	6	6
7	5	5	5	5	6	6	6	6	6	6	6	6
8-12	5	5	5	5	5	5	5	5	5	5	5	5
13	4	4	4	5	4	4	5	4	4	4	5	5
14-17	4	4	4	4	4	4	4	4	4	4	4	4
18	4	3	4	4	4	4	4	4	4	4	4	4
19	0	1	1	1	2	2	2	3	3	3	3	3.6

Property placed in service from 5/6/85 to 12/31/86, Accelerated

Year	Jan	Feb	Mar	Apr	May	Jun	Jul	Aug	Sep	Oct	Nov	Dec
1	8.8	8.1	7.3	6.5	5.8	5.0	4.2	3.5	2.7	1.9	1.1	0.4
2	8.4	8.5	8.5	8.6	8.7	8.8	8.8	8.9	9.0	9.0	9.1	9.2
3	7.6	7.7	7.7	7.8	7.9	7.9	8.0	8.1	8.1	8.2	8.3	8.3
4	6.9	7.0	7.0	7.1	7.1	7.2	7.3	7.3	7.4	7.4	7.5	7.6
5	6.3	6.3	6.4	6.4	6.5	6.5	6.6	6.6	6.7	6.8	6.8	6.9
6	5.7	5.7	5.8	5.9	5.9	5.9	6.0	6.0	6.1	6.1	6.2	6.2
7	5.2	5.2	5.3	5.3	5.3	5.4	5.4	5.5	5.5	5.6	5.6	5.6
8	4.7	4.7	4.8	4.8	4.8	4.9	4.9	5.0	5.0	5.1	5.1	5.1
9	4.2	4.3	4.3	4.4	4.4	4.5	4.5	4.5	4.5	4.6	4.6	4.7
10-19	4.2	4.2	4.2	4.2	4.2	4.2	4.2	4.2	4.2	4.2	4.2	4.2
20	0.2	0.5	0.9	1.2	1.6	1.9	2.3	2.6	3.0	3.3	3.7	4.0

Property placed in service from 5/6/85 to 12/31/86, Straight-line

Year	Jan	Feb	Mar	Apr	May	Jun	Jul	Aug	Sep	Oct	Nov	Dec
1	5.0	4.6	4.2	3.7	3.3	2.9	2.4	2.0	1.5	1.1	0.7	0.2
2-13	5.3	5.3	5.3	5.3	5.3	5.3	5.3	5.3	5.3	5.3	5.3	5.3
14-19	5.2	5.2	5.2	5.2	5.2	5.2	5.2	5.2	5.2	5.2	5.2	5.2
20	0.2	0.6	1.0	1.5	1.9	2.3	2.8	3.2	3.7	4.1	4.5	5.0

The Alternative Minimum Tax

You really have to compute your depreciation **two** ways:

- The **regular** way described in the tables above
- The Alternative Minimum Tax (AMT) way.

In fact, your state may have its own regular and AMT ways as well. California is one that does. Then you have to calculate it **four** ways.

Here's an article from my newsletter on the subject of how to calculate AMT depreciation.

JOHN T. REED'S
Real Estate Investor's Monthly

Volume 4, Number 3   **April 1989**

AMT Lessons Learned

Even if you've already turned in your 1988 tax return, you can probably benefit from some things I learned about the Alternative Minimum Tax (AMT). You may find that you should file an **amended** return for 1988 and/or 1987. And at the very least, you may learn a trick you can use in the future.

Depreciation

One of the biggest pains since the Tax Reform Act of 1986 (TRA '86) is figuring depreciation. Because now you've got to do it at least **two** ways. And in many, states, like California, you have to do it **four** ways: regular federal, AMT federal, regular California, and AMT California.

When you have to calculate the four depreciation methods on each piece of personal and real property you own...under time pressure... the task can feel overwhelming. In fact, taken one at a time, the calculations are no big deal. Plus, it's far easier to calculate all of the depreciation deductions for the entire life of the property at one time than it is to get your head back into previous calculations every year.

You should set up a spreadsheet on your computer which calculates all the depreciation deductions...for the life of the property...all four ways. Then at tax time, calculate only the deductions for the properties you acquired **that year**. To get the rest of this year's deductions, simply pick the 1988 figure off all the lifetime deduction sheets you created in previous years. If you don't have a computer (masochist), you should create a **form** which you fill out on each new personal or real property acquisition. Keep the spreadsheets or forms in a depreciation loose leaf binder with a divider for each real property.

Here's a five-year personal property spreadsheet using the Modified Accelerated Cost Recovery System (MACRS) which came in with the TRA '86.

	A	B	C	D	E	F
1	Property:	Refrigerator Apt. 209				
2	Year Acquired	1988	Cost:	$463.26		
3		Regular		AMT		
4	Year	200% db	Cumulative	150% db	Cumulative	Excess deprec.
5	1988	$92.65	$92.65	$69.49	$69.49	$23.16
6	1989	$148.24	$240.90	$120.45	$189.94	$27.80
7	1990	$88.95	$329.84	$83.39	$273.32	$5.56
8	1991	$53.37	$383.21	$83.39	$356.71	($30.02)
9	1992	$53.37	$436.58	$83.39	$440.10	($30.02)
10	1993	$26.68	$463.26	$83.39	$523.48	($56.70)

Column B shows the MACRS deductions which are part of what you put on your IRS Schedule E (line 21 of the 1988 Schedule E). Column D shows the deductions you are allowed to take for Alternative Minimum Tax purposes. And Column F is the difference between the two. In 1988, that difference became part of the number you entered on line 4j (Deprecia-

tion of property placed in service after 1986) of Form 6251 (Alternative Minimum Tax).

On the next page is the same spreadsheet only with the computer **formulas** instead of the answers they produce.

I did this on the Microsoft® Excel program. Lotus and other spreadsheets are similar. For you non-computer masochists, "= tells the computer that what follows is a formula to be calculated, * means multiply by, and entries like D2 refer to what's entered at column D, row 2. For example, the com-

mand "=.15*D2 means multip y the number in location D2 by .15. Or .15 x $463.26 = $69.49.

The numbers D2 is multiplied by in column B (.2, .32, etc.) come from any tax book including my *Aggressive Tax Avoidance For Real Estate Investors* (eighth edition). I got the numbers D2 is

(Continued on page 210)

Inside:

John T. Reed's *Real Estate Investor's Monthly* (ISSN: 0887-1922) Subscriber Service and Address Changes: P.O. Box 27311, Concord, CA 94527 800-635-5425; FAX, 510-820-1259. Editor: John T. Reed, 342 Bryan Drive, Danville, CA 94526 510-820-6292. $125/year. Copyright 1991 John T. Reed. All rights reserved.

	A	B	C	D	E	F
1	Property:	Refrigerator Apt. 209				
2	Year Acquired:	1988	Cost:	$463.26		
3		Regular		AMT		
4	Year	200% db	Cumulative	150% db	Cumulative	Excess depre
5	=b2	=.2*D2	=B5	=.15*D2	=D5	=B5-D5
6	=b5+1	=.32*D2	=C5+B6	=.26*D2	=E5+D6	=B6-D6
7	=b6+1	=.192*D2	=C6+B7	=.1475*D2	=E6+D7	=B7-D7
8	=b7+1	=.1152*D2	=C7+B8	=.1475*D2	=E7+D8	=B8-D8
9	=b8+1	=.1152*D2	=C8+B9	=.1475*D2	=E8+D9	=B9-D9
10	=b9+1	=.0576*D2	=C9+B10	=.1475*D2	=E9+D10	=B10-D10

spreadsheets would use the different mathematical formulas which were used to compute depreciation before the TRA '86, i.e. 15-, 18-, and 19-year Accelerated Cost Recovery System and even useful lives and so forth if you still have any pre-1981 basis.

If you did your Form 6251 right for 1987 and 1988, good. If not, get a 1040X (Amended Return) or two and correct it.

multiplied by in Column **D** (.15, .26, etc.) from the **first** edition of *Aggressive Tax Avoidance...*

Here is the spreadsheet for residential real property:

	A	B	C	D	E
1	Real Property:	123 Elm Street		Land:	$16,000
2	Month and year acquired:		Jun-88	Improvements:	$137,000
3		MACRS %	Regular Fed.	Fed. AMT	Excess
4	Year		deduction	40-year S/L	depreciation
5	1988	1.97	$2,698.90	$1,853.64	$845.26
6	1989-2014	3.64	$4,986.80	$3,425.00	$1,561.80
7	2015	3.39	$4,644.30	$3,189.77	$1,454.53

You should have a row for each year. I collapsed years 1989 through 2014 into one row here to save article space. The MACRS % figures in Column B come from the June (month of acquisition) column of the tax tables in any tax book. In Column D, I used the Column B figures to prorate the first and last years in which only partial deductions are allowed.

The AMT

Here are some formulas I developed with the help of CPA Bob Baldassari (703-698-6260) to fill out the 1988 AMT Form (6251).

Line 4j (Depreciation of property placed in service after 1986) = F5 on the personal property spreadsheet above plus E5 on the real property spreadsheet (You should have a spreadsheet on each piece of personal and real property you owned in 1988. The total excess depreciation for all those spreadsheets goes on line 4j. Line 4j prevents you from getting the front-end-loaded benefits of accelerated depreciation.)

Line 4p (Adjusted gain or loss) = gain on property disposed of in 1988 computed using your **AMT** federal deductions minus gain computed using your **regular** federal depreciation deductions. (This is typically a **negative** number and should be **entered** as a negative number on your Form 6251 thereby **reducing** the amount of alternative minimum tax you owe for this year.)

Line 4s (Passive activity loss) = Line 15 of Form 8582 (Passive Activity Loss Limitations) minus Lines 4j and 5e of Form 6251. If you don't subtract Lines 4j and 5e you are double-counting them.

Line 5e = same as line 4j only for property placed in service before 1987. That means your

Form 8801

Real estate investors learned to hate the AMT in the last two years. But if we hate the AMT, we love the "Credit For Prior Year Minimum Tax" which you claim on Form 8801.

Basically, the AMT, which seems to **increase** your tax liability, only **accelerates** tax that you would pay in the future to the present. Having done that, it would be double taxation if they didn't give you credit for the tax you had already paid when the future arrives.

In '87, I had a $7 regular tax liability and a $6,675.86 AMT liability. But in '88, I got the $6,675.86 back...in the form of a Credit For Prior Year Minimum Tax. I did not have to pay any AMT in '88 because I deeded a property back to a seller (See "Arbitration" article in this issue) last year. By giving me $145,000 of passive income, that "sale" enabled me to escape the AMT in '88. If you pay AMT due to passive losses or accelerated depreciation...then have a year in which you pay no AMT, you can generally get a credit on your taxes during the no-AMT year for the AMT you paid in prior years. The Credit For Prior Year Minimum Tax goes on your 1040 at line 45 and reduces your tax payable. JTR

	A	B	C	D	E
1	Real Property	123 Elm Street		Land:	$16,000
2	Month and year acquired:		Jun-88	Improvements:	$137,000
3		MACRS %	Regular Fed.	Fed. AMT	Excess
4	Year		deduction	40-year S/L	depreciation
5	1988	1.97	B5/100*$E$2	=(B5/$B$6)*($E$2/40)	C5-D5
6	1989-2014	3.64	B6/100*$E$2	=(B6/$B$6)*($E$2/40)	C6-D6
7	2015	3.39	B7/100*$E$2	=(B7/$B$6)*($E$2/40)	C7-D7
8	2016	0	B8/100*$E$2	=(B8/$B$6)*($E$2/40)	C8-D8

16

First-Year Expensing

You can expense (deduct all in one year) the first $10,000 (married filing jointly) you spend on qualifying property. This is property that you would otherwise have to depreciate over five or seven years.

What's eligible?

The Code defines Section 179 property as Section 38 property. No kidding. Wait. It gets worse. When you look up Section 38 property, you learn that Section 38 property is defined at Section 48(a) of the Internal Revenue Code. Really.

In plain English, the real estate investment-type property eligible for first-year expensing is:

Eligible for first-year expensing

- Coin-operated vending machines and coin-operated washers and dryers [IRC § 48(a)(3)(C)]
- New elevators and escalators [IRC § 48(a)(1)(C)
- Personal property in non-residential real estate (hotels and motels are non-residential real estate) [IRC § 48(a)]
- Rental furniture even if in an apartment but only if owned by a furniture rental company and not by the apartment owner (Revenue Ruling 81-133)

Not eligible for first-year expensing

- Personal property used in or in connection with apartments [IRC § 48(a)(3)]

- Real property [IRC § 48(a)(1)(A) and (B)]
- Property used less than 50% for business in **any** of the years you own it [IRC § 179(d)(10)]
  (Computers do **not** have to pass the 50% test if used only at regular business establishment.)

Coin-operated washers and dryers **are** eligible if they are used in an apartment building.

Definition of apartment building

Whether you can first-year expense depends on the length of time people normally **stay** in your building—**not** the length of the **lease**. The cut-off is 30 days. If the normal length of stay is 30 days or longer, it's an apartment building for first-year expensing purposes. Less than 30 days, it's a hotel or motel and all its personal property items are therefore eligible for first-year expensing. [Regulation § 1.48-1(h)(1)(i) and (2)(ii)]

Starting in 1991, there's a new definition of what property's eligible. Section 179 property is now defined as Section 1245(a)(3) property which is depreciable. Section 1245(a)(3) property is personal property or other property which is used to furnish "...communications, electrical energy, gas, water, or sewage disposal services." [§ 1245(a)(3)(A)+(B)(i)]

This suggests you can do first-year expensing on many items of personal property in residential buildings—like refrigerators. The restriction against apartment owners using § 179 appears to have been eliminated by the Omnibus Budget Reconciliation Act of 1989 which substituted § 1245(a)(3) for § 38 in the definition of eligible property.

Limits on the deduction

If you acquire more than $210,000 worth of eligible property in a year, you may **not** claim **any** first-year expensing. That's so only **little guys** can use this provision. Between $200,000 and $210,000, you lose one dollar of first-year expensing for every dollar by which you exceed $200,000.

Also, you can only deduct the first-year expensing from the **taxable income** of the business in question (not counting the first-year expensing deduction). If your business (that is, your rental property) has **no** taxable income or has a tax loss, you must carry forward the undeducted amount until you have taxable income from that business to deduct it from. That would typically be after you've raised rents significantly or sold the building.

When the taxable income of the building is less than the first-year expensing you could otherwise claim, you deduct enough to zero out the income from the rental property in question and carry the rest forward.

Because of the annual $10,000 limit and the other limits, you may wish to **stagger** eligible purchases over two years instead of buying all the items you had planned to buy in one year.

No proration

You do **not** prorate first-year expensing. That means you get the **full** deduction even if you place the property in question in service on the **last day** of the year.

Recapture

If your business use of property on which you claimed first-year expensing **falls below** 50% in any later year, the income you sheltered by first-year expensing becomes "recaptured" or taxed. That's also true if you sell the property by installment sale.

17

Depreciation Examples

Rental house

You buy a rental house on April 15, 1987. Purchase price is $100,000. But that's not your basis. Your basis includes other things, too.

Here's your closing statement:

Disclosure/settlement statement

Contract sales price	$100,000.00
Settlement charges to borrower	$2,596.00
County taxes	$157.60
Gross amount due from borrower	$102,753.60

Settlement charges

Items payable in connection with loan:
Loan origination fee	$425.00
Credit report	$22.80

Items required by lender to be paid in advance:

Interest	$451.40 -c
Hazard insurance premium	$400.00 - e

Reserves deposited with lender:

Hazard insurance	$38.08
County property taxes	$414.12

Title charges:

Title insurance	$301.60 -B
Closing fee	$35.00 -B
Document preparation fee	$50.00 -B
Attorney's fees	$300.00 -

Government recording and transfer charges:

Recording fees: Deed $3.00 Mtge $5.00	$8.00 -B+ L

Additional settlement charges:

Survey	$150.00- B
Total settlement charges	$2,596.00

Remember that the settlement statement is not the only place where you may find items which are included in your basis. You should also look in your check book for the months leading up to the closing. In this case, the check book reminds you that you paid your attorney $100 up front and that you paid a $50 loan application fee. Your total loan charges are:

Loan charges

Loan application fee	$50.00
Loan origination fee	$425.00
Credit report	$22.80
Attorney fee associated with loan	$50.00
Recording fee for mortgage	$5.00
Total	$552.80

It's a 30-year loan so these fees must be amortized over 30 years. That's $552.80 ÷ 30 = $18.43 a year. Since you bought the property April 15th, you can only deduct 8.5 months worth of amortization the first year or 8.5 ÷ 12 months per year = 71% x $18.43 = $13.05. If you pay off the loan or get rid of the property, you can deduct all of the remaining, unamortized loan charges that year.

Now the real and personal property basis. It is composed of the following in this example:

Real and personal property basis

Contract sale price	$100,000.00
Title insurance	$301.60
Closing fee	$35.00
Document preparation	$50.00
Attorneys fees associated with purchase	$350.00
Recording fees for deed	$3.00
Survey	$150.00
Total	$100,890.20

Now we break this number down into personal property and real property. We do **not** break it down into land and improvements until **after** we have taken out the personal property.

Rental house personal property

In a typical rental house, the personal property you'd get would be:

• Range
• Refrigerator
• Dishwasher
• Wall-to-wall carpet
• Drapes or blinds.

None of this stuff is eligible for **first-year expensing**—unless this is a resort area house and the tenants normally stay for less than 30 days—in which case it's **all** eligible. For this example, I'll assume it's a regular house where the tenants normally stay for months or years.

The seller says the frige is two years old and cost $800 when new. You estimate it's now worth $500. The seller says the range and dishwasher came with the house when it was built four years ago. You figure they're now worth $200 and $175 respectively. The carpet and drapes are also original. You estimate their current value as $1,000 and $400 respectively.

The law is not clear. But it appears that the appliances are five-year property and the carpet and drapes seven-year property. The following deductions over the life of the investment would apply:

FRIGE

Year	% from table		Basis		Deduction
1	20.00%	x	$500	=	$100.00
2	32.00	x	$500	=	$160.00
3	19.20	x	$500	=	$96.00
4	11.52	x	$500	=	$57.60
5	11.52	x	$500	=	$57.60
6	5.76	x	$500	=	$28.80
Total	100.00%				$500.00

RANGE

Year	% from table		Basis		Deduction
1	20.00%	x	$200	=	$40.00
2	32.00	x	$200	=	$64.00
3	19.20	x	$200	=	$38.40
4	11.52	x	$200	=	$23.04
5	11.52	x	$200	=	$23.04
6	5.76	x	$200	=	$11.52
Total	100.00%				$200.00

DISHWASHER

Year	% from table		Basis		Deduction
1	20.00%	x	$175	=	$35.00
2	32.00	x	$175	=	$56.00
3	19.20	x	$175	=	$33.60
4	11.52	x	$175	=	$20.16
5	11.52	x	$175	=	$20.16
6	5.76	x	$175	=	$10.08
Total	100.00%				$175.00

WALL-TO-WALL CARPET

Year	% from table		Basis		Deduction
1	14.28%	x	$1,000	=	$142.80
2	24.49	x	$1,000	=	$244.90
3	17.49	x	$1,000	=	$174.90
4	12.49	x	$1,000	=	$124.90
5	8.93	x	$1,000	=	$89.30
6	8.93	x	$1,000	=	$89.30
7	8.93	x	$1,000	=	$89.30
8	4.46	x	$1,000	=	$28.80
Total	100.00%				$1,000.00

DRAPES

Year	% from table		Basis		Deduction
1	14.28%	x	$400	=	$57.12
2	24.49	x	$400	=	$97.96
3	17.49	x	$400	=	$69.96
4	12.49	x	$400	=	$49.96
5	8.93	x	$400	=	$35.72
6	8.93	x	$400	=	$35.72
7	8.93	x	$400	=	$35.72
8	4.46	x	$400	=	$17.84
Total	100.00%				$400.00

The total personal property depreciation deductions for the first year of ownership of this rental house are:

Year 1 personal property deductions

Frige	$100.00
Range	$40.00
Dishwasher	$35.00
Carpet	$142.80
Drapes	$57.12
Total	$374.92

The total value of the personal property is:

Total value of personal property

Frige	$500.00
Range	$200.00
Dishwasher	$175.00
Carpet	$1,000.00
Drapes	$400.00
Total	$2,275.00

So your basis in the **real** property only is $100,890.20 - $2,275 = $98,615.20. **Now** we break it into land, land improvements, and structure.

The improvement ratio

The local property tax bill says the land is worth $20,000 and the improvements, $51,000 giving an improvement ratio of $51,000 ÷ $71,000 = 72%.

The typical real estate investor stops here. He multiplies his basis by the tax assessor's improvement ratio and concludes he can depreciate $100,000 x 72% = $72,000 over 27.5 years. That gives him annual deductions of $72,000 ÷ 27.5 = $2,618.18.

Let's see if we can do better.

Bank's appraisal

Digging into the available evidence further, we find that the bank's appraisal valued the land at $25,000 and the improvements at $75,000—a 75% improvement ratio.

Insurance company replacement cost

The fire insurance company said current replacement cost of that type home in that location was $51 per square foot. The house has 1,750 square feet, indicating a replacement cost of 1,750 x $51 = $89,250—an improvement ratio of 89.25%.

That's three different improvement ratios: assessor, bank, insurance company.

The fire insurance company's ratio is the best for tax purposes.

But, there's a difference between replacement cost and market value. Market value is what the law requires. Proper appraisal technique requires that you subtract depreciation (not the tax kind of depreciation, but the real deterioration of the property over time) from the replacement cost to arrive at the current value of the improvements.

Most of the building depreciates very slowly. The plumbing, foundation, walls, etc. aren't much different from the day they were installed. Most rapid depreciation takes place in the roof, flooring, appliances and so forth. And often they've been replaced since the building was built.

In this example, we make a rough estimate that the depreciation has been 9% of the purchase price. Subtracting 9% from the 89% replacement cost improvement ratio gives us an improvement ratio of 80%. And, that's the one we'll use.

How do you explain to the IRS and/or a court why you rejected the other two?

Bank and assessor don't care about land value

Neither the bank nor the local assessor has any incentive to estimate the separate values of the land and improvements accurately.

The assessor works for the government. The government cares only about the **total** assessment because that's what they tax.

Same thing for the lenders. They care only about the **total** value of the collateral for their loan because that's what they foreclose on in the event of a default. They can neither foreclose on separately, nor sell separately the land.

Habit is about the only reason assessors and bank appraisers even bother to break down the value into land and improvements. That's the way they've always done it. That's the way the appraisal forms were designed a hundred years ago, so they continue to break down the value into land and improvements. But neither the assessor nor the appraiser spends much time worrying about the break down. There's no reward for accurate break down. Nor is there any punishment for an inaccurate break down. His job is to get the **total** right.

That's not the case for the insurance company. They pay claims. A guy's house is damaged by fire. The insurance company has to repair it. Bids are obtained and checks are written. If the insurance company inaccurately estimates that replacement cost, they suffer financially. So they are intently interested in the correct land/replacement cost breakdown.

80% x $98,615.20 = $78,892.16.

Land improvements

Land improvements on the property include:

- Landscaping
- Driveway
- Walkway
- Sprinkler system
- Fence
- Finish grading under the above.

We take a photo of the house and its landscaping to a local nursery and ask what the landscaping including finish grading would cost installed. They say about $2,000. We ask them to jot that down on a piece of their stationery and buy some supplies for their trouble.

Then we go to the library and look at one of the construction cost books that comes out every year. The 1988 edition of the *National Construction Cost Estimator*, for example has the following figures:

- Finished concrete paving: $3.95 per square foot
- Typical lawn sprinkler system: $.45 per square foot
- 42-inch high chain link fence: $4.61 per linear foot

Measuring the property we find we have 500 square feet of paving, 8,000 square feet of yard, and 300 feet of chain link fence. So the cost of the land improvements would be:

- Landscaping: $2,000
- Paving: 500 x $3.95 = $1,975
- Sprinkler system: 8,000 x $.45 = $3,600
- Fence: 300 x $4.61 = $1,383
- Total $8,958

The land improvements depreciation deductions from the table would be:

Year	% from table		Basis		Deduction
1	5.000%	x	$8,958	=	$447.90
2	9.500	x	$8,958	=	$851.01
3	8.550	x	$8,958	=	$765.91
4	7.695	x	$8,958	=	$689.32
5	6.926	x	$8,958	=	$620.43
6	6.233	x	$8,958	=	$558.35
7-15	5.905	x	$8,958	=	$528.97
16	2.951	x	$8,958	=	$264.35
Total	100.000				$8,958.00

Structure depreciation schedule

The structure basis would then be $78,892.16 - $8,958 = $69,934.16. The depreciation deductions would then be:

Year	% from table		Basis		Deduction
1	2.58%	x	$69,934.16	=	$1,804.30 (April acquisition)
2-27	3.64	x	$69,934.16	=	$2,545.60
28	2.78	x	$69,934.16	=	$1,944.17
total	100.00%			=	$69,934.16

Your total deductions for the rental house

Year	Frige	Range	DW	Carpet	Drapes	Land Imp.	Structure	Total
1	100.00	40.00	35.00	142.80	57.12	447.90	1,804.30	2,627.12
2	160.00	64.00	56.00	244.90	97.96	851.01	2,545.60	4,019.47
3	96.00	38.40	33.60	174.90	69.96	765.91	2,545.60	3,724.37
4	57.60	23.04	20.16	124.90	49.96	689.32	2,545.60	3,510.58
5	57.60	23.04	20.16	89.30	35.72	620.43	2,545.60	3,391.85
6	28.80	11.52	10.08	89.30	35.72	558.35	2,545.60	3,279.37
7				89.30	35.72	528.97	2,545.60	3,199.59
8				28.80	17.84	528.97	2,545.60	3,121.21
9-15						528.97	2,545.60	3,074.57
16						264.35	2,545.60	2,809.95
17-27							2,545.60	2,545.60
28							1,944.17	1,944.17

In contrast, the deductions for the **typical** investor would be:

Year	Frige	Range	Dishwasher	Carpet	Drapes	Real property	Total
1	0.00	0.00	0.00	0.00	0.00	1,857.60	1,857.60
2-27	0.00	0.00	0.00	0.00	0.00	2,620.80	2,620.80
28						2,001.60	2,001.60

The correct approach loads more deductions onto the **front end** of the 28 years thereby **increasing the present value** of the deductions. The correct approach also increases the **total** amount of the deductions as a result of **separating** out the personal property **before** making the land/improvements breakdown and as a result of justifying a **higher improvement ratio**.

Since you'll probably not own the property more than five to seven years, the present value difference is even greater.

Non-residential property

You would depreciate a non-residential property the same way except that you would take advantage of first-year expensing on the first $10,000 of personal property. And, of course, you'd have to use the 31.5-year table instead of the 27.5-year table on the real property.

When you exchange out of properties you owned before 1981

When you exchange out of a property you did not own until **after** 1980, your basis in the new property comes under the depreciation rules in effect on the day you completed the exchange. But if you owned the old property **before** 1981, it's more complicated.

Because of a part of the Economic Recovery Tax Act of 1981 called the "**anti-churning** rules," you must depreciate pre-'81 basis carried forward in an exchange using the pre-'81 depreciation rules. Namely, you pick a "**useful life**" and a value for each **component** of the building and depreciate them accordingly. [IRC § 168(f)(5)(A)(i)]

PART FOUR: EXPENSES

18

Expenses

In Reed's Rules, I told you that you **don't want** deductible expenses which result from actual cash payments. Depreciation's different because it's mostly just a **paper** loss. Avoid **payments**, whether you can deduct them or not.

But, once you've had to make a payment, for gosh sake make sure you get the deduction that's coming to you. Or to paraphrase Confucius, if expenditure inevitable, relax and deduct it. Because they are careless, many real estate investors make deductible payments which they do **not** deduct.

The main reason is records. In order to deduct a payment, you must remember it. In order to remember it, you must have a written record of it. And if the IRS should ever challenge a payment, you need a record to prove the deduction was legal.

Some payments are easy to keep records of—like your phone bill. The phone company sends you a bill every month. You pay by check. And, you probably keep the phone bill and the check and the check register.

But what about cab fares, taxes, and insurance paid by a mortgage company, items paid at closing on a property, supplies you bought at the local lumber yard, business mileage on your car, etc.?

Losing a record of a ten dollar payment is like losing $3.10 in cash if you are in the 31% bracket. You'll probably forget about the payment by the time taxes are due. Failure to deduct that $10 will raise your taxes $3.10. So, what appears to be a mere scrap of paper (receipt) is really the same as money.

The receipt habit

If you are not already, get into the receipt habit.

Asking for a receipt is not enough. The receipt must be complete for tax purposes. Most receipts do **not** have enough information for tax purposes.

Most receipts tell you:

• Date
• Amount paid
• Name of seller.

That's not enough. You also need:

• Product or service purchased
• Business purpose.

That means you need to acquire two habits: asking for the receipt and then adding the missing information to it on the spot—what the law of evidence calls a "recorded recollection" or "record of a regularly conducted activity." [F.R.E. 803 (5)and (6)] If you wait to do it later, you'll probably forget. Every time you do that, you've thrown money away.

Sometimes, getting a receipt is awkward or impossible—like when you tip a bellhop. In those cases, make a note to yourself as soon as possible. Reed's handy dandy business trip checklist (coming up in a couple pages) will also help you make sure you don't forget tips paid while traveling.

Log books

Other times, there's no one to get a receipt from, as in keeping track of business use of your car or computer.

A simple copy book thrown into your car or kept handy to your computer is all you need. They are not required by law. They were briefly. But Congress repealed that requirement. But they are almost required in that IRS will disallow or reduce car or computer deductions at the drop of a hat then demand that you prove the use you claim. The log book is the simplest way to do that.

All is not lost if you do not have a log book, however. You can reconstruct business travel from receipts and your appointment calendar. For example, your calendar may say on March 12th,

Bill Henderson 11:00

Henderson is your attorney. You **always** go to his office. He **never** comes to yours. His office is 15.8 miles from your office. Therefore, you made a 15.8 x 2 = 31.6 mile business trip.

Or you have a receipt from Sears for two cans of off-white latex paint and a roller and pan. That reminds you that you went to Sears, bought the paint stuff, then went to your Yale Avenue property to paint the upstairs apartment. You can reconstruct the mileage for that two-stop trip from a map or from another trip to Sears and the property on which you recorded the odometer readings.

Use pocket folders to organize receipts

Get pocket folders from your stationery store for your receipts. Pocket folders are manila folders—with an accordion pleat down each side. You mark the folders for your various categories of expense like:

Supplies '88

Plumbing '88
Gas '88

If you have more than one property, you may want to have a set of pocket folders for each property. Then you would add the name or initial of the property to each folder like:

C Supplies '88

where C stands for Cottonwoods Apartments. This system was a great help in my TCMP audit.

How to search for deductible expenditures

Your records are like a pile of gold mine ore. You need to sift through them for valuable nuggets. Here's a check list to make sure you don't overlook anything.

1. Business and/or investment check registers.

2. Personal checking account register.

3. Receipts.

4. Credit card statements (the total finance charge paid for the year is often listed in the January or February statements of the following year.)

5. Annual mortgage or other loan statements.

6. Settlement statements on properties bought, sold, or exchanged during the year and loans obtained or paid off during the year.

7. W-2 and 1099 forms on income you've received.

8. Loan payoff statements.

9. Property tax bills.

10. Insurance policies (where premium is typed).

11. Loan amortization schedules.

12. Tax returns from past years (Federal, state, and local). (I once overlooked the interest I paid on an entire second mortgage. A Realtor® who looked at two years of my income tax returns spotted the dramatic drop in interest expense and asked why. I submitted an amended return and got the deduction.)

13. Monthly bank statements.

14. Purchase orders.

15. Accounts receivable and sales journal.

Your tax notebook

Each year, I create a three-ring, two-inch capacity, loose-leaf notebook to do my taxes. I use clear overlay binders which have clear plastic covers open at the top. You write "1988 Taxes" on spine and cover sheets and insert them. Inside is a set of dividers which are labelled:

- "Returns" (filled-out IRS and California returns)
- "Records checked" (list of what you've already checked so you don't go over it again)
- "Schedule A & B"
- "Schedule C"
- "Schedule E"
- "Form 4562" (Depreciation and amortization)
- "Statements" (This requires a 9" x 12" manila envelope which holds W-2s, 1099s, mortgage statements, etc.).

Your basis notebook

You should also have a binder to hold records of capital assets which are depreciable or for which you have to keep track of your basis like your home. You would divide it into such categories as:

- Home
- Elm Street land (Elm Street is one of your rental properties)
- Elm Street improvements
- Elm Street personal property
- Elm Street land improvements
- Home office
- Home office personal property.

You would not mark the basis notebook "1988" or whatever—because it covers all the years you've owned the various properties listed in it.

Under the home section, you should have your closing statement and other receipts relating to the cost of the home. Whenever you improve the home, you add records of the cost of the improvement to the home section because they increase your basis—which, in turn, reduces the tax you'd have to pay on any gain when you sell that home—or a subsequent home if you avoid taxes on sale through the two-year reinvestment rule.

Under "Elm Street land," you would note the value of the land and any evidence you found to support it.

Under "Elm Street improvements," you would list the original value of the improvements and any later improvements you add. I recommend that you calculate the depreciation schedule for the **entire** 27.5- or 31.5-year depreciation period the year you acquire the property. The reason is it's fresh in your mind then. And it's a pain to go back and try to recalculate it each year.

If you have a computer, you would simply use a spread sheet program to generate the whole depreciation schedule. You'd stick that printout in the basis notebook and each year, when you were doing your taxes, you'd look up this year's deduction for that property and put it on your tax return. So, the only depreciation calculations you'd do each year would be on properties you bought that year.

Treat the personal property and land improvements sections the same way. You'll end up with a sheet for each building, building improvement, land improvement, and item of personal property. Here's an example:

Personal property depreciation schedule from basis notebook

ITEM: GE Frige   DATE PURCHASED: August 12, 1987

Year	Basis	% For year	Deduction	Adjusted Basis EOY
1987	$439.00	20.00	$87.80	$351.20
1988		32.00	$140.48	$210.72
1989		19.20	$84.29	$126.43
1990		11.52	$50.57	$75.86
1991		11.52	$50.57	$25.29
1992		5.76	$25.29	$0.00

Once you've set up one of each depreciation schedule, you can easily use your computer's copy command to produce different schedules for different properties. If you don't have a computer, you can do it by hand. That's pretty backward, though. These days, computers are so cheap and real estate so expensive that it's hard to justify not having a computer.

MacInTax®

I do my taxes on the MacInTax® (4820 Adohr Lane, Suite F, Camarillo, CA 93010) computer program—which I highly recommend if you have a Macintosh computer. In fact, if you are a professional tax preparer, you ought to go buy a Macintosh™ just so you can use the MacInTax® software.

With MacInTax®, you see the actual IRS or California tax return forms on the screen in front of you. You simply fill in the blanks. Wherever math is required, the program does it. The computer beeps at you (literally) if you make an obvious mistake and puts an explanation of why it beeped on the screen. Whenever the tax return requires that you list an answer "here and on line such-and-such on Schedule so-and-so," the program does that for you.

At every blank where it makes sense, you can itemize. You type the appropriate command and a blank list appears. You give it a name at the top and enter the various expenses that make up the category in question. The itemization automatically totals and inserts the total in the appropriate blank in your tax return. If you later try to change that entry, the computer will beep at you to remind you to make any changes on the **itemization** for that blank. You can **print** the itemizations. In fact, my tax notebook consists mostly of MacInTax® itemization sheets.

My IRS auditor loved them. She kept asking, "How did you arrive at this figure?" Whereupon, I'd turn to that section of my tax binder and whip out the appropriate itemization sheet. After I did that several times, she said, "This is fun!" Here's a sample.

```
┌──────────────────────────────────────────────────────────┐
│ ▤ ▦    Schedule E(1)/Line 15-B Itemization  ▤         │
├──────────────────────────────────────────────────────────┤
│ Itemization of:  L utilities                         ⇧  │
│   9  Items                    Total      8,386 77      │
│              Description                  Amount       ▓ │
│ a office elec...........................    515 18     ▓ │
│ b lights................................    770 06     ▓ │
│ c vacancy elec..........................    888 82     ▓ │
│ d mgr elec..............................  1,106 86     ▓ │
│ e gas...................................    399 28     ▓ │
│ f water................................. 3,028 79     ▓ │
│ g phone.................................    630 61     ▓ │
│ h trash.................................    877 84     ▓ │
│ i phone to..............................    169 33  ⇩  │
│ ◁                                            ⇨  ▨     │
└──────────────────────────────────────────────────────────┘
```

MacInTax® prints the entire IRS or California income tax forms on blank paper. So you need no IRS or CA forms. That saves scrambling for forms at tax time.

Another neat thing about MacInTax® is that it lets you play "what if." For example, if you want to know precisely to the penny how much a particular building is saving you on taxes, run MacInTax® twice: once with the building on your Schedule E and once without it. The difference between your tax payable with and without is the precise amount it saved you.

Unfortunately, IRS does not tell the world what its forms will look like until about November of the tax year they apply to. As a result, MacInTax® cannot start work on its annual update until then. So, it's hard to use MacInTax® for planning because it always contains last year's law. If Congress would ever leave the law alone for a year or two, you could use MacInTax® for planning. But, speaking as the author of a tax book that comes out annually, I can tell you that Congress has not left the tax law alone for a single year since at least 1981

Travel and entertainment expenses for the real estate investor

Real estate investors have four kinds of travel expenses:

• Looking **for** properties to acquire,
• Looking **after** properties they've already acquired,
• Education,
• To confer with your attorney, accountant, trustee, or investment counselor.

Travel costs you incur while looking **for** properties to buy are **not** deductible unless

• You actually negotiate to buy the property,
• Negotiations break down and you do not buy the property.

If the deal goes through, you must add the travel costs to your basis. Revenue Ruling 77-254; *Price*, TCM 1971-323; *Feed*, 52 TC 880; *Goodson*, 5 TCM 648; and *Domenic*, TCM 1975-94.

Travel expenses to look *after* properties are deductible

You can deduct either actual car expenses or the IRS mileage limit if your rental properties are a trade or business, which most are. Only limited partners and owners of net leased properties would be prohibited from using the mileage allowance. But, since the mileage allowance is set artificially low, not being able to use it is not much of a restriction.

If you use the mileage allowance, you cannot deduct depreciation, first-year expensing, or operating expenses. But you can still deduct parking fees, tolls, and the business portion of interest on the car loan above and beyond the mileage allowance.

The mileage allowance rate was 26¢ a mile for all miles in '90. (Rev. Proc. 89-66) **Actual** expenses should be much higher and therefore, the better way to deduct car expenses. Hertz Rent A Car figured it cost 44.6¢ a mile to operate a car in the average city in the early eighties. The American Automobile Association figured 25-26¢ a mile in '87.

Use the auto expense **check lists** in either J.K. Lasser's *Your Income Tax* or in the Prentice-Hall or CCH *Federal Tax Guides* to make sure you don't overlook any deductions.

You need to add the **origin** and **destination** of the trip to most travel receipts to make them pass tax muster.

Some of you will be travelling by plane, train, or whatever to properties or education events like seminars or conventions. For those expenses, here's my handy dandy check list:

Business Trip Check List

Start date _____ End date _____
Origin _____ Destination _____
Business Purpose _____

Date	Item	Amount
	home to airport	
	bridge toll	
	baggage tip at home airport	
	air fare	
	baggage tip at destination airport	
	airport to hotel	
	baggage tip curb to lobby	
	baggage tip lobby to room	
	rental car	
	hotel	
	baggage tip room to lobby	
	baggage tip lobby to curb	
	hotel to airport	
	baggage tip at home airport	
	airport to home	
	bridge toll	
	airport parking	
	laundry and cleaning	
	breakfast 1st day (unless on hotel bill)	
	lunch 1st day (unless on hotel bill)	
	supper 1st day (unless on hotel bill)	
	breakfast 2nd day	

and so on

I have this check list in the form of a computer spread sheet which automatically totals the amount and puts the information in neat form. I put that summary print out and the related receipts in a number 10 business envelope marked "2/12/88 trip to Dallas" or whatever and put it in the pocket folder labelled "Travel '88."

Meals

A lot of investors think that if they drive over to their income property in the next county, they can deduct the lunch they have there. Sorry, but you cannot. You have to stay "**overnight away from home**" in order for your meal to be deductible. And in accordance with the Tax Reform Act of 1986, only **80%** of the meal is deductible.

You can deduct the car expense of driving to the next county—whether you stay overnight or not.

Meals you eat at real estate **seminars** and **conventions** are deductible if you have trade or business real estate (apartments, rental houses, office buildings, etc.) but **not** if you are a passive investor (limited partner, owner of net-leased building). But again, you have to stay away from home overnight to deduct.

Standard meal deduction

You have the option of deducting a **standard meal rate** instead of your actual expenses. If you are frugal, the standard rate might give you a higher deduction.

The standard meal allowance is the meals and incidental expenses per diem rate allowed to employees of the federal government. That rates varies by county and is published periodically under section 301-7.3 of the IRS regulations also in title 41 of the *Code of Federal Regulations* also at ¶274.76 of the *Prentice-Hall Federal Tax Guide*.

Entertainment

Entertainment generally means having a meal with **someone else**—on you. 80% of it is deductible if the meal is directly related or associated with the active conduct of your trade or business. There is no requirement that you be away from home overnight. **Spouses'** meals may also be deducted as part of business entertainment. You have to **discuss** business during the entertainment. You have to have a **specific** expectation that business will result. Conducting business must be the **main reason** for the entertainment.

The legal requirements for deducting entertainment are not strict. The problem is that IRS hates this deduction and demands more proof than in other, similar situations.

What you need on entertainment receipts

- Names of persons entertained
- Business relationship with entertainees
- Business purpose of the entertainment
- Date
- Location
- To whom paid
- Amount
- Business discussed during entertainment

American Express and some other credit card companies print a place for most of this information on the back of the "cardholder copy." Fill it out **on the spot** so you don't forget.

If you get into a dispute with IRS and do not have receipts, you should still be able to prove your deductions from the following:

- Your appointment calendar
- Your telephone log and/or bills
- Statements from those who were at the entertainment function
- Your car log book
- Correspondence files
- Credit card records.

Combined business and pleasure trips

When you take a trip which combines business and pleasure, you must prorate

- Meals
- Hotel
- And so forth.

But if the **primary** purpose of the trip was business, you can deduct the **entire** cost of getting there and back.

For example, if you attend a convention in Hawaii for three days then spend two days sightseeing. Meals and lodging for the three convention days are deductible; but not those for the two days of sightseeing. However, the whole plane fare to and from Hawaii is deductible.

Spouse expenses are deductible only if the spouse plays a major role in the business and in the business part of the trip. But if your spouse's expenses are not deductible, make sure you still deduct the single room rate rather than half the double room rate. Sometimes the single rate is only a couple dollars less than the double rate.

Repairs versus improvements

For tax purposes, repairs are better than improvements. Because you deduct repairs all at once. But, you must depreciate improvements over 27.5 or 31.5 years.

Whether a particular expenditure is a repair or improvement is judgmental.

The distinction was spelled out in *Illinois Merchants Trust Co.*, 4 BTA 103:

> *A repair is an expenditure for the purpose of **keeping the property in ordinarily efficient operating condition**. It does **not add to the value** of the property, nor does it **appreciably prolong its life**. Expenditures for that purpose are distinguishable from those for **replacements, alterations, improvements, or additions** which prolong the life of the property, or make it adaptable to a different use.*

The *Realty Bluebook* has a section which lists many of the most common expenditures. Each one is identified either as a repair or an improvement. The *Realty Bluebook* is not law, but it's a useful guide.

General plan of improvement

Some repair items become improvement items if they are done as part of a "general plan of improvement." Paint, for example, is generally considered to be a repair, even though it lasts more than one year. But if paint is done as part of a general plan of improvement, you have to depreciate it over 27.5 or 31.5 years.

So you should avoid doing repairs as part of a general plan of improvement on investment or business property. As much as possible, have your repairs done at separate times by separate contractors. Or at the very least, have the contractor list the repairs on a separate invoice.

That's for your investment/business property. On your **home**, you want just the opposite.

Repairs are deductible on business/investment property. But not on your home. (Fix-up costs within 90 days of sale of your home may be deducted from the sale price to reduce your gains tax.) You can't deduct improvements to your home either, or depreciate them. But you **can** add improvements to the basis of your home. That will reduce your gains tax if you ever sell your home in a taxable transaction. (That's rare. Most people avoid tax on a home sale by reinvesting within two years or via the over 55 $125,000 one-time exclusion.)

So on your residence, try to lump repairs in with improvements so you can add them to basis. The big case on that was *E. Russell Jones v. U.S.*, 279 F. Supp. 772. You can deduct normal maintenance expenses incurred **during** a general plan of improvement. (*W.A. Stoeltzing*, 266 F2d 374. Also *Moss v. Comm.*, 831 F2d 833.)

The costs of preparing a house to rent it must be amortized. They cannot be deducted in one year. *Odom*, #82-1999 (4th Circuit, 4/15/83)

Investment periodical **subscriptions are still deductible** unless you are purely a passive investor like a stockholder, a limited partner, or an owner of a net-leased building. The Tax Reform Act only made investment subscriptions undeductible for the passive guys. The media reports did not make that clear.

Asbestos

Asbestos removal may be deductible as a repair. See an article on that subject at 70 *Journal of Taxation* 290.

Interest

Whether interest is deductible depends on the purpose of the loan. Expenditures made within 30 days before or after receiving the loan are treated as the purpose of that loan. (IRS Notice 89-25)

Miscellaneous

You do not count rental income for self-employment (social security) tax purposes. [IRC § 1402(a)(1)]

If you use both Schedule C and Schedule E, there is a danger of counting, and being taxed on, the same income twice. Be careful.

Vacation homes which you rent out

Allocate the **variable** expenses according to the number of days the house is **used**.

Allocate the **non**-variable expenses according to the number of **days in the year** (365 or 366).

What are variable expenses? Expenses that vary according to the use of the property, namely, utilities. Interest, property taxes, insurance, and so forth are not variable.

Why? You can always deduct interest and property taxes on a second home if you itemize. But if you use the vacation home more than 14 days per year, you can only deduct expenses up to the amount of taxable income the property generates.

So you want as little interest and property taxes as possible included in the rental period expenses. That's because you can deduct it on Schedule A (Itemized Deductions) if it's not in the rental use period. But, if it is in the rental use period, it crowds out some depreciation deductions—which cannot be deducted elsewhere. *Bolton*, 77 TC 104, aff'd CA-9, 82-2 USTC ¶9699

Under prior law, you were almost always better off taxwise to use your rental vacation home less than 14 days per year so you could deduct its losses from other income. That's still true if you have not used up your $25,000 exemption from the passive loss limits. But if you are over the $25,000 passive loss limit, you are probably better off flunking the 14-day test—in other words, use your vacation home more than 14 days. Then your entire mortgage interest and property tax bills for the year will be deductible under the no-limit-on-first-and-second-homes rules. A prorated portion of the remaining depreciation and operating expenses can then be deducted from the home's rental income—with any excess carried forward until you sell the property.

Vacation home rent is tax-free income if rented for less than 15 days per year.

Charge market rent

Risicato let his Mom pay rent only now and then. Later he rented the place to a non-relative for less than market value. Result: No deductions at all! IRS said he lacked a profit motive. Tax Court agreed. (TC Memo 1984-238)

19

How to Maximize Your Home Office Deduction

Most real estate investors can and should claim a home office. If you only own such passive interests as limited partnership or REIT shares or net-leased property, you cannot deduct a home office to manage those interests.

The Code criteria you must meet to deduct a home office are that it must be:

- Used exclusively for that purpose
- Used on a regular basis
- Your principal place of business or a place of business which is used by clients or customers in meeting or dealing with you in the normal course of your business.

In Letter Ruling 8350008, IRS added the requirement that your home-office-based management activities be:

- Continuous,
- Systematic, and
- Substantial.

But the Tax Court disagreed with that letter ruling in *Hazard*, 7 TC 372 and *Wasnok*, 71,006 P-H Memo TC.

On the other hand, the United States District Court for the District of New York agreed with IRS's letter ruling in *Union National Bank*, 8 AFTR 2d 5133.

The home office does *not* have to be a separate room

Weightman claimed part of his bedroom as a home office. He lost in court because he did not prove it was his principal place of business. He was a college professor and the IRS said the college was his principal place of business.

But the court rejected the IRS's argument that it had to be a separate room. The Court noted that the actual wording of Section 280A of the Code is "portion of the dwelling unit." *Weightman*, 81,301 P-H Memo TC and McCue, TCM 1983-580

The IRS capitulated on this issue in Proposed Regulation 1.280A-2(g) where they said,

> *the phrase 'a portion of the dwelling unit' refers to a room or other separately identifiable space; it is not necessary that the portion be marked off by a permanent partition.*

The *Scott* decision and the Tax Reform Act of 1986

There was a dispute between the Tax Court and the IRS over what income you could deduct home office expenses from. IRS said you could only deduct home office expenses from the net taxable income from the home office business. The Tax Court said (*Scott*, 84 TC 683) you could deduct home office expenses from **any** income.

The Tax Reform Act of 1986 resolved that dispute by making the IRS version law.

So you can only deduct home office expenses from the net taxable income (before home office expenses are taken into account) of the home office business. If that limit prevents you from deducting all the home office expenses you have, you carry them forward until the home office business generates enough net taxable income to absorb the deductions.

What to deduct

You can deduct home office expenses whether you own a home or rent it. Here is a list of expenses that might apply to your office:

Home office expenses

- Rent
- Property taxes
- Mortgage interest
- Insurance
- Electricity
- Water
- Sewer
- Gas
- Amortization of loan fees
- Heating oil
- Trash collection
- Maid or cleaning service
- Repairs
- Telephone (but not monthly fee)
- Burglar alarm system
- Depreciation
- Homeowners association dues
- Mortgage insurance premium

How to allocate

You allocate by the most favorable of these two formulas:
- % = number of rooms for office ÷ number of rooms in dwelling unit
- % = square feet used for office ÷ total square feet in dwelling unit.

Insurance

Do not allocate insurance according to area. Rather ask your agent what your insurance would be if you did **not** have a home office and that room were not there at all. The difference between your premium **with** the office and with**out** that space is the proper amount to deduct.

My insurance company charges an extra **surcharge** for home offices. And they recommend higher than normal contents insurance to reflect the higher value of business equipment and furniture. These extra charges relate **only** to the office and therefore should **not** be prorated.

Electricity

Prorate electricity according to **use**, not area. Business machines like computers and photocopiers use electricity. Rooms and square feet do not. Taking into account business machine use of electricity should give you a higher deduction than prorating by rooms or area.

Water and sewer

Even though the office may not contain any plumbing fixtures, it contributes to water use. If you worked elsewhere, you water use (for drinking and flushing) would be less.

Heat and air-conditioning

I think you can justify allocating more than floor area warrants to home office for climate control. Having a home office causes you to have the climate control working during the day. Whereas if you worked elsewhere, you would probably adjust the thermostat accordingly when you left for work and returned.

Trash removal

The office floor area may be only 15% of the house area. But you probably generate a disproportionate quantity of trash from there. If so, and if you pay separately for trash removal, deduct the disproportionate amount as an office expense.

Maid service

If maids clean the whole **house** once a week, prorate according to the floor area of the office. If, however, someone cleans **only** the office, deduct the **whole** amount. If the maid pays any extra attention to the office, allocate disproportionately to reflect that.

Repairs

If you repair the office only, deduct **all** of the cost. If you repair an interior part of the house other than the office, deduct **none** of the cost. If you repair the outside of the house, like the roof, prorate the cost according to office area.

Telephone

You can deduct business calls. But because of the Technical And Miscellaneous Revenue Act of 1988, you cannot deduct a prorata portion of the monthly fee for phone service on the first phone.

Depreciation

If you are a **tenant** in your home, you can**not** deduct depreciation on your home office structure. You can, however, depreciate your furniture and equipment if you own it even though you rent your office.

If you own your home, calculate your basis as if the entire building were depreciable investment property. Remember that your home office is **non**-residential real estate—even though it is in a residential building. It's an **office** and offices are non-residential. That means you have to use the **31.5-year** recovery period.

Amortization of loan fees

The points and other expenses you pay to got your home mortgage must be allocated partly to the residence and partly to the office. You can deduct the points paid on a home purchase mortgage in the year you pay them. But you must amortize the points and all other loan costs over the life of the loan on the home office portion.

Sample home office deductions

You buy a six-room, $120,000 home on February 12th. You pay $4,000 in loan fees to get a 30-year mortgage. One room serves exclusively as the office in which you manage your rental properties. It's floor area is 20% of the area of the house. You allocate $100,000 of the purchase price to depreciable improvements.

Here's how to arrive at your home office deductions and where to put them on your return.

Sample home office deductions

Item	Total	Office %	Office Deduction
Rent	$0.00	0%	$0.00
Property taxes	2,000.00	20*	400.00
Mortgage interest	13,000.00	20*	2,600.00
Homeowners ins.	500.00	20	100.00
Office insurance	185.00	100	185.00
Electricity	556.24	25	139.06
Water	160.00	20	32.00
Sewer	0.00	0	0.00
Gas	652.73	25	163.18
Heating oil	0.00	0	0.00
Trash collection	125.00	25	31.25
Maid service	440.00	25	110.00
Repairs	0.00	0	0.00
Total			$3,760.49

* The other 80% of these expenses is deducted on Schedule A (itemized deductions).

In the first two editions of this book, I said to put all home interest and property taxes on Schedule A (itemized deductions) rather than Schedule C. I saw no difference between putting it on Schedule A or C. It was deductible either place—and simpler to put it all on one schedule. But reader Carmen Conicelli, Jr. of North Wales, PA wrote to say that it can make a difference if you have excess medical deductions. Then, you're better off putting as much on Schedule C as possible.

As a result of the Tax Reform Act of 1986, you may have to carry home office deductions forward to future years. But it's better to carry forward than not to deduct at all. At the very least, those carried forward deductions will probably reduce your taxes in the year of sale.

Depreciation of the sample property

Your basis is $120,000. $100,000 of that is depreciable improvements. And the floor area of the office is 20% of that or $20,000.

You bought in February, so according to the depreciation table, your depreciation deductions are:

Year	% for the year	Basis		Deduction
1	2.78	x $20,000	=	$556.00
2-31	3.17	x 20,000	=	634.00
32	2.12	x 20,000	=	424.00

You put the depreciation of the home office on Schedule C.

Amortization of the loan fees on the sample property

Allocate 20% of the $4,000 in loan fees to the home office or 20% x $4,000 = $800.00. Then amortize that over the life of the loan—30 years, $800 ÷ 30 = $26.67 per year. And prorate the first year according to the half-month convention. That is, assume you got the loan half way through February. That would allow you to claim 10.5 months worth the first year or 10.5 ÷ 12 = 88% x $26.67 = $23.34.

If you actually kept the loan the full thirty years, you would deduct the $26.67 - $23.34 = $3.33 in the 31st year. More likely, you would pay off the loan or sell the property with the loan transferred to the new owner before the 31st year. In that case, you would deduct the unamortized balance of the loan fees in the year you paid off or transferred the loan. For example, let's say you refinanced and paid off this loan after five years. By then, you would have amortized a total of

Year	Amortization	Cumulative total
1	$23.34	$23.34
2	26.67	50.01
3	26.67	76.68
4	26.67	103.35
5	26.67	130.02

The unamortized balance after five years would be $800.00 - $130.02 = $669.98—which you would deduct **in toto** the year of the refinancing.

Total sample deductions for first year

Depreciation	$556.00
Amortization	$23.34
Other	$3,760.49
Total	$4,339.83

If you are in the 31% bracket, that deduction will save you $4,339.83 x 31% = $1,345.35 the first year and more per year thereafter. Or, if you bump up against the passive loss or home office limitations, the deduction will save you the same cumulative amount—only in the year of sale instead of annually. Either way, you would not leave that much money lying on the table so you should not be talked out of claiming your home office deduction.

IRS wants to intimidate you out of deducting home office expenses

Line G of the 1986 and previous Schedule Cs asks you,

Did you deduct expenses for an office in your home?

In my opinion, this is, in part, an attempt to intimidate you out of taking the home office deductions you are entitled to. Don't let them scare you off. Section 280A of the Internal Revenue Code authorizes the home office deduction. And IRS has no authority to deny it unless you don't meet the criteria set forth in the Code.

Arguments against the home office deduction

I get the impression that most tax advisers recommend against claiming the home office deduction. Here are the arguments they use.

Attract IRS attention

There is no automatic audit trigger. The home office deduction is certainly not one. I know at least one person who has been answering "yes" to the "Did you deduct expenses for an office in the home?" question ever since IRS starting asking it. And that person has not been audited at all in those years.

Loss of the two-year reinvestment rule on part of the house

If you sell your house and buy another of equal or greater value within two years, you pay no tax on the gain at that time. But your home office is like a separate non-residential structure, for tax purposes. So you could only defer the gain on the home office portion of a sold house by doing a tax-free **exchange**—which is precisely what you should do if the tax payable on the sale would exceed $2,000.

Presumably, your new home will also have a home office. So arranging such an exchange should be no big deal.

Kill off the home office in the year of sale

There's another way to avoid paying gains tax on the home office portion in the year of sale. Kill off the home office that year. Revenue Ruling 82-26 created that solution.

It says that if you've claimed a home office for years—but **not** in the year of sale—it's as if you've **never** claimed a home office as far as the two-year reinvestment rule is concerned.

How do you **not** claim a home office in the year of sale? Deliberately flunk the exclusive use test is probably the simplest way. Invite a few friends over to have a party in the office. Of course, you can still claim a home office in the house you are moving **to**—even in that same year.

Killing the office this way makes sense if you sell the house toward the beginning of the year. Because you are only losing a few months worth of home office deductions. If you sell the house toward the end of the year, you should either claim the home office deductions and pay the capital gains tax on the office portion. Or you should exchange the home office if the tax payable would be greater than $2,000.

If capital gains tax is	and home office deduction on old house will	then
less than $2,000	save more than capital gains tax	claim office
less than $2,000	save less than capital gains tax	kill office
more than $2,000		claim office and exchange

Two '82 cases confuse the home office issue

The Tax Court decided two pertinent cases in 1982. In *Cristo*, TC Memo 1982-514, they denied a home office deduction to a real estate investor. He owned one 8-unit apartment building. The Court said the home office was not his principal place of business—the apartment building was. They said the home office was not the "focal point" of his business.

I think they're out of line with that "focal point" stuff. That phrase does not appear in the Internal Revenue Code. The Court can add phrases like that when the law is vague. But I submit that the phrase "principal place of business" is clearer than "focal point."

The Seventh Circuit Court of Appeals (Illinois, Indiana, Wisconsin) **reversed** the Tax Court in a 1986 case (*Meiers*, 57 AFTR 2d 86-642). They rejected the Tax Court's "focal point" test as:

not fair to the taxpayer and did not carry out the apparent intent of Congress.

Then, in *Soliman* (94 TC # 3), the Tax Court said the focal point test would **not** apply where:

1. The administration of the taxpayer's business is essential, and
2. The home office is the only available office space in which to do it.

Meiers ran a laundramat, not a real estate investment. But the principles appear to apply to real estate. In fact, I'd say real estate investors would have an easier time than laundramat owners convincing a court that their home office was their principal place of business. The Seventh Circuit said major consideration should be given to:

• "The amount of time spent" in each location
• The "importance" of what is done in the home office
• The "business necessity" of the home office
• How much the home office cost to establish.

The other 1982 case was *Barnes*, TC Memo 1982-439. That case seemed to support the *Curphey* decision I told you about in the beginning of the book. Barnes owned a two-family and a 6-unit building. He lost the case because he did not have proper receipts. But the Court said that his home office was indeed his principal place of business.

What if there will *not* be a home office in your new home?

If you plan not to have a home office in the next home, you could exchange your current home office for a separate business or investment property. It wouldn't have to be your office. That's a bit complex, but it can be done without any great difficulty.

For example, you have a $100,000 home containing a $20,000 home office. You want to buy a new home and a $100,000 duplex. You exchange your old home to the duplex owner in return for the duplex. He, in turn, sells the home to the person who has already agreed to buy it. And you buy your new, office-less house separately. If your equity in your old home was more than you needed for the duplex, the duplex seller would give you not only the duplex but also cash. You could receive that cash tax-free if you reinvested in a new home within two years. So the exchange would move your home office equity to the duplex tax-free and the two-year reinvestment rule would allow you to move any residence gain to the new home tax-free.

Phone calls may not be enough

The Code says you're eligible for the home office deduction if you "meet or deal with" customers in your home office. Unfortunately, both the IRS and the courts have decided to ignore the phrase "...or deal with." *Green*, 707 F 2d 404 and *Frankel*, 82 TC 26.

Income cannot be passive

Businesspeople can claim a home office. **Investors cannot.** But owners of income properties are generally considered to be in a "trade or business," not investors for tax purposes. A **stock market** investor was denied home office deductions in *Frick*, TC Memo 1983-733. The same fate would likely befall a very passive investor like a **limited partner** or an owner of **net leased** property or **raw land**. At one time in the early '80s, a property was considered to be net leased if the total deductions for operating expenses, other than property taxes, interest, and depreciation, were less than 15% of rental income or if the lessor was guaranteed a specific return or was guaranteed against loss.

182

PART FIVE:
DEALER PROPERTY

20

Dealer Property

A sword of Damocles hangs over the heads of virtually all real estate investors. That sword is the possibility that IRS might label a property you own as dealer property—and get a court to agree with them.

Why is dealer property so bad?

There are two provisions of the Internal Revenue Code which you cannot take advantage of on dealer property:

- Depreciation
- Exchanging.

These, I hope you recognize, are two of the most important breaks in the tax code.

The definition of dealer property

IRC section 1221 defines a capital asset. A capital asset is the opposite of dealer property. A capital asset is what you **want** your properties classified as. Section 1221 says:

> ...*a capital asset...does not include--*
> *(1)stock in trade of the taxpayer or other property of a kind which would properly be included in the inventory of the taxpayer if on hand at the close of the taxable year, or property held by the taxpayer primarily for sale to customers in the ordinary course of his trade or business;...*

The key words for real estate investors are property held by the taxpayer primarily for sale to customers in the ordinary course of his trade or business.

Unfortunately, whether a property is dealer property is highly judgmental. As with other judgmental areas, you have to turn to the relevant court decisions to try to understand it.

Here are the factors which various court decisions have identified and the citations.

Frequency of sales

The more frequently you sell property, the more likely a court will decide you own dealer property. This is probably the most important of all factors in determining dealer status.

Question: How long must you wait before you sell to avoid dealer status?

Answer: There is no absolutely safe time period.

Question: You say frequency of **sales**. Does that mean you can't be declared a dealer if you **exchange**?

Answer: No. Quite the contrary. You can't exchange dealer property. The courts decide **first** whether the property in question is dealer property. **Then** they decide whether the exchange is valid.

Question: If I have frequent sales, does that mean I have no chance to avoid dealer property?

Answer: No. Here are some cases where the taxpayer had relatively frequent sales and still avoided the dealer property designation.

A land trust which sold 536 parcels of land during a nine-year period was allowed to pay tax at capital gains rates. The Court of Appeals said the total parcel was so **big** (over a million acres) that the taxpayer had no choice but to subdivide. *Chandler*, 226 F 2d 403

Taxpayer built a number of homes during World War II and sold them after the war. Court of Appeals said the houses were capital assets not dealer property. *Goldberg*, 223 F 2d 709

Arthur Smith inherited a parcel of land, which he subdivided and sold as lots. The Court of Appeals was impressed with the fact that Smith **inherited** the land rather than acquiring it on his own initiative. Not dealer property. *Smith*, 224 F 2d 253

Ayling bought a house but had to buy an adjoining parcel of land to get it. The taxpayer wanted to sell the land in one lump but the prospective buyer wanted to build low priced homes. Ayling thought these homes would reduce the value of his home so he subdivided the land and sold lots with **deed restrictions** preventing low-priced homes. He sold 13 lots in four years. The Tax Court allowed capital gains treatment. (*Ayling*, 32 TC No. 59)

The Fifth Circuit Court of Appeals (AL, FL, GA, LA, MS, TX) said Byram was not a dealer. Even though he sold seven properties in one year—six of which had been held for six months or less.

Forty-five sales in seven years, but not a dealer. (*Williams*, 53 AFTR 2d 84-884)

Primary purpose

IRC Section 1221 uses the word "primarily." If you interpret that literally, it means that if you had **multiple** purposes for owning the property, and the **secondary** purpose was to make dealer profits, it would not be dealer property.

In fact, that's what happened in *Malat v Riddell*, 383 US 569.

Another example where the court said the dealer aspects were substantial but not dominant was *Municipal Bond Corporation v. Comm.*, 341 F 2d 683.

Substantial improvement and subdivision

Substantial improvements and/or subdividing tend to make a property look like a dealer property to a court.

That happened to *Gerson A. Bush* (TC Memo 1977-75) in a case involving an apartment building. Another case where substantial improvements were a factor was *McManus v Comm.*, 583 F 2d 443.

Heebner bought land, arranged financing, put up buildings, and turned them over to buyers. The Tax Court said he was a dealer. 280 F 2d 228

Question: Are improvements always fatal?

Answer: No. Moore made same improvements which were **required** by a local ordinance before he sold. The court said that didn't mean it was dealer property. 30 TC 1306

The *Goldberg* and *Ayling* cases mentioned in the "frequency of sales" section also show that making substantial improvements is not always fatal.

Sales solicitation

In several cases, the courts decided that a taxpayer was or was not a dealer in part because of how hard he tried to sell the property. This seems a bit kooky to me. I should think that both investors and dealers would make an effort to present their property to prospective buyers.

Advertising got the taxpayer in trouble in *Tidewell v. Comm.*, 298 F 2d 864. **Listing** the property with a real estate agent, putting for sale signs on it, and advertising were strikes against the taxpayer in the *Municipal Bond Corp.* case mentioned in the "primary purpose" section above.

The fact that the offer was **unsolicited** helped *Starke* avoid dealer property status. 312 F 2d 608

But on the other hand, the lack of advertising didn't prevent *Gates* from being declared a dealer. The court said it was a "seller's market." 52 TC 898

Using a Realtor® was not fatal to *Au*, (Claims Court, 84/519 P-H Federal Taxes).

Intent

What you intended to do when you acquired the property is an important factor in determining whether it's dealer property.

I attended a seminar at a national real estate convention not too long ago. In that seminar, a nationally known real estate author was asked how he avoided dealer status. "Just write into your purchase agreement that you are acquiring the property for investment purposes," he said.

He's nuts.

Not that there aren't thousands of real estate investors and tax advisers who believe that nonsense. And it would be nice if it were true. Trouble is there hasn't been a single court case in which the wording of a purchase agreement or any other document was taken seriously in determining the investor's intent.

In other words, judges know that talk is cheap.

Can't do any harm to put that wording into your purchase and exchange agreements. But it's also a total waste of time as far as I can tell.

That's not to say that your intent is irrelevant. Not at all. The courts are interested in evidence of your intent. It's just that they do not find your own words on the subject very persuasive.

I mentioned that the court in the *Smith* case (in the "frequency of sale" section) was favorably impressed by the fact that Smith inherited the property. That suggested "innocent" intent at the time of acquisition.

If you can point to "changed conditions" as a reason for selling it helps to establish that your intent at the time of acquisition was not to be a dealer. (*Dillon v. Comm.*, 213 F 2d 218)

More questions and answers on dealer property

Q: How can I be sure to avoid dealer property?

A: Never sell or exchange.

Q: How long do you have to hold a property to avoid the dealer designation?

A: The longer, the better. But forever is the only **sure** dealer-avoiding holding period.

Q: Is there a maximum number of properties you can sell in a year before they call you a dealer?

A: No.

Q: But I've heard that if you sell five or fewer parcels in a year, you're guaranteed not to be a dealer. Isn't there something in the law about that?

A: That's IRC section 1237. Only non-dealers can qualify for it. So it provides no guarantee beyond regular dealer law.

Q: Are you automatically a dealer if you have a real estate license?

A: No. You're not automatically a dealer under any circumstances. It's always judgmental no matter how many strikes are against you.

The notion that a real estate license causes you to be called a dealer comes from the *Culley* case (29 TC 1076). The fact that Culley had a license was held against him in a dealer determination. But it is only one factor—and a lightweight one at that. Don't avoid getting a license or get rid of the license you have to avoid dealer status.

Q: If I do **not** have a license, will that prevent me from being declared a dealer?

A: No. At least it didn't help *Gault*, 332 F 2d 94.

Q: Who would be an example of someone who is generally considered to be a dealer?

A: The prime example is a home builder. People who subdivide land or convert apartments to condominiums are also generally considered to be dealers, but not always. A dealer is generally a person who makes his living by selling many properties he owns.

Q: Are you automatically a dealer when you buy raw land because the only purpose for holding it is resale since it has no income?

A: No. That falls into the category of speculation which is OK as far as dealer property is concerned. You can buy the property for use in your trade or business (like an apartment rental business), or for production of income, or for speculation.

Q: Can I avoid the dealer label if I sell the property to someone else and they subdivide it?

A: Maybe. If the person or organization to whom you sell the property is **your agent**, it won't work. (*Boyer*, 58 TC 316) By agent I don't mean real estate agent. I mean anyone who is acting on your behalf. It was a corporation in *Brown v. Comm.*, 448 F 2d 514.

Q: If I'm found to own dealer property in one transaction, does that mean everything I do is dealer property?

A: No. It's not once a dealer, always a dealer. You don't have to wear a scarlet "D" for the rest of your life just because you did one dealer transaction.

You can own both dealer and non-dealer property at the same time. *Pritchett* did that by identifying some of his property as investment property on his books and records and by consistently **segregating** it from his dealer property. 63 TC 149. *Crabtree* was a dealer but that did not mean his home had to be taxed as dealer property when he sold it. 20 TC 841

Q: So the fact that I'm a dealer on one property does not affect another property I own, right?

A: Wrong. The courts may look at your other activities. *Rockwell* lost a dealer case because a large fraction of his total income was from sales of real estate. (512 F 2d 822) *Glover* stated in his tax return that he was a dealer. The court agreed. ¶ 55,329 P-H Memo TC. *Mitchell* avoided the dealer label by proving that he was not in the business of selling real estate. 47 TC 120

Q: If I bought a property for dealer purposes, can I change my mind and make it an investment property?

A: Yes.
Bynum, 46 TC 295.
Malat v. Riddell, 383 US 569
Dressen, 17 TC 1443
Maddux Construction Company, 54 TC 1278
Oace, 39 TC 743
Howell, 57 TC 546
Westchester Development Co., 63 TC 198
Casalina, 60 TC 72
Biedermann, 68 TC 1

Q: If I'm not a dealer, can it hurt me that my business associates are dealers?

A: Yes. In *Brady*, 25 TC 682, a joint venture's purpose for owning some dealer property tainted the members of the joint venture.

Q: This whole question of dealer property is pretty ambiguous, isn't it?

A: You can say that again.

PART SIX:
INSTALLMENT SALES

21

Installment Sales

The Revenue Act of 1987 more or less restored the pre-Tax-Reform-Act-Of-1986 rules for installment sales.

You automatically get installment sale treatment if you receive more than one payment in more than one year. You can elect out of installment sale treatment in the year of the sale.

Installment sales after the Revenue Act of 1987

Here's the article I wrote on the Revenue Act of 1987's changes in the installment sale rules.

Installment Sales Are Back

The wicked proportionate disallowance witch is dead for sales after 8/16/86. So sayeth the Revenue Act of 1987 which Reagan signed 12/22/87. The diagram below explains the details.

abolish **all** installment sales just to stop tax-free hypothecation. New IRC § 453A(d) makes hypothecation proceeds taxable when received as if they were payments received on the installment note

(6)] which prohibited the use of the installment sale election when computing your Alternative Minimum Tax (AMT) liability.

Under RA '87, you can again use the installment method when computing your AMT [**new IRC** § 56(a)(6)] for sales after 1986.

Property on which you took back mortgage is	Installment sale rules which apply	**Authority** [all cites refer to the Internal Revenue Code (IRC) **after** incorporation of the Revenue Act of 1987]
Personal use property i.e. your principal or second or third or fourth or whatever residence	Pre-Tax Reform Act of 1986 rules, i.e., you pay tax on installment payments as you receive them	IRC §453A(b)(3)
Trade, business, or income property Sale price* $150,000 or less		IRC § 453A(b)(1) same as pre-RA '87
Sale price more than $150,000 but seller** takes back $5,000,000 or less in mortgages during the year in question		IRC § 453A(b)(2)(B) for sales after 8/16/86
Sale price more than $150,000 and seller** takes back **more than** $5,000,000 in mortgages during the year in question	First $5,000,000 of mortgages taken back: Pre-Tax Reform Act of 1986 rules; Above $5,000,000: must pay **interest** on deferred tax at the year-end IRS underpayment rate***	IRC § 453A(a)(1) & (b)(2)B) for sales after '8/16/86
Residential lots, timeshare, or farm notes not bank-guaranteed	Must pay interest on deferred tax at the IRS underpayment rate	IRC § 453A(b)(4) for sales after 12/31/87
Dealer property	No installment sale treatment allowed…pay tax as if all payments were received in the year of sale	IRC §453(b)(2)(A) for sales after 12/31/87
* Chopping up a deal into sub-$150,000 pieces is not allowed [IRC § 453A(b)(5)].	** The "seller" is you and any entities you control [IRC § 453A(b)(2)(B)].	*** IRS underpayment rate is currently 11% [IRC § 6621(a)(2)].

Hypothecation of seller mortgage now taxable

Hypothecation is pledging a mortgage you took back from another borrower as security for a loan **to** you. IRS hates hypothecation because it lets people report income on the installment method …but get all or most of the money up front by borrowing against the installment note. It was IRS hatred of hypothecation that inspired the Tax Reform Act of 1986's proportionate disallowance rules.

Now, in RA '87, Congress has discovered that they don't have to

(mortgage you took back). Furthermore, pledging a mortgage you took back as security for a loan you **already** have makes the proceeds of the loan you already have taxable in the year you pledge the new mortgage as security. That's effective 12/17/87.

Installment sale method OK for AMT

After rendering installment sales virtually unusable a year ago, Congress twisted the knife. By including in the Tax Reform Act of 1986 a provision [**old** IRC § 56(a)

New rules should break ice

The absence of installment sales froze much of the income property market. The new rules should thaw it out. Sellers who want too high a price can now save face by hiding their price cut in the form of a better-than-market seller loan. You can get the cash flow you need by getting those favorable terms.

I have not changed my opinion that you should never take back a loan as a seller. Use installment sales only as a **buyer**. JTR

Don't do installment sales

Real estate investors have long regarded installment sales as one of the main tax saving devices available to them.

I've got news for you. Installment sales have nothing to do with **saving** taxes. Do an installment sale and you will **pay** taxes—not save them.

You should **never** do an installment sale. I've been saying that since the late seventies.

The installment sale is not now and never was a tax-saving device. If you want to save taxes when you get rid of a property, **exchange**.

Yes, it defers taxes—but it defers *income*, too

Installment sale advocates say that installment sales defer taxes and that deferring the payment reduces its present value. Just so.

But in order to defer the taxes, you have to defer the **income** you receive. And since **you** get more (72% at least) of the income in question than the IRS (28% at most), **you** are more the victim of the deferral's reducing the present value than the IRS.

Installment sales are a classic example of cutting off your nose to spite the IRS.

'But don't you save by avoiding raising your bracket in the year of sale?'

This is the main argument people cite to push installment sales. The answer is that **some** people will pay tax at lower rates if they do an installment sale rather than a cash sale. But that doesn't mean those people should do installment sales. **Nobody** should do installment sales. Not even those few who save as a result of lower brackets. There are at least six reasons:

- Spreading out the income does not lower your bracket if you are **already** in the **maximum** bracket.
- Any small tax savings you might realize is far outweighed by the **opportunity cost** of having your money tied up for years.
- Instead of **reducing** your tax rate by doing an installment sale, why not **eliminate** the tax altogether by exchanging.
- The alternative minimum tax may wipe out or more than wipe out the savings.
- Losses carried forward under the passive loss limits may reduce your tax on sale so much that there's little or nothing left to save via an installment sale.

Installment sales don't help max bracket investors

If you are in the 15% bracket, an installment sale could keep you from hitting the 28% bracket in some sale situations. But if you are **already** in the 28% bracket, what bracket-lowering can spreading out the income from a sale accomplish? If you get it all this year, IRS will take 28%. And if you get half this year and half next year, they'll **still** take 28%. If you get a dollar a year for a million years, they'll **still** take 28%.

The only people who benefit from spreading are those who are **below** the maximum bracket both before **and after** taking into account the annual **installment payments** (not the cash sale lump sum).

Nickel and dime tax savings; huge opportunity cost

Let's assume that you are in a lower bracket and that an installment sale will truly save you taxes. Are the savings worth the cost?

If you receive, say $100,000 of gain in a lump, you'll pay about $28,000 in taxes. You may reduce that through an installment sale—by maybe $5,000. And that's it. Just a one-time savings. But you forego the return you could have earned on the $72,000 after-tax proceeds. At 20% that's $72,000 x 20% = $14,400—**a year!**

Exchange

If you do an installment sale, you pay tax. If you exchange, you don't.

To a simple minded fellow like me that means I exchange. I don't sell—on an installment basis or otherwise.

Actually, you can do **both** in the same deal. That is, you can do an exchange in which you take back a mortgage on the property you get rid of. But you **shouldn't**. In a combination exchange/installment sale, the installment sale wipes out the benefit of exchanging on the amount of the installment note. In other words, the installment portion of the deal will be taxed. It's as if you did **two** deals: one a taxable sale and one a tax-free exchange.

Carried forward losses

The new passive loss limits may cause you to carry forward losses which you could not deduct while you owned the property. But when you **sell** the property, you can deduct those carried forward losses from the gain on resale. By the time you get done doing that, there may be little or no benefit to doing an installment sale.

Mind-boggling calculations

The calculations to determine whether an installment sale will save you taxes are mind-boggling. You have to calculate your tax the **regular** way then the **AMT** way for **both** the installment sale and cash sale alternatives—for **each year** the installment note will be outstanding.

You also need to choose a **discount rate** and make assumptions about your future balance sheet and income tax situation. The calculations are so mind-boggling, and would only apply to a narrow group of investors with the same assumptions and situation, that I will not do them here. I doubt that anyone has **ever** done the calculations. So when someone says installment sales will save you taxes, he doesn't know for sure what he's talking about.

Ever since the first edition of this book in 1981, I have been defying people to come up with an example which bears some resemblance to a real world deal and in which the investor will earn a higher after-tax rate of return on equity by doing an installment sale instead of a cash sale. No one has done it. No one has even tried.

Why is hypothecation taxable?

To understand the Revenue Act of 1987 hypothecation rule, it helps to know why it was passed.

Home builders were selling houses and taking back mortgages. Then they would immediately pledge the mortgages they took back as security for loans. Borrowing against a loan owed to you is called hypothecation.

The builders had the best of both worlds, they sold their properties and reported the sales on an **installment** basis—but they got the money **up front**. In other words, the builder got his money out immediately. But the IRS had to wait for theirs.

The Revenue Act of 1987 hypothecation rule was meant to stop that.

The rule

You may have seen the bumper sticker which says,

I owe, I owe, so it's off to work I go.

As a result of the Revenue Act of 1987, one could create a similar installment seller's bumper sticker:

I owe, I owe, so pay tax triggered by the hypothecation rule I must.

I don't agree with Congress's creating that sticker, but I will defend to the death their right to stick it.

Under the hypothecation rule, it's a "crime" to pledge an installment note as security for a loan. In other words, if you borrow against any note you hold—even one you took back years ago—you are, in effect, deemed to be one of those no good, hypothecating builders.

Doesn't matter that you've never built anything. Doesn't matter that the money you owe is a mortgage you got four years ago on a different building.

It's an *'election'*

Installment sales are an **election**, you know. You do **not** have to elect installment sale treatment just because you do an installment sale. You can do an installment sale and report it as a **cash** sale and pay taxes accordingly.

I do **not** recommend installment sales with or without the election. But you might want to point out that installment sale reporting is optional to a seller who is willing to take back a loan but is afraid of the complexity of the rules.

How to do an installment sale

Having said all of the above against installment sales, I will now tell you how to do them. For two reasons:

- Many of you will ignore my advice and do an installment sale anyway.
- You need to understand installment sales when you want the seller to do one.

Installment sales are covered by section 453 of the Internal Revenue Code. Installment sales were dramatically revised by the Installment Sale Revision Act of 1980, the Tax Reform Act of 1984, the Tax Reform Act of 1986, and the Revenue Act of 1987. So make sure you are looking at a **current** version of the law.

Low interest rate loans

There are two limits on how low the interest rate can be on seller financing for tax purposes:

Amount of seller loan	Minimum interest rate
$2.8 million or less	Lower of 9% or AFR
More than $2.8 million	AFR

This applies to sales of **real estate** and **used personal** property. A 6% minimum interest rate applies to sales of up to $500,000 of land per year between family members.

AFR stands for Applicable Federal Rate. That is an interest rate announced by the IRS monthly. Actually, twelve AFRs are announced every month. One for each of four types of compounding:

- Annual
- Semiannual
- Quarterly
- Monthly.

And there are three different terms:

- Short-term (not over three years)
- Mid-term (over three but not over nine years)
- Long-term (over nine years).

Four types of compounding times three different terms equals twelve AFRs.

No problem *above* minimum

If your seller financing is at an interest rate **above** the government minimum, you ignore all this AFR stuff. It's only when your interest rate is **below** the government minimums that you must use the government limits to report the deal for tax purposes.

Whenever you use a below-market rate...

There are two very important caveats when you do a deal with a below-market interest rate.

From the **seller's** point of view, the **sale price** must be **increased** above the cash value of the property.

From the buyer's point of view, the loan documents must provide for a prepayment discount which enables the buyer/borrower to, in effect, buy the loan from the seller at the loan's then fair market value rather than have to buy it (pay it off) at full face value.

Why you need a prepayment bonus

The buyer must get that prepayment bonus unless he is absolutely sure he will not pay the loan off one day before it's due date. Hardly any buyer would wait until the absolute last day on a loan large enough to require refinancing or sale to pay it off. And the best laid plans oft times go awry. So get the prepayment bonus.

If you do **not** get it, here's what you're doing. Let's say the **market** interest rate for a mortgage like the seller is taking back is 12%. And he's taking back a 9% mortgage. If you were forced to get a 12% institutional mortgage, you'd be willing to pay $1,050,000. But at 9%, you agree to pay $1,200,000. Down payment is $300,000 and seller carries back $900,000 for ten years at 9% interest only at monthly payments of 9% x $900,000 = $81,000 ÷ $6,750.

Then, for some reason, you decide to pay the loan off after **two** years. Maybe you become disabled and your spouse does not want to manage the property. Maybe it goes up in value and you decide to sell or refinance. Maybe you get an inheritance. Who knows.

Without a prepayment bonus, you'd have to pay the full $900,000. At the two-year point, the present value of the remaining payments on the mortgage, discounted at the market rate of 12% is:

n = 96 payments
i = 12% ÷ 12 months per year = 1%
PMT = $6,750/month

PV = $415,312.00

+

n = 96
i = 1%
FV = $900,000 (balloon payment on interest only loan)

PV = $346,250.67
Total present value = $761,562.67

PV, FV, PMT, i, and n are entry keys on a financial calculator. See my book, *How to Use Leverage to Maximize Your Real Estate Investment Return* for a detailed explanation of how to use a financial calculator.

The present value (assuming a 12% discount) of the remaining mortgage payments including the $900,000 balloon payment is only $761,562.67. So if the market interest rate on such loans is still 12% at the two-year point, $761,562.67 is the most the seller would be able to sell the loan for. In fact, it would probably sell for much less because the buyers of used mortgages expect returns in the 18% to 25% range.

If the market value of the loan is less than $761,562.67, why should **you** have to pay $900,000 for it?

To put it another way, you agreed to pay a **premium** of $1,200,000 - $1,050,000 = $150,000 for the property in return for a **ten**-year, 9% mortgage. Which is OK. But if the seller had insisted on a **two**-year pay off date, you would **not** have agreed to the $150,000 premium. If, in fact, you do pay off the mortgage in two years, you have bamboozled yourself out of $900,000 - $761,562.67 = $138,437.33.

How you must report below-minimum rate deals

Roughly speaking, you have to report **below**-minimum rate deals as if they were **at** the minimum rate.

First, you have to compute what Treasury Regulations call the "unstated interest." You do that with this formula:

> *Unstated interest = face amount of the loan - present value of all payments discounted at the applicable minimum rate (9% or AFR)*

IRS used to provide tables for doing this calculation. But the calculation was simpler then. With dozens of interest rates going out to two decimal points, I presume that we are now supposed to use a financial calculator.

Example

Seller takes back a loan with the following terms:

Face amount	$1,000,000
Interest rate	8%
Term	10 years
Amortization	none
Balloon payment	$1,000,000
Semi-annual payment	$40,000

The present value of all the payments discounted at 9% semi-annually is:

n = 20
i = 4.5%
PMT = $40,000

PV = $520,317.50

+

n = 20
i = 4.5%
FV = $1,000,000

PV = $414,642.90
Total present value $934,960.40

So the unstated interest in this deal is $1,000,000 - $934,960.40 = $65,039.60.
To calculate the portion of each payment which is unstated interest, you use this formula:

Interest portion = payment amount x unstated interest ÷ face amount of the loan

For the semi-annual payments in this example, that would be $40,000 x $65,039.60 ÷ $1,000,000 = $40,000 x .0650396 = $2,601.60. For the balloon payment, that would be $1,000,000 x .0650396 = $65,039.60.

In effect, the law says the seller did not take back a $1,000,000 at 8%. Rather the seller took back a $934,960.40 loan at 9% for tax purposes. The effect is that $65,039.60 of what would have been a $1,000,000 principal payment (balloon payment) becomes interest. That means the seller must report it as interest income and the buyer may deduct it [unless it's for personal use. IRC § 1275(b)(1)]—even though the loan documents say that the $65,039.40 is a principal payment.

Sale price and buyer's basis are lower

Also, the seller's sale price (for tax purposes) will be smaller by $65,039.60. And the buyer's basis will be smaller by the same amount.

I've met some sophisticated real estate investors who knew about imputed interest but who disputed my claim that the sale price and buyer's basis also had to be changed.

They're wrong. Number one, logic requires it. Either the interest rate is 8% and the price is $1,200,000 or the interest rate is 9% and the price is $1,134,960.40. But to say the the interest rate is 9% and the price is $1,200,000 defies the laws of mathematics. It's like saying that 5 + 2 = 7 and 3 + 4 = 7 therefore 5 + 3 = 7.

And if logic's not enough, try Internal Revenue Code sections 1274 and 1274A, Revenue Ruling 82-124, and Regulation 1.483-2(a)(1)(i).

Different deals come under different rules

There are two main Internal Revenue Code sections when it comes to imputed interest: 483 and 1271 through 1274. Sections 1271 through 1274 are also known as the Original Issue Discount rules or OID rules. Some below-minimum rate deals are covered by 483, others by 1271 through 1274, and still others are exempt from both.

For example, if the sale price is $3,000 or less and the price is fixed, it doesn't matter what the interest rate is. Sales of principal residences are exempt from the OID rules but they are not exempt from section 483. Same goes for any sale in which the payments total less than $250,000.

That $250,000 cutoff point applies to the **arithmetic** total of all payments, **not** the present value of all payments. And all payments means down payment, interest payments, principal payments, assumptions or subject tos, and the fair market value of any property given as part of the purchase price. In other words, **everything**.

Neither section 483 nor the OID rules apply to assumptions or subject tos.

Accrual and cash accounting

Accrual accounting means you count income when you **earn** it and expenses when you **incur** them. Cash accounting means that you count income when you **receive** it (or have the right to receive it) and expenses when you **pay** them. That lets you sock it to the tax man.

Seller takes back a loan but accrues interest. Seller is on a cash basis accounting system for tax purposes so he gets to deduct the interest as it accrues—even though he hasn't paid a cent! Nice work if you can get it. But you can't get it anymore. Not since the 1985 Simplification of Imputed Interest Rules.

For deals entered into after June 30, 1985, both the buyer and the seller in a seller-financed deal have to use the same accounting for the seller loan. Furthermore, they both have to use the **accrual** method unless the seller loan amount is $2,000,000 or less (not $2.8 million which is a figure that often comes up as a result of a related law) and if the seller is **not a dealer**.

And, if the buyer later sells the property to another buyer who assumes or buys subject to the original seller's loan, that **new** buyer must also use the same accounting method as the **original** seller and buyer.

This will tend to make it hard to persuade sellers to agree to accruing interest except on non-dealer loans of $2,000,000 or less.

Buydowns

As far as I can tell, the imputed interest rules do not apply to buydowns.

I have long opposed taking back mortgages. Instead, I recommend that you either sell for a low enough price to get all cash for your equity or do a buydown. As a practical matter, buydowns are better. Because buyers just do not have the imagination to see the benefit of a low price when they have to get their own financing.

You probably already know that you can take back a below-market interest rate mortgage then sell it to a third party at a discount. In a buydown, you simply do that **before closing**.

VA mortgages are buydowns. The VA interest rate is typically set below the market rate for VA loans for political reasons. The discount at which you sell the loan is called "points."

FHA deals used to be the same. But now the FHA interest rate is whatever you can get from the lender. FHA simply insures the loan. It no longer regulates the interest rate.

Builders frequently do conventional buydowns to sell houses in times of high interest rates. They typically advertise a below-market rate loan—with an asterisk. The asterisk refers you to the small print where you learn that rate goes up to market in three years or some such.

As with VA loans, the builder simply pays points to the lender to increase the lender's yield up to market rate.

Buydowns are better than price cuts

A buydown is the same as a price cut. Sell your house conventionally for $60,000 and you get $60,000. But sell your house for $60,000 to a VA buyer and you only get $60,000 less the points you have to pay.

Theoretically, buyers should have no preference for a full-price/bought down below-market interest rate and a discount price/market interest rate. Theoretically, the two are exactly, mathematically equal.

But in reality, buyers don't think that way. They'd much rather pay full price and get the below-market interest rate. Even though they know in their heart of hearts that they are paying the points themselves in the form of a higher purchase price.

Case history

Don't believe me? Try it both ways. I did. I offered an apartment complex for sale. Realtor ® said it would sell for $720,000—if I took back a 75% of value, 12%, seven-year wraparound second mortgage. Interest rates at the time were about 14% for loans like that.

I said, "What price if I refused to take back a mortgage at all?"

"$600,000."

"OK," I said. "I'll list it for $600,000."

I did and it expired unsold after six months with no offers.

Then I offered it for sale for $740,000 and promised the buyer a 75%-of-value, seven-year, 12% wraparound second mortgage. It sold for $720,000 on those terms. Did I take back that mortgage? No way. In effect, I bought it down from an institutional lender. Cost me $60,000 in points when all was said and done. But my net of $660,000 was $60,000 more than my previous listing price—and I paid no $30,000 commission on the deal.

Buydown $90,000 better than discount price

I increased my net proceeds by $60,000 plus a $30,000 commission by the simple device of arranging the financing for the buyer.

Those buyers could have bought the property for $600,000 previously. Then turned around and sold it for a net of $660,000 without paying a commission as I did. Nice money for a couple months work. Alternatively, the Realtor ® could have arranged the same financing and thereby gotten a $30,000 commission instead of an expired listing.

Most sellers of big ticket items do buydowns

Look at what other sellers of expensive products do, Expensive products like new homes, vehicles, appliances, etc. Do they ever advertise below-market interest rates? You bet. I already mentioned builders. And in 1985 and 1986 Detroit auto makers made news—and enormous sales gains—with their 7.7% and 8.8% financing. They bought down those loans.

I suspect that builders, auto makers, and others who make their living selling big ticket items have learned from experience that providing below-market interest rate financing produces a bigger bottom line than cutting the price by the amount of the buydown points. Apparently, because buyers are lazy and have no imagination. Just as tenants cannot see a clean apartment-to-be when you show them a dirty apartment, neither can prospective investors see that a $600,000 get-your-own-14%-mortgage is a better deal than a $720,000 I'll-get-you-a-12%-mortgage deal.

Note that buydowns must be disclosed to lenders

This is not a tax matter. But you should know that if a deal involves two or more new institutional mortgages—and one is being bought down—that fact must be disclosed to the other lender. It is a "material fact" and concealing material facts is a federal felony if the lender who is kept in the dark is federally related. Buydowns also require buyers to reduce their basis (Letter Ruling 8942001).

Do the OID rules affect buydowns?

The OID rules do not appear to affect buydowns. Section 1274(c)(1) of the Internal Revenue Code says

> ...this section shall apply to any debt instrument given in consideration for the sale or exchange of property...

The phrase "in consideration for the sale or exchange of property" means it only applies to loans taken back by a seller. A buydown is not a loan taken back by a seller. However, Section 1275(d) gives IRS broad authority to issue regulations. Those regs may put buydowns under the OID rules.

There's another code section which may cover buydowns

So far, I've told you about section 483 (the 9%/AFR rule) and sections 1271 through 1275 (OID rules). Now let me tell you about section 7872 "Treatment of loans with below-market interest rates."

Most of the articles I've read about the law discuss this section as if it only applied to gift loans and demand loans—loans commonly made between family members, employers and employees, and corporations and shareholders as a tax avoidance device. But I see some **other** things in that section.

Subsections 7872 (c)(1)(D) and (E) say this section covers:

> (D) TAX AVOIDANCE LOANS.—Any below-market loan [one] of the principal purposes of the interest arrangements of which is the avoidance of any Federal tax.
> (E) OTHER BELOW-MARKET LOANS.—To the extent provided in regulations, any below-market loan...if the interest arrangements of such loan have a significant effect on any Federal tax liability of the lender or the borrower.

Tax avoidance principal purpose

If one of the principal purposes of the buydown is tax avoidance, the buydown comes under section 7872's imputed interest rules. How do you tell if tax avoidance is one of the loan's principal purposes? Good question.

The fact that the buyer's tax picture is better if the buydown is ignored suggests that it **might** be one of the principal purposes. Any written evidence that tax avoidance is a principal purpose of the buydown—like words to that effect in a limited partnership prospectus—would probably hurt.

But other than those two observations, I don't know whether buydowns come under the tax avoidance principal purpose part of the law.

'Significant effect on any Federal tax liability?'

What about subparagraph E? The significant effect subsection.

I'll tell you right away that buydowns **do** have a significant effect on the buyer's Federal tax liability. If the buydown points were deducted from the sale price, the buyer would have a lower basis and therefore lower depreciation deductions.

Subsection E starts with the words, "To the extent provided in regulations." Regulation section 1.7872-5T(c)(3) says,

> *Among the factors to be considered are--*
> *(i)   whether items of income and deduction generated by the loan offset each other;*
> *(ii) the amount of such items;*
> *(iii) the cost to the taxpayer of complying with the provisions of section 7872 if such section were applied;*
> *(iv) any non-tax reasons for deciding to structure the transaction as a below-market loan rather than a loan with interest at a rate equal to or greater than the applicable Federal rate and a payment by the lender to the borrower.*

The regs that are out so far do not mention buydowns.

Make sure you get a higher price if you cut the rate

If you loan someone money at a below-market interest rate, you **must** recoup the present value of the interest rate subsidy you're giving by getting a higher price for the property.

You need to understand excess loans over basis

If you do installment sales, you need to understand "excess loans over basis."

Frequently, when you get rid of a property, the buyer takes over one or more existing loans. The law calls this "loan relief." Loan relief is considered **income**—which makes sense. When someone takes over a $100,000 loan which you owed, you're $100,000 better off. (Actually, the amount by which you are better off is the cash resale value of the loan that was taken over—but the law does not look at it that way.)

But if you give up $100,000 worth of **property** at the same time, you're **not** better off. The two cancel each other out.

Now I must remind you that tax law has a strange view of the value of your property. In the law's eyes, your property is worth what you paid for it less all depreciation you've claimed or were allowed to claim. The law does **not** see your property as being worth its fair market value.

Your cost less the depreciation you've claimed is your "adjusted basis" or just "basis."

The phrase "excess loans over basis" refers to situations where you sell a property and the existing loans which the buyer takes over exceed the adjusted basis of the property. This is most likely to happen when you've owned the property for some time and have refinanced, or where you've used the combination of high leverage and aggressive depreciation.

No matter how it happened, excess loans over basis are considered a payment received in the year of sale. That means you'll have to pay tax on it.

Example

You sell a property for $145,000. The buyer gives you $30,000 in cash and takes over an existing loan of $115,000. Your basis in the property is $65,000.

In this case, you have $50,000 of excess loans over basis:

Existing loan	$115,000
Basis	$65,000
Excess loans over basis	$50,000

As a result, although you've only received $30,000 in cash, you're going to be taxed as if you had received $30,000 + $50,000 = $80,000 in cash. That increases your tax bill and thereby reduces the amount of money you have available for investment in another property.

How to avoid 'the heartbreak of excess loans over basis'

Turns out there is a way to avoid the "heartbreak of excess loans over basis." The *Stonecrest* case (24 TC 659). Although the more recent *Hunt* (80 TC 62) and *Professional Equities* (89 TC 165) cases are more broadly applicable and therefore probably more important.

In the *Stonecrest* case, IRS said Stonecrest owed more taxes because of excess loans over basis. Stonecrest said excess loans over basis did not apply in this case and won.

Stonecrest sold property on a **wraparound land contract.** A wraparound land contract is a financing device. This is not a book on real estate finance, so I don't want to spend much time on it. Here's a brief explanation.

The wraparound land contract

Normally, when you buy a property, you get a deed. In legalese, that's called "legal and equitable title." With a land contract, you only get "equitable" title. That means you get everything but the deed.

The seller keeps the deed until you pay off the money you owe him. It might help if you think of it as a mortgage taken back by the seller. Only instead of having a mortgage for security, the seller has the deed. And instead of giving you a mortgage cancellation when you pay off the loan, he gives you the deed.

Example of a wraparound

The adjective wraparound refers to an arrangement best described by example.

You're selling a million dollar property. There's an existing loan of $491,900 at 8% with 21 years left. The buyer has $200,000 to put down and you take back a mortgage or a land contract for the remaining $308,100. You and the buyer agree that you will take back a wraparound land contract for $800,000 at 12% interest for 21 years. The land contract is junior to the existing financing.

The buyer will make monthly payments to you of $8,709.60 ($800,000 loan at 12% for 21 years).

You will continue to make payments on the underlying $500,000 loan. That loan, which was originally for $550,000 at 8% for 30 years requires payments of $4,035.71 per month.

So you will receive payments of $8,709.60 per month. Then you will deduct $4,035.71 and send it to the lender on the existing first mortgage and pocket the difference, $4,673.89.

The reason for the name "wraparound" is that the $800,000 land contract seems to wrap around the smaller $491,900 first loan.

In any event, Stonecrest did a wraparound land contract. That was important to the outcome of the case. Actually, there were five characteristics which the Court cited in the Stonecrest decision.

1. The taxpayer (seller) continued to make the monthly payments on the underlying loan.

2. The transaction was a land contract.

3. The buyer did not assume the existing loan.

4. The taxpayer (seller) remained liable on the loan.

5. The seller's payments to the underlying lender were not dependent upon the buyer's paying the seller.

Because of these factors, the court said the buyer did not really relieve the taxpayer (seller) of the existing loan. Therefore the taxpayer should not have to pay tax on the excess loan over basis.

In *Hunt*, 80 TC 62, a taxpayer won an excess loans over basis case using a wraparound **mortgage, not** a land contract.

Voight blew it

There was another case on this subject (*Voight*, 68 TC 10). There the taxpayer also tried to avoid the excess loans over basis problem. But he blew it because

1. The buyer paid the underlying lender direct.

2. The buyer personally guaranteed the seller's loan.

These two cases tell you what to do and what not to do to solve an excess loans over basis problem.

Note: The IRS did not acquiesce to these court decisions. That means they did not agree with them and as a result, you may be challenged if you set up a wraparound land contract or mortgage to avoid excess loans over basis. In February of 1981, the IRS issued temporary regs which prohibited avoiding excess loans over basis by using a wraparound land contract [TD 7768 Reg Section 15A.453-1(b)(3)(ii)]. The Tax Court explicitly rejected that regulation in *Professional Equities, Inc.*, 89 TC 165, and the IRS acquiesced in IRB 1988-37.

The 'heartbreak of excess loans over *value*'

Some people used to think that loan amounts which exceeded the market value of a property didn't count for excess loans over basis purposes. That notion applied to non-recourse loans wiped out by foreclosure, deed in lieu of foreclosure, abandonment, and selling at a loss.

Wrong.

In *Tufts*, the U.S. Supreme Court said the value of the property is irrelevant—even if it's a non-recourse loan. In other words, you have to pay tax on excess loans over basis even if the loan total exceeds the value of the property.

The investment interest limitation

Interest on passive rental property activities in which you "actively participate" or trade or business activities (other than rental properties) in which you "materially participate" is **never** limited by the investment interest limitation. In other words, stuff that's subject to the passive loss limits is **not** subject to the investment interest limitation. Since real estate investor's properties are almost **all** subject to the passive loss rules, they are rarely affected by the new, Tax Reform Act of 1986 version of the investment interest limitation.

PART SEVEN:
PASSIVE LOSS LIMITATIONS

22

Passive Loss Limitations

The $25,000 exemption for 'active participants'

For certain small investors, the passive loss limits do **not** apply at all. You are one of them if:

- You "**actively participate**" in the management of the rental property.
- Your rental property losses are **$25,000** or less.
- You own a **10%** or greater interest in the property.
- You are **not** a **limited partner** in the property.
- Your **adjusted gross income** (not counting rental property losses) is **$100,000** or less.

Definition of an 'active participant'

The Internal Revenue Code does not define "active participation." But the Senate Finance Committee Report on the Tax Reform Act of 1986 does. It says you must:

> participate, e.g. in the making of management decisions or arranging for others to provide services (such as repairs), in a significant and bona fide sense. Management decisions that are relevant in this context include approving new tenants, deciding on rental terms, approving capital or repair expenditures, and other similar decisions.

Forget the 'material participation' test

A great many articles on the new tax law's effect on real estate have talked about the law's "material participation" test. I don't know why. It only applies to businesses **other than** rental property. Because section 469(c)(2) of the Internal Revenue Code says that:

The term 'passive activity' includes any rental activity.

In other words, no matter how many hours you devote to managing your rental properties, they are **still** passive activities subject to the passive loss limitations.
The Senate Finance Committee Report says you must be:

involved in the operations of the activity on a regular, continuous, and substantial basis, in order to be materially participating.

On February 19, 1988, IRS issued temporary regulations further defining "material participation." They said you "materially participate" in a trade or business (but not rental property) if **any** of the following are true (from regulation section 1.469-5T):

1. You participate in the business more than **500 hours** per year, OR
2. Your participation is substantially **all** the participation there is by anyone, OR
3. You participate at least 100 hours per year and **no one else** participates more than 100 hours per year, OR
4. You participate in more than one "**significant participation**" activity and the total hours you spend on all those activities exceeds 500 hours. (A "significant participation" activity is one in which you participate more than 100 hours but do not meet the "material participation" criteria on that one activity.), OR
5. You participated in the business in question more than 500 hours per year for **any five** of the last ten years, OR
6. The activity in question is a "**personal service**" activity and you participated in it more than 500 hours per year in any three years prior to 1987. "Personal service" activities means the following fields:

  - Health
  - Engineering
  - Accounting
  - Performing arts
  - Law
  - Architecture
  - Actuarial science
  - Consulting
  - Any business in which capital is not a "material income producing factor."

  (This is the anti-Yuppie section of the reg.), OR
7. You participate more than 100 hours per year and your praticipation is "**regular, continuous, and substantial.**"

Limited partners *can* 'materially participate'

Limited partners "materially participate" if they pass either of the following two tests:

1. They participate more than 500 hours per year, OR
2. They meet the criteria described in numbers 5 or 6 above.

You plus spouse = one taxpayer

For purposes of this reg, you add the hours you and your spouse participate together to see if you pass the test. For example, if **you** participate 200 hours and your **spouse** participated 312 hours, you would have a total of 512 hours—thereby passing the 500-hour test.

No logbook required

Reg section 1.469(f)(4) says you do not need to keep a log book . You can prove the hours by "any reasonable means" like appointment books, calendars, etc.

What the passive loss limitation says

The rule is that you can deduct passive losses like those from rental property from passive income—like a business in which you do not materially participate. But you **cannot** deduct passive losses from nonpassive income like:

- Salary or wages
- Interest
- Income from a business in which you "materially participate"
- Commissions
- Dividends

Understanding Congress's motivation may help you to understand the passive loss limits. Congress is saying, in effect:

"You real estate investors have been telling us on your tax returns that you were **losing** money. Mainly due to depreciation.

"Who do you think you're kidding? Everybody knows your properties are appreciating. So here's what we're going to do. You can deduct depreciation and other 'losses' from the **income of the property in question**. And if you have any losses left over you can deduct them from the taxable income generated by **other** rental properties or other passive income generators like a business in which you do not materially participate.

"And if you **still** have rental property losses which you can't deduct, you can **carry** them **forward** into future years. Finally, if you dispose of all your interest in the property in question—and you **still** have a loss—then and only then—we will let you deduct that loss from **any** kind of income you want to deduct it from."

Definition of 'rental activity'

According to IRS regulation section 1.469(f)(4), what you do is a "rental activity" if:

payments are principally for the use of tangible property.

But there are six **exceptions** to that rule [Reg. section 1.469-1T(e)(3)(ii)]. Your property is **not** a "rental activity" if:

1. The average period of customer use is **seven days** or less (e.g. hotel and motel rooms)
2. The average period of customer use is more than seven days but not more than thirty days AND "**significant personal services**" are provided (e.g. maid service) Telephone, cable tv, janitorial, improvements, and replacements are **not** personal services according to §1.469-1T(e)(3)(iv)(B).

3. The average period of customer use is greater than thirty days but "**extraordinary personal services**" are provided (e.g. hospitals and nursing homes).
4. The rental is **incidental** to non-rental activities. (e.g. An accounting firm owns and occupies an office building which it moves out of and rents briefly while waiting to sell it.)
5. The rental is used by customers during defined business hours as invitees or licensees (e.g. **golf club memberships**).
6. You rent property to a partnership, S Corporation, or joint venture in which you own an interest and which is **not** in the rental property business.

Rent from a property which is all or mostly **land** is **not** passive income unless the depreciable portion of the property exceeds 30% of the original basis of the property. That affects farms and houses or other property on extremely expensive land like view lots. [reg. §1.469-2T(f)(3)]

Dealer property is not "rental activity." But don't be too quick to declare yourself a dealer. Dealers cannot deduct depreciation or exchange. Without depreciation, you probably have little or no tax loss on the property. So the passive loss limits probably no longer restrict you.

Owner occupancy should be more popular

The passive loss limits change the economics of renting versus owning. Under the prior law, tenants were indirectly subsidized by their landlord's ability to deduct depreciation and other losses from other income. That made renting relatively attractive.

Under the passive loss limits, owner occupancy of properties becomes relatively more attractive. Because homeowners can still deduct interest and property taxes. But landlords who hit the passive loss limits can't deduct depreciation or other losses.

Businessmen who own their business real estate can deduct depreciation and other expenses without limit. But if that same building were owned by a **landlord**, it becomes "rental activity" subject to the passive loss limits.

Phase-out of the $25,000 exemption above $100,000 AGI

If your adjusted gross income (AGI) not counting rental property income or losses is $100,000 or less, you get to deduct up to $25,000 in rental property losses from nonpassive income. Once you go **over** $100,000, you start to lose the $25,000 exemption at a rate of 50¢ worth of exemption lost for every dollar by which your AGI exceeds $100,000. For example, if your AGI is $120,000, you lose $120,000 - $100,000 = $20,000 x 50% = $10,000 of the $25,000 exemption. In other words, your exemption is $25,000 - $10,000 = $15,000, not $25,000. When your AGI hits $150,000, you lose **all** of the $25,000 exemption because $150,000 - $100,000 = $50,000 x 50% = $25,000.

As I explained in the Reed's Rules For Understanding Income Taxes chapter, this phase-out between $100,000 and $150,000 AGI caused the marginal tax rate in that income range to be 57.75% in 1987 and 49.5% thereafter for taxpayers with $25,000 or more in rental activity losses.

Note: If you are **married and file separate tax returns** and are not living apart you get **no** exemption from the passive loss limits no matter what your AGI is. Not $25,000. Not $12,500. Not nothing.

$25,000 limit applies to tax credits, too

If a building is eligible for the rehab investment tax credit, your ability to use that credit is restricted by the $25,000 limit. You can only claim credits up to the "deduction equivalent" of the $25,000 deduction limit. IRC section 469(j)(5) defines "deduction equivalent" as:

*...the amount which (if allowed as a deduction) would reduce the regular tax
liability for such taxable year by an amount equal to such credits.*

In other words, first you figure your deduction limit. Let's say it's $15,000 because your AGI is $120,000 as calculated in the example above. Next figure how much a $15,000 deduction would reduce your taxes by calculating your tax with and without the $15,000 deduction. The difference in tax payable is the maximum credit you can claim in the year in question.

Five-year phase-in of passive loss limits

The passive loss limits apply fully to properties placed in service after October 22, 1986. That's the day President Reagan signed the Tax Reform Act of 1986 into law.

Properties placed in service on or before October 22, 1986 are subject to the passive loss limits according to a five-year phase-in schedule as follows:

1987 35%   **1988** 60%   **1989** 80%   **1990** 90%   **1991** 100%

The percentages refer to the portion of your passive losses which are subject to the limits each year. This phase-in schedule is what makes the Tax Reform Act of 1986 retroactive. In previous tax law changes, people who had already bought property relying on the tax law in effect at the time of purchase were grandfathered in.

If 'Cash flow is king,' the problem is solved

In theory, the change in the tax law ought to reduce the prices of investment real estate by about 15% to 25%. Such lower prices increase the cash flow return which replaces the return that used to come from tax savings. In reality, the buyers have gone along with that. But the sellers have not. They are refusing to sell their properties for such "low" prices. As a result, the market is dead (except for pride-of-ownership properties which are sold on the basis of looks, not economics).

Example

When cash flow is king, buildings would sell for about a 10% cap rate. That means a property with $100,000 annual net operating income would sell for $1,000,000. With $250,000 down, the mortgage would be $1,000,000 - $250,000 = $750,000. At 10% interest for 30 years, the annual payment would be $6,583.02 x 12 = $78,996.24.

So the taxable income (loss) would be:

net operating income	$100,000.00
interest	$74,996.90
depreciation (residential)	$29,090.91
Taxable income (loss)	($4,087.81)

With 4% inflation, the second year taxable income would be:

net operating income	$104,000.00
interest	$74,389.73
depreciation (residential)	$29,090.91
Taxable income (loss)	$519.36

The loss you could not deduct the first year (assuming you were not eligible for or had used up the $25,000 exemption) is **carried forward**, not forgotten about. So in the second year of owning the property in this example, you could deduct $519.36 of your first-year loss. If 4%

inflation continued on your net operating income, you'd wipe out the rest of the first-year loss in the third year.

May make sense to shift debt to home

Until the "cash-flow-is-king" millennium arrives, you may want to shift debt from investment property. You can deduct first and second **home** mortgage interest on a loan of up to $1,000,000 if you use the proceeds to "acquire, build, or substantially improve" your residence. Plus you can deduct the interest on an **additional** $100,000 of mortgage(s) above your "acquire, build, or substantially improve" amount for **any** purpose as long as the total mortgages on which you deduct interest do not exceed $1,000,000. (There is no $1,000,000 limit on mortgages which you took out before October 14, 1987 or future refinancing of pre-October-14, 1987 loans up to the principal balance at the time of refinancing. But if you extend the **term** of a pre-October-14, 1987 mortgage when you refinance, the $1,000,000 **will** apply.)

But **investment** property deductions are limited by the passive loss limits. In Letter Ruling # 8816006, IRS approved using a home equity loan to build a small commercial building. For most people, debt on your home is more likely currently deductible than debt on your rental property.

Deducting points

On a straight refinancing, the points would **not** be deductible. Although, in 1990, the Eighth Circuit allowed points to be deducted when a taxpayer replaced a three-year balloon mortgage with a 30-year mortgage and did not get a lower interest rate. (*Huntsman*, 90-1, USTC ¶ 50,340)

But if you were interested in **moving**, you could sell your old home and buy a new one with a larger loan and equal or smaller equity. That would give you tax-free net sale proceeds from the old house which you could use to pay down the mortgage on the investment property. Since the points on the new home were for "purchase or improvement" of a residence, they would be deductible.

Is resale gain passive income?

Generally, resale gain on a rental property is passive income. But not if the value of the property in question is more than 120% of its adjusted basis, AND

> 1. *It was used in a non-passive activity more than 80% of the time you owned it OR*
> 2. *It was used in a non-passive activity for any part of the two-year period that ended on the day you got rid of it [Reg. §1.469-2T(c)(2)(iii)]*

If you are the one who **developed** the property, you must rent it out for at least **two years** in order for the resale gain to be passive income [reg. §1.469-2T(f)(5)]

This appears to apply to **both** business property and to your **residence**. If you owned a residence or business property for five years and it was not rented out for four of those five years, the resale gain would not be considered passive income. To make it passive, you'd need to rent it out and wait until either the rental period equalled either: 1. 20% of the total holding period OR 2. two years—whichever came first.

Credit For Prior Year AMT

Because of the Tax Reform Act of 1986, many real estate investors have had to pay alternative minimum tax (AMT). If you pay AMT due to passive losses or accelerated depreciation—then have a year in which you pay **no** AMT, you can generally get a credit on your taxes during the no-AMT year for the AMT you paid in prior years. Calculate it on Form 8801 and claim it on Form 1040.

PART EIGHT: EXCHANGING

23

Why You Should Exchange Rather Than Sell

Bill Tappan, author of *Real Estate Exchange and Acquisition Techniques*, says, "The only time you sell rather than exchange is when you are getting out of real estate altogether."

I say, "You exchange rather than sell whenever the tax payable on the sale would exceed $2,000." $2,000 is my rough estimate of the incremental cost of exchanging.

The cost of exchanging

You'll probably need more **attorney time** to do an exchange. You may also have to spend a little more time holding the hand of the other parties to the deal if they are not experienced with exchanges. And you may even have to contribute a couple hundred dollars to the fee to pay their attorney to assure them that the exchange will not hurt them.

And you may need to spend a little extra time explaining the transaction to the title company, real estate agents, and so forth.

All told, I figure the incremental out-of-pocket expenses and the value of the incremental time you'll have to spend are about $2,000.

When does the tax payable exceed $2,000?

The tax payable in a sale of investment real estate virtually always exceeds $2,000. With the maximum tax rate on long-term capital gains at 28%, you would only need a gain of $2,000 ÷ 28% = $7,142.86. That ain't much. Unless your properties are in Texas or some similar depressed area.

Exchanging more popular due to Tax Reform Act of 1986?

A number of articles have said that exchanging would or should become more popular as a result of the Tax Reform Act of 1986. The reason is that the maximum tax rate on long-term capital gains is now 28% instead of 20%.

I am bemused and annoyed by this line of reasoning.

I have been advocating exchanging since 1979. The long-term capital gains tax rate **then** was 28%. Yet I was virtually alone in pushing exchanges.

Why is the 28% rate that everyone thought was a good deal **then** suddenly so high that one ought to exchange to avoid it? Everything is relative. The maximum ordinary income rate in '79 was **70%**. And there was a **60%** long-term capital gains **exclusion**. People looked at the comparison and said, "Boy, long-term capital gains rate sure are better than ordinary rates. Let's pay long-term capital gains rates."

Why not 0%?

But I have a simpler mind. A sort of zero-base perspective. I said, "Why pay **any** tax at all if you can avoid it by exchanging?" Nobody ever gave me a satisfactory answer.

In one article I wrote in my newsletter, **Real Estate Investor's Monthly**, I said the logic of saying there will be more exchanges now that the capital gain tax rate has gone from 20% to 28% is like saying, "Now that we've moved from a 20-story building to a 28-story building, fewer people will be jumping off the roof."

In fact, what has inspired tax writers to finally notice that the tax rate on exchanges has always been 0% is the elimination of the long-term capital gains exclusion—the elimination of the difference between tax rates on long-term capital gains and ordinary income. What finally penetrated the thick skulls of the non-exchangers was the "horror" that they would have to pay tax at **ordinary** income rates on their capital gains. Never mind that the rate is precisely the same as the long-term capital gains rate was back when they were selling rather than exchanging.

Some state and local jurisdictions levy transfer taxes and income taxes on exchanges which are tax free under federal law; e.g., New York City.

I started out thinking selling was best

You ought to know how I came to be such a strong advocate of exchanging. In 1978, I decided to teach a nationwide seminar on real estate tax law and finance. In preparing the student loose leaf binder, I quickly realized that I would have to cover exchanges. When I got to that part of the preparation, I figured the first question my students would have would be, "When do you exchange and when do you sell?"

I had already taken CCIM courses in which exchanging and selling were presented as equal alternatives with no preference for one over the other. We were left with the impression that sometimes it made sense to sell and less often it made sense to exchange. But we were not told how to tell **when**.

I got out my tax books and began searching for the author's opinions on when to exchange. None of them gave an opinion. They just discussed both exchanging and selling without ever saying when each is appropriate. Then I got out my calculator and began trying to calculate the crossover point when it was better to exchange. Very quickly, I pushed back from the table and said to myself, "Heck, you don't need a calculator. It's simpler than that. If you exchange, you pay no tax at all. If you sell, you pay tax. Paying no tax is better than paying some tax. Therefore, you always exchange."

I asked friends in real estate if I was missing something. They all felt I must be. Always exchanging didn't sound like it **could** be the right advice because they had never heard it before. But when I asked them to point out the error or omission in my logic, they could not.

Later, I figured out that there are some incremental hassles and costs to doing an exchange over doing a sale. Thus, my *de minimus* exception for deals where the tax payable is less than $2,000.

EXCHANGE!!! DOGGONE IT!!!

My advice to exchange is such an important part of this book that I am now going to make absolutely sure that you do not miss the point. Imagine that my hand is reaching out of the pages of this book. It's grabbing you by the lapel and a loud voice is booming,

> **"DON'T YOU EVER SELL AN INVESTMENT PROPERTY AGAIN! DO YOU HEAR ME?! ONLY A CLASS A TURKEY WOULD SELL AND PAY ALL THOSE TAXES!"**

Apparently that gets the message through. Jane Bryant Quinn quoted that passage in her column in *Newsweek*—years before the recent rise in popularity, to her credit. I also heard a real estate teacher quote it in his cassette on exchanging.

Stick to your guns

You exchange even though the guy who's buying your property doesn't want to exchange. You exchange even though the guy whose property you are acquiring doesn't want to exchange. You exchange even though the real estate agents involved don't want to exchange.

You're **not** taking a poll or a vote on how many people in the deal want to exchange. You **are** exchanging. And anybody who insists that you sell and pay all those taxes should be shown the door. That includes your tax adviser.

Exchanging is the only way to go. Selling is out of the question—unthinkable.

You'd be out of the club

If I had a junior real estate investors club and you were in it, I'd revoke your secret decoder ring if you sold rather than exchanged.

If West Point were a real estate academy, selling a property instead of exchanging would get you six months of walking the area and reduction to the grade of cadet private.

In most cases, selling rather than exchanging is the equivalent of lighting your barbecue with ten thousand dollar bills.

If I asked you to give me $15,000 in cash for no reason, you'd think I was crazy and instantly refuse. But most real estate investors would let me talk them out of exchanging even if it meant paying $15,000 more in taxes to Uncle Sam.

Balking at exchanging is unacceptable

The proper response to someone who balks at going along with your exchange is, "Are you crazy?" A bit more tact would help. But anyone who expects you to throw away thousands of dollars for no reason most certainly is making a crazy, unreasonable request.

I don't want to belabor the point. But I am acutely aware of the enormous resistance and inertia I'm up against when I tell someone who has never seen an exchange to start exchanging. If you invest in the West where exchanging has long been common, you won't have much difficulty becoming an exchanger. But elsewhere, you will need extraordinary fortitude to stick to your exchange guns when all the other parties in the deal start verbally beating up on you for wanting to do an exchange.

But you **must** stick to your guns. I did in 1978 when I exchanged four New Jersey properties for one in Texas. The Texas seller knew all about exchanges and uttered not a peep of protest—even though he had to take title to my four New Jersey properties and then sell them to the New Jersey buyers I had lined up.

One of the New Jersey buyers made no protest because he was an easy-going guy. But every other New Jersey participant had to be coaxed or cajoled to the closing. I felt like I had been through the wringer. But I saved tens of thousands of tax dollars and, indeed, could not have afforded the 36-unit apartment building I bought in Texas had I not exchanged. In other words, it was **worth** the extra trouble.

Many people in the deal may resist the exchange

Especially in the East, many, if not all, of the participants in the deal will resist exchanging. There are three reasons for this:

• Ignorance of how to do an exchange.

• Laziness or human inertia.

• Fear of complications or reduced income.

Californians are the main exchangers

California is the exchange capital of the U.S. I live in California. But I've never done an exchange here. I exchanged New Jersey property for Texas property in one deal and Texas property for other Texas property in another deal.

The farther east you go, the fewer exchanges there are. Eastern real estate agents, accountants, and attorneys frequently respond to client inquiries about exchanging by saying, "We don't do those here. That's a California thing." As if avoiding taxes were some kooky California quirk like est seminars or hot tubs.

Why are exchanges popular in the West but not the East? I don't know for sure. My guess is that Californians and other Westerners are less bound by "the way we've always done things" than Easterners. More willing to evaluate something on its merits even if it's new.

And exchanges are hardly new. The right to exchange has been in the Internal Revenue Code since **1921**. Income tax law is uniform nationwide. So there's simply no excuse for the failure of Eastern real estate agents, accountants, and attorneys to acquire exchange expertise and urge their clients to exchange whenever permitted and whenever the tax payable on the sale would exceed the cost of exchanging. I think a case can be made that the difference between the incidence of exchanging in the West and East is due to **malpractice** by Eastern real estate agents, accountants, and attorneys.

By the way, I think exchanges ought to be far more prevalent in the **West** than they are. Bruce Makar of Coldwell Banker, the nation's largest real estate investment brokerage firm, told me that less than one in five investment deals in California was an exchange. In contrast, Jim O'Brien couldn't recall a single exchange in the four years he headed Coldwell Banker's Washington, DC office.

You'll probably have to contend with ignorance of exchanges

Ignorance of exchanges is the rule rather than the exception in most parts of the country. Although in the West, there will probably be one or more people in the deal who have participated in an exchange—and their lack of resistance tends to convince the inexperienced parties to make no protest. In the East, however, typically **no one** in the deal has ever seen an exchange. So there you usually get a reverse synergy in which each party's fear of the unknown feeds on the others' fear.

Fortunately, this is changing. I've had a little to do with it as a result of my proselytizing exchanges in about 40,000 copies of this book and in years worth of newsletter articles read by tens of thousands of real estate investors. Also, a number of other real estate writers like Bill Tappan have made exchange expertise accessible to the public by writing readable laymen's books on the subject. And then there are adult education-type speakers here and there opening minds. Jane Bryant Quinn's aforementioned article in *Newsweek* helped. As did an article I wrote for *Changing Times* magazine in 1981. Finally, there has been the recent burst of exchange publicity due to the Tax Reform Act of 1986—for the wrong reasons, but overdue good advice nevertheless.

Many tax advisers oppose exchanges

Paradoxical as it may seem, tax advisers frequently oppose exchanging. I believe their opposition, which they purport is based on their expertise, is, in fact, based on the opposite—their ignorance of the legal and practical aspects of exchanging. And their unwillingness to admit that ignorance to their client.

Many tax advisers have an inordinate fear of IRS

Exchanging avoids all tax on resale. That's a lot of money in most cases. So much that it seems too good to be true to some—including tax advisers.

Avoiding that much tax seems like something that will aggravate the IRS. And indeed, it appears the IRS is overly grouchy about exchanges. Unfortunately for IRS, your right to do a tax-free exchange is clear cut.

In addition, there are a lot more penalties than there used to be—for both taxpayers and tax preparers. And the penalties are often a percentage of the tax owed. So screwing up an exchange can trigger a large penalty depending on the nature of the screw-up. But that's simply an argument for not screwing up—not an argument for abandoning your right to exchange and paying an unnecessary tax that far exceeds the penalty.

Doing it right is not difficult. The few exchanges that are disallowed by the courts usually contain some glaring error. And often, the courts will allow an exchange that **does** contain a glaring error. If anything, the courts have been generous in their willingness to overlook sloppiness in tax-free exchanges.

But the ignorant tax adviser is taking the attitude,

> *I don't know the requirements of an exchange. I could research it. But that would take time. And if I try to do it and screw up, I may have to pay a big preparer penalty. Plus, my client will have to pay a big back tax plus interest plus penalty. He may sue me for malpractice—and win. Better I should talk him out of the exchange.*

Looking out for themselves rather than you

This attitude is the "When in doubt, don't" or "suspenders and belt" approach to tax advice. To put it another way, when it comes down to the adviser having to risk screwing up a relatively easy technique and paying for the screw up—or you paying far more taxes than you need to—you are going to pay in far too many cases.

Some advisers also fear their ignorance becoming apparent to you or to their peers involved in the deal or to a future IRS auditor. They'd rather try to talk you out of the whole idea.

Extra time learning about exchanges

Real estate agents, accountants, and attorneys who have no exchange education or experience have to take time to learn about them. Time is money. Real estate agents don't bill by the hour, so they are extremely resistant to having to do anything other than their normal routine.

Accountants and attorneys usually bill by the hour. But billing you for their learning a subject they ought to know already is arguably improper. And even if it is allowed by their code of ethics, the client is likely to complain if he gets a big bill. So accountants and attorneys have incentive to shrink from learning a new trick (exchanges) because the time spent on such learning probably cannot be fully billed to the client. And in the East, it's unlikely the adviser will soon get the opportunity to use the newly learned expertise to help **other** clients. So few are the requests for exchanges.

The solution is to use one of the advisers I recommend in the tax adviser chapter of this book. They already know exchanges.

Why real estate agents often resist exchanges

Real estate agents are paid by the deal. The less time they spend on each deal the more deals they can do and the more money they make. As a result, real estate agents want simple deals. Exchanges are pretty simple. But they are more complex than straight sales. And to an agent who has never seen an exchange, they sound like they are infinitely more complex than a straight sale.

That makes the agent think not only that the deal will increase the number of hours he has to spend on the deal and thereby reduce his income per hour—it also makes him fear that the deal will fall through entirely. Because experienced agents know that complexity not only takes more time—often, it kills the deal altogether.

So agents who do not have exchange experience believe they have two strong reasons to try to talk you out of doing an exchange. And even agents **with** exchange experience may try to talk you out of the exchange.

One complication of exchanges is a higher degree of attorney involvement. Real estate agents dislike attorney involvement because attorneys often kill deals or at least prolong them. Although if you ask the typical real estate agent if he recommends that you get an attorney, he will recite the "party line," which is somewhere between, "That's your decision" and "We recommend it."

Agents also have some of the same fears as tax advisers. Namely that you or someone else in the deal will discover their ignorance of exchanges. Or that something will go wrong and you'll sue them.

Some real estate agents *want* to do exchanges

Not all real estate agents oppose exchanges. Opposition is more likely in the East than the West. On the other hand, some agents are **eager** to do exchanges.

Among real estate agents, commercial investment deals are more prestigious than selling houses. And any agent who tries to learn about commercial investment real estate soon hears about exchanges.

Doing exchanges is a sort of rite of passage into the commercial investment real estate world.

Other agents would like to do an exchange for the experience or to add another trick to their bag. While I commend such agents for their willingness to learn a new trick, I do not recommend that you let them acquire such education at your expense. Better you should use an experienced agent.

Some agents—and this is a recent phenomenon—use their willingness to exchange and exchange expertise as a selling point. Often, their business phone number ends in 1031—the section of the Internal Revenue Code which covers exchanges. They may also put the word exchange in their company name and/or feature their exchange expertise prominently in their promotional literature. Generally, I welcome such agents and expect they'd be good ones to use in an exchange. But talk is cheap. It may be that they've done few, if any, exchanges. Ask them how many they've done before you hire them.

C.C.I.M.s

Ostensibly, a C.C.I.M. is a Realtor ® who specializes in commercial-investment real estate. Usually, that's true. But some C.C.I.M.s may have picked up the designation even though they concentrate on other activities. Other C.C.I.M.s specialize in commercial-investment real estate but may only do commercial leasing or whatever.

In any event, you should write for a free C.C.I.M. Designation Roster to the Realtors ® National Marketing Institute, 430 North Michigan Avenue, Suite 500, Chicago, IL 60611.

Not proof positive of exchange competence

I won't guarantee that all C.C.I.M.s will do the job you need on an exchange. But it's probably the best starting point. In order to become a C.C.I.M., you must complete courses and examinations on material which prominently features exchanges. C.C.I.M.s also must have a certain amount of experience in commercial-investment transactions.

But the fact that someone has a C.C.I.M. designation does not mean that he has ever **done** an exchange. It may not even mean that ever **wants** to do an exchange. C.C.I.M.s are real estate agents and are therefore subject to the same fears of extra effort and greater likelihood of the deal falling through. Although they at least should know far better than the average agent that exchanges are no big deal thereby minimizing those fears.

On the other hand. the fact that an agent does **not** have a C.C.I.M. does not prove that he is not a competent commercial-investment agent and exchanger. I used to be a real estate agent. I was a C.C.I.M. **candidate** for a couple years. But never a C.C.I.M. And Realtor ® Bill Tappan who wrote the book, *Real Estate Exchange and Acquisition Techniques*, is one of the leading authorities in the nation on exchanging and has participated in many of them. But he is not a C.C.I.M.

Demand to know why when an adviser you trust recommends against an exchange

Now that you know the reasons why tax advisers and agents may be motivated to talk you out of an exchange, you'll be better able to resist such selfish advice. If your tax adviser or real estate agent advises against your exchanging, demand that they explain the basis for their opposition. If the explanation does not hold water, replace the agent or adviser.

Here are the arguments I've heard against exchanging. And the flaws in each.

Argument # 1. "Exchanging is more trouble than it's worth."

The person who makes that argument must do two things:

1. Specify the "trouble," and
2. Calculate the value of the exchange in the deal in question.

What trouble?

People who have participated in an exchange before rarely give you a problem about the exchange. And some people who have never been in an exchange are, nevertheless, no problem.

So the people problems, if any, generally come from a percentage of the inexperienced people in the deal. Title and escrow company personnel in almost every part of the country have done exchanges so they are rarely a problem. And when they are, you can easily fix it by switching to another company which **does** have exchange experience.

That leaves the suspicious buyers, sellers, attorneys, and agents. The trouble you must put up with in an exchange is convincing those turkeys that the exchange is really none of their business and will not affect them in any way. As I've said before, this mainly occurs in the Midwest and East, not in the West.

Convincing the balkers takes time. But before you throw up your hands and pay all that tax, let's analyze just how much more time. Reassurance should take at most, one or two extra meetings with the balking party or parties. If one of those parties still refuses to cooperate, find another deal or walk around him.

Extortion

On one occasion, a buyer of a building I was exchanging demanded that I pay him $2,500 to cover the costs of the extra attorney bills he would run up as a result of my complicating exchange. I said that $2,500 would probably pay for the extra attorney time required by **25** exchanges, not one. Eventually, he agreed to accept $200 to pay for a couple hours of checking with his attorney about the exchange.

Even that was $200 too much. But it was the extortion that often comes up in exchanges. One of the non-exchanging parties figures out that you are saving tens of thousand of dollars—or more—by exchanging—and figures since he's "helping" you do the exchange, he's entitled to a share of the savings. In fact, he's not helping you. He's doing a real estate deal in which he's either buying or selling real estate and all he's entitled to is the purchase or sale he agreed to.

I was outraged to find that at least one book on real estate investing actually **advocated** trying to squeeze the exchanger. On page 102 of Tony Hoffman's book, *How to Negotiate Successfully in Real Estate*, he says,

> *Many times the seller will tie the property into a 1031 tax-deferred exchange…*
> *With this in mind, you can take advantage of the seller by just recognizing his vulnerability.*
>
> *A day or two before closing, and even on the day of closing, you have the power to demand and receive concessions, providing you don't go overboard."*
> *Take advantage of the situation. Pick up a little extra on the deal.*

Hoffman rationalizes this unethical recommendation by saying,

> *Don't feel bad or upset about using eleventh hour tactics to win a point. The seller would do it to you if he could.*

Mr. Hoffman can speak for himself. I do not use eleventh hour tactics. And I try to identify and steer clear of the kind of people who do by checking the other party's references before I enter into agreement with him. You should, too. But, in spite of such precautions, you may find yourself confronted with such extortion in **any** real estate deal and it's more likely in an exchange because more is at stake.

You should note that Tony Hoffman's company, National Superstar, Inc. declared Chapter 11 bankruptcy in Los Angeles at the end of 1986.

In another deal I did, the attorney for one of the **other** parties handed **me** a bill for his services at closing. I promptly told him that I paid for **my** attorney, **not** other people's attorneys. In the ensuing heated argument, he cited several reasons why I owed him the money including the rhetorical question, "How much are you saving in taxes as a result of this exchange?" I did not pay it.

$2,000 worth of 'trouble'

As I said earlier, I figure the trouble of an exchange totals about $2,000. That includes:

- Extra attorney fees for your attorney
- Extra attorney fees for others' attorneys
- Extra time spent by you
- Unavoidable petty extortion payments.

If anyone tells you that figure is too **low**, ask to see the list of expenses on which they base their, higher figure.

What an exchange is worth

So much for the "trouble." Now what's the exchange—and the "trouble"—worth?

It's worth the taxes you save. Roughly speaking, that's 28% of the gain. On a $100,000 gain, exchanging saves you roughly $28,000.

The value of your time

Now let's compare that savings to the "trouble." Let's say that $500 of the $2,000 goes for out-of-pocket costs.

If you make $50,000 a year at a forty-hour-a-week job, that's $25 per hour before taxes. In the example above—where the exchange saves $28,000—a guy whose time is worth $25 per hour can afford to spend $28,000 - $500 (out-of-pocket costs) =$27,500 ÷ $25/hour = 1,100 hours!

That's how much time you could afford to spend to do an exchange that saved you $28,000 if your time were worth $25 an hour. 1,100 hours is 27.5 weeks of full-time, 40-hour-a-week effort. More than six months doing nothing but spending time persuading the other parties in the deal to go along with the exchange.

I'd say the extra time required by the exchanges I've been in was more in the 5 to 10 hours range—maybe 20 in an unusual case. But certainly nothing resembling 1,100 hours.

Even at $100 an hour, a $28,000 savings would enable you to spend $28,000 - $500 = $27,500 ÷ $100/hour = 275 hours—which is **far** more than you would ever need.

If it did only take 10 extra hours, your compensation for those extra hours in this example would be $27,500 ÷ 10 hours = **$2,750 per hour!**

Unless you can devote those same hours to an activity that earns you **more than** $2,750 an hour, you are **crazy** to sell rather than exchange. And the statement that, "Exchanging isn't worth the trouble" is absurd when you look at what exchanging is really worth in dollars.

Argument # 2. "Exchanging doesn't *eliminate* the tax. It only defers it. So why not pay it and get it over with?"

In every audience, when you use the phrase, "tax-free exchange," some pedant pipes up, "You mean 'tax-**deferred**,' don't you?"

No. I mean tax-**free**. Because I figure I'll exchange forever, as many other real estate investors have.

You *can* take it with you

They say, "You can't take it with you." But there is one thing you **can** take with you when you die—your personal income tax liability.

The reason is something I talked about in the chapter on basis. You'll recall that an heir's basis is the **fair market value of the property at the time of death**. That's called, "stepped-up basis."

Suppose I exchange for a lifetime and own $5,000,000 worth of property with an adjusted basis of just $500,000. If I sell, the gain would be $5,000,000 - $500,000 = $4,500,000.

But if I die without having sold the property, my heirs get the property. What's their basis? $5,000,000. The fair market value at the time of my death.

And if the heirs sell the property the day after I die for $5,000,000, what's their gain?

Sale price	$5,000,000
Basis	-5,000,000
Gain	$0

So that's why I say the exchange is "tax-free" rather than "tax-deferred." If you never pay it, it's tax-free. You're not going to exchange a couple times then sell. Remember, the rule is you exchange rather than sell whenever the tax payable is greater than $2,000. If it's already **greater** than $2,000 **now**, what do you think the chances are that it will ever be **less** than $2,000 later?

Argument # 3. "But that means that once you start exchanging, you can never stop."

Not true. You can stop exchanging and start selling any time you get the overwhelming urge to pay a lot of taxes.

Argument # 4. "If you keep exchanging, you'll eventually have no depreciation deductions to speak of. So there's a point at which it makes more sense to sell so you can increase your depreciation deductions."

That's my "favorite" anti-exchange argument. Doesn't it sound logical and erudite? It's baloney. But it sure sounds good.

I once tried to write an article on that subject. Trouble was I could **not** come up with a set of numbers consistent with sensible investing that would prove it's correct.

Example

The reason it's not true is that you generally exchange **up**. That is, you increase your loan-to-value ratio when you exchange. You may have bought a building for $500,000 with $100,000 down five years ago. Now it's worth $750,000 and the loan is paid down to $375,000. Your loan-to-value ratio is now $375,000 ÷ $750,000 = **50%**. Your equity is $750,000 - $375,000 = $375,000.

If you exchange, you would typically again borrow $4 for every $1 of equity so you'd be buying a building worth 5 x $375,000 = $1,875,000 with $375,000 down and mortgage of 4 x $375,000 = $1,500,000. The new loan-to-value ratio would be $1,500,000 ÷ $1,875,000 = **80%**.

Basis in new less than if bought

True, you'd have to carry forward your old basis. That would make your basis in the new property **less than** the purchase price of $1,875,000 by the amount of gain you avoided tax on by exchanging.

Let's say in five years, you claimed 3.64% depreciation per year for a total of 5 x 3.64% = 18.20% and that 85% of the property or 85% x $500,000 = $425,000 was depreciable improvements. That means your cumulative depreciation deductions were 18.2% x $425,000 = $77,350. And your adjusted basis in the old building would now be $500,000 - $77,350 = $422,650.

So the gain, if you sold, would be $750,000 - $422,650 = $327,350. That's called **"unrealized gain"** in an exchange. And your basis in the new property will be the price of the new property—less any unrealized gain in an exchange that acquires it. In this case, $1,875,000 - $327,350 = $1,547,650.

Another way to calculate the basis in the new building is to add the old basis carried forward, $422,650, plus the amount by which your mortgage amount goes up or $1,500,000 - $375,000 = $1,125,000 for a total basis of $422,650 + $1,125,000 = $1,547,650. Voila!

Exchange allows you to buy bigger building

Would your depreciation deductions in the new building be **bigger** if you **bought** it rather than exchanged into it? Of course. Then, your basis would be the full $1,875,000 purchase price, not the purchase price reduced by the unrealized gain or $1,547,650.

However, if you had **not** done the exchange, you would not be able to **afford** to buy the building. Remember, exchanging saves a lot of taxes. By exchanging, you move **all** your equity from the old building to the new. If you had **sold** the old building, you would have had to pay a lot of your old equity to **IRS**.

At 28%, the tax on a gain of $327,350 would be 28% x $327,350 = $91,658!

If you had sold and paid the tax, you'd only be able to go shopping for the new building with $375,000 - $91,658 = $283,342 in your pocket. Used as a 20% down payment as above, that would buy you $283,342 ÷ 20% = $1,416,710 worth of real estate. Which is **less real estate and even less basis** than you could afford if you **exchanged** out of the old building ($1,875,000 and $1,547,650 respectively).

So even though your basis is less than the **purchase price** of your new building by the amount of the gain that you avoid tax on, you more than make it up in being able to afford a **much bigger building** as a result of avoiding the taxes.

The learned journals are full of baloney

I have seen several articles in scholarly real estate journals purporting to show why you are better off selling than exchanging. But they all contain the same fatal flaw. They compare the depreciation basis if you exchange into a building with the depreciation basis you'd have in the **same building** if you sold then bought. Thereby ignoring the fact that the sale requires you to pay taxes and **prevents** you from affording to buy the **same building**. In other words, they compare selling/buying with exchanging—**including** selling's advantage (entire purchase price is new basis)—but **excluding** exchanging's advantage (tax avoidance)—which is the **whole reason** for exchanging!

Argument # 5. "What if you need cash?"

Refinance. (Interest is only deductible if loan is spent on business or investment purposes.)

Argument # 6. "What if you can't refinance?"

By the time you get done paying a real estate commission, the income taxes on the sale, and deducting the cost of the buy down you had to do (taking back a mortgage doesn't get you cash), you ain't gonna get much cash out of a sale. If you've got enough equity that you can extract it by **selling**, then you must have enough equity that you can extract some by **refinancing**.

Refinancing and buying down are the same thing. If you can do one, you can do the other. If there's absolutely no financing available for either refinancing or a buy down, then you'll either have to heavily discount the sale price or take back a mortgage. Both either dramatically reduce or wipe out the cash you get to walk away with.

Argument # 7. "What if you don't want to own real estate anymore?"

That's the only time you would sell rather than exchange according to Bill Tappan.

But I even wonder about that. Why would you want to get out of real estate?

I suspect that it's **tenants**, not real estate, that most people want to get away from. In other words, **management hassles**. You don't need to get **out** of real estate to get away from management hassles.

Net-leased property and land

You can and should exchange your management intensive properties for properties which require **little or no management**. Like **net-leased** property (tenant takes care of maintenance and other expenses). Examples would be industrial and retail buildings. Tenant turnover is low. Virtually all maintenance is the tenant's responsibility—to obtain as well as pay for. The tenant also pays the expenses direct through separate utilities meters or by sending the money to you to forward as in the case of property taxes or insurance. So your management duties are extremely few and sufficiently simple that they could be farmed out to a bank trust department or some such.

You could also exchange management intensive property like apartments or office buildings for **raw land** which requires almost no management. (Exchanging improved property for raw land may trigger tax if you claimed accelerated depreciation on the old property.)

Be your own tenant

You could exchange your rental properties for property in which **you** are your own tenant. That assumes you have some other business that needs to rent or own space. If it's a small business, you could buy a "Taj Mahal" as a way of absorbing the maximum amount of exchange proceeds from your old management intensive properties.

In order for your expenses of your new business quarters to be deductible, they must be "ordinary and necessary." Some might wonder if a "Taj Mahal" is ordinary and necessary. I suspect you'd not be challenged unless you got ridiculous. I know of no court decisions where a business was denied deductions due to the lavishness of its quarters.

Exchange to rental house then move in

Finally, you could exchange your rental property for a **single-family house**—which you rent out initially—then **move into** after five or six years. If your intention was to move in at the time you exchanged, it would not qualify as a tax-free exchange because you did not hold the house for "trade or business or for investment." But if you did rent it out for five or six years, IRS would probably not notice, let alone challenge your exchange because of your subsequent move-in. And if they **did** challenge, you could probably win by citing the five or six years you rented it out as evidence of intent to rent it.

Moving into a former rental house is not a taxable event (unless IRS could use it to prove lack of investment intent). So you would have converted your investment equity into home equity tax-free. That would get rid of tenants—but you'd still have some real estate.

So you see what I mean when I express skepticism that you really want to "get out of real estate." Real estate is so vast—and the number of different ways to hold property and different property types and uses so numerous—that just about any problem you might try to solve by getting **out** of real estate could be solved with**in** real estate.

Charitable remainder trust

There is a non-exchange way to get out of real estate tax-free: the charitable remainder trust. That approach is beyond the scope of this book. The basic idea is you deed free-and-clear real estate to a trust. You retain a **life estate** in the income of the trust; a charity gets a **remainder** interest in the trust. The trust immediately sells the property and invests the sale proceeds in securities or a mortgage taken back on the sale or whatever.

Your deeding the property to the trust is tax free. So is the trust's sale of the property. You get the income from whatever the trust invests the sale proceeds in as if **you** had sold and reinvested the proceeds is bonds or whatever. You can specify that your heirs also get income for a period of years after you die if the charity in question will agree. You're actually giving very little to the charity in present value terms.

For more information on charitable remainder trusts, see "How to get out of real estate tax free" in the August 1990 issue of my newsletter, **Real Estate Investor's Monthly.**

It has been pointed out to me that selling your property for nothing down and taking back an interest-only mortgage has the same effect as the charitable remainder trust; tax-free sale and taxable income. Except, you could leave the principal balance of the note to your relatives.

Sell personal property

Don't exchange if the property's fair market value is less than your tax basis in it. That's often true of **personal property** like cars, computers, refrigerators, ranges, etc. You are better off **selling** those items and claiming a loss. In a real estate deal, you would typically **sell** the personal property which comes with the building to the buyer with whom you are exchanging the real property. Be careful. IRS may disallow the loss deduction claiming you exchanged the personal property as well as the real property. (Rev. Rul. 61-119)

24

How to Do an Exchange

The name's the problem

To most people, an exchange sounds like a deal between two people who happen to want each other's property. They then trade properties of exactly equal value. That is **not** how exchanges are done.

The **two**-way trade image the word exchange conjures up is probably the main reason so few exchanges are done. Investors have the mistaken idea that an exchange would be extremely difficult to arrange. Because of the need to find an incredible coincidence.

You do **not** need to find a perfect match. You don't need to find **any** match at all. Exchanging is the same as selling one property then buying another except for a few extra clauses in the purchase agreements. And the timing must be right.

But aside from the extra clauses, and the need to meet two deadlines, an exchange is about the same as any other sale and purchase.

It's very important that you understand and believe that.

Exchanges need a new name

Have you ever heard of Arnold Dorsey?

I didn't think so. He didn't become famous until he changed his name—to Englebert Humperdinck. He sings, of course. But he doesn't sing any better now than he did when his name was Arnold. He gets paid a lot more though.

Exchanges have a similar problem—wrong name.

So for the sake of improved understanding, the exchange should be renamed an "interdependent sale and reinvestment."

Here's what Section 1031 says

Here's my translation of Section 1031 into plain English:

"If you exchange one property for another, you don't have to pay any tax. Both the property you start with and the one you end up with must be for your business or investment. Both must be the same kind of property (I'll explain shortly). This doesn't apply to inventory or dealer property. Not only are you not taxed on any gain in an exchange, but you are not allowed to deduct any loss either. You have to identify the property you want to acquire by midnight of the 44th day after you close on the property you got rid of. And you must close on the new property within 180 days. You have to file for an extension if the first closing is after October 15th and you are a calendar year taxpayer."

Don't try to use my plain English translation in court. But it's pretty accurate.

What 'like kind' means

A lot of people who think they know what "like kind" means are dead wrong. They think it means you must exchange residential property for residential property or land for land. No. No. No. A bill to substitute "similar use" for "like kind" **failed** to pass Congress in 1989.

"Like kind" was defined in Treasury Regulation Section 1.1031 (a)-1(b) and by the Tax Court in *Koch*, 71 TC 5.

The Regulation says,

> *...the words 'like kind' have reference to the nature or character of the property not to its grade or quality.*

Koch says,

> *...like kind does not mean identical...consideration must be given to :*
>
> • *the respective interests in the properties*
> • *the nature of the title conveyed*
> • *the rights of the parties*
> • *the duration of the interests*
> • *any other factor bearing on the nature or character...*

Does that help you understand it? Me neither.

The best way to understand like kind is by examples of what is and what is not like kind.

Real property versus personal property

You cannot exchange real property for personal property or vice versa.

That's pretty simple. But you may not have considered some of the things which fall into the personal property category.

Furniture and appliances. When you buy **real estate**, you usually get a bunch of **personal property** along with it. Refrigerators in apartment buildings and so forth. That's good because personal property is depreciated over five years instead of nineteen. And personal property in non-residential property is eligible for such tax breaks as **first-year expensing** and **short** **recovery periods.**

But getting a mixture of personal and real property complicates your exchange a little. No big deal though. You just do **two** exchanges. You exchange the personal property in the old property for the personal property in the new property and the old real for the new real. If the value of the personal property is not the same in each property, allocate an appropriate amount of any new cash coming into the deal—or any step up in loan balances—to the purchase of the personal property in the new property. [Proposed Reg. § 1.1031(a)—3(c)(5)]

Foreign real estate. You cannot exchange U.S. property for foreign property and vice versa. This change came as a result of the Omnibus Budget Reconciliation Act of 1989.

What is like kind?

Now let me tell you what **is** like kind.

Co-op to condo. You can convert a co-op to a condo tax-free according to eight letter rulings.

Tenant in common. A tenant-in-common relationship is like a partnership in many ways. But there's one important difference. You can exchange a tenant-in-common interest, sometimes referred to as an "undivided interest," for other property.

The IRS approved a tenant in common exchange in Revenue Ruling 73-476. And the courts approved the following tenant in common exchanges:

Commissioner v. Crichton, 122 F 2d 181
Starker v U.S., 602 F 2d 1341

The tenant in common form of ownership crops up most frequently in inheritances. If your parents die and leave real estate to you and their other children, you'll probably get a tenant in common interest.

If you are in a partnership, you and your partners may want to convert it to a tenancy in common. Then you or another "partner" can exchange out. The wording of the deed determines whether it's a tenant in common or some other form of group ownership.

But watch out for substance over form

You need to know the doctrine of "**substance over form**" if you plan to convert a partnership to tenants in common then exchange. The doctrine of substance over form says that the law is interested in what something **is**, not what you **say** it is on the forms you used. If your "tenancy in common" has more of the characteristics of a partnership than of a tenancy in common, it **is** a partnership for tax purposes. In *Chase* (92 TC 874), the Tax Court applied the substance-over-form rule and disallowed an exchange done by a partnership that converted to tenants in common.

Regulation section 301.7701-3(a) says a tenancy in common will not be treated as a partnership merely because a property is maintained and rented. But tenants in common may be treated as a partnership if they actively carry on a trade or business. The distinction there is not real clear to me.

- **Improved real estate versus unimproved.** You can exchange raw land for improved real estate and vice versa. With one complication. If you exchange improved real estate for raw land, any recapture tax due on the improved real estate must be paid at that time. Specifically, you must pay recapture on the amount by which your recapturable depreciation exceeds the market value of the improvements portion of the new property. So says section 1250(d)(4) of the Internal Revenue Code. That's only when you exchange improved property on which you claimed accelerated depreciation for property with little or no improvements value like raw land or a farm.

...ter rights. According to Revenue Ruling 55-749, perpetual water rights are ...l estate that they can be exchanged for real estate and vice versa. The reason ... the duration of the rights—one of the considerations mentioned in the *Koch*

...sed property. You can exchange a new building for used and vice versa.

- **Mineral rights.** Sometimes, mineral rights are like kind with real estate. It depends on whether the rights in question are considered real property under the law of the state in question. There must be an absolute, unconditional transfer of the rights to minerals until they are exhausted.

- **Leases of 30 or more years.** Revenue Ruling 60-4 says that a leasehold which at the time of its sale has 30 years or more to go is real property for exchange purposes. Regulation section 1.1031 (a)-1(c) also covers this.

- **Remainder estates.** Rev. Rul 78-4 and Technical Advice Memorandum 8950034 say remainder estates are like kind to real property for exchange purposes.

The Omnibus Budget Reconciliation Act of 1989 added a requirement that property exchanged between certain **related parties** (brothers, sisters, spouse, ancestors, and lineal descendants) must be held for at least two years after the exchange.

A 1031 exchange isn't much different from a 1034 exchange

You'll recall that section 1031 of the Internal Revenue Code covers exchanges of investment or business property. Section 1032 covers exchanges of stock for property. Section 1033 covers exchanges of condemned or destroyed property (called "involuntary conversion"). And section 1034 covers exchanges of principal residences (called "the two-year reinvestment rule").

All of these forms of exchange have similar IRC section numbers because they are similar transactions. Most people have never heard of sections 1032 and 1033. But they have heard of the two-year reinvestment rule. It's just that they don't think of reinvesting the proceeds from the sale of a home as an exchange.

Sections 1034 and 1031 are quite similar. The main difference is that with 1034, you don't have to do anything at the time you sell the home. You just have to buy another home of equal or greater value within two years.

But with a 1031 (investment property) exchange, the documents which state the terms of the "sale" of your old property must **require** you to put the "sale" proceeds into the new property. Or, to put it another way, the "sale" documents must say that the "sale" of the old property is an interdependent part of a transaction which includes the acquisition of the new property. Thus the name "interdependent sale and reinvestment."

So about all you have to do to have a tax-free exchange is sell your old property and buy a new one and put a clause in each agreement saying that the two are interdependent and meet the legal deadlines. In addition, the "sale" proceeds of the old property must be held in a **special escrow** if the exchange is not simultaneous. As with the sale of a house, you have to go even or up to avoid tax. Although the calculation is a bit different. I explained the exchange calculation in the chapter on how to calculate your basis.

It's simple

I explained the mechanics of an exchange to a Realtor® once and he said, "You mean it's that simple? I thought doing an exchange meant you had to wait for a situation that was about as common as a collision of worlds."

You do **not** have to acquire a property whose owner happens to want your property. Nor do you have to find a property which has the same value as yours. Both are absolutely irrelevant to doing an exchange.

You can exchange into **any** property you can afford to buy. In fact, by exchanging, you'll be able to afford to buy a **more** expensive property than if you sold—no taxes to pay, remember. And you can exchange **out** of any property for which you can find a **buyer**. It's that simple.

The two-way exchange

When someone who does not know real estate thinks of an exchange, they'll probably assume it's a two-way exchange.

In a two-way exchange, you want my property and I want yours. If the equity in each is not exactly the same, the one with the lower equity gives the other some cash to make up the difference.

Two-way exchanges **should** be as rare as four-leaf clovers—or that collision of worlds the Realtor® envisioned. Here's why.

When you go out to buy or exchange into a piece of real estate, you ought to have very **specific criteria** as to the property and terms you want. Heck's bells, man, you're about to spend a significant part of your life savings. My acquisition criteria usually run a full, typewritten page. Only a **few** buildings meet my criteria. The chances that the owner of a building which I want would also want my building are about nil.

So the only way a two-way exchange can take place, aside from an incredible coincidence, is if one or both parties have **extremely broad acquisition criteria**.

Actually many investors do two-way exchanges

Many investors do two-way exchanges. One of my seminar students had done a number of different exchanges—all two-way.

Exchange groups around the country hold monthly or weekly meetings to arrange two-way exchanges. They sit around a table and one guy says, "I've got two building lots in Tulsa." Another pipes up, "Would you take a vacant gas station in Tacoma?"

These guys are real estate brokers. The properties they are talking about are their listings. Members of these groups seem to have a great deal of *esprit de corps*. They think they are the leading edge of the world of real estate exchanges.

They're nuts. Or at least their clients are. These brokers are simply churning junk properties. Trading one client's dog for another's white elephant. The clients apparently think they're benefiting on the theory that the devil you **don't** know (the property you're acquiring) is better than the one you **do** know (the one you're getting rid of).

I said earlier that two-way exchanges involve either the incredible coincidence or the extremely broad acquisition criteria syndrome. The exchange groups might have you believe their meetings make "coincidences" more likely. Wrong. These exchange groups do deals because one or both parties have extremely broad acquisition criteria.

Broad acquisition criteria is a formula for poor return

NFL football coaches do not build champion football teams by telling their scouts to go down to the corner and bring back 44 guys who weigh more than 200 pounds. Rather, they have highly selective criteria. They don't want just **anybody** for the team. They want the best men they can find—given who they already have, their strategy, and their budget.

By the same token, you don't get champion returns in real estate investing by acquiring whatever comes up at the monthly exchange group meeting. You should have some **formula** to succeed at real estate.

William Nickerson wrote the book, *How I Turned $1,000 Into $5,000,000 in Real Estate in My Spare Time*. His formula was to buy buildings in need of cosmetic renovation, renovate, raise rents, and exchange up. From 1975 to 1983, I bought apartment buildings with **below-market rents**, raised the rents to market, and exchanged up. (In '83, I could no longer find apartment buildings with below-market rents in Texas.)

You can skin the real estate investment cat dozens of ways. But all require care in picking property. You can't profitably renovate a building which is already renovated. You can't raise rents on a building which is already at market.

Don't reject two-way exchanges totally. But make sure it's the **other** guy who has the broad acquisition criteria that made the two-way exchange possible—that you're getting a property that meets sensible acquisition criteria.

The three-way exchange

When people who know what they're talking about say the word "exchange," they are talking about a **three**-way exchange—**not** a two-way exchange. Here's an example.

You own a 4-unit apartment building. You'd like to exchange for something bigger.

Bill Buyer wants to buy your 4-unit. He does not own anything you want to acquire.

Steve Seller owns a 10,000 square foot strip shopping center which you want. He does **not** want your 4-unit apartment building. He just wants to sell for some cash down and take back a mortgage for the rest.

You deed your 4-unit to Bill Buyer. He pays the cash to Steve Seller or your intermediary. Steve Seller deeds the strip center to you and leaves with cash.

Constructive receipt

Constructive receipt is the main way to blow an exchange. It's a legal phrase. You have constructive receipt when you have the **right** to receive money—whether you **actually** receive it or not. And receiving money—actually or constructively—is fatal to an exchange. You must receive **property only,** not money or mortgages you took back.

That means the documents must require that the "sale" proceeds from the "sale" of your old property go into the new property. Furthermore, you must not—at any moment prior to the expiration of the legal deadlines—have the unilateral right to take the money instead of the property.

When you sell your **residence** and buy another within two years, it does not matter what you do with the money in the interim. You can carry it around in your pocket, put it in your bank account, spend it on lottery tickets—anything you want. But when you **exchange** investment property, you must put an **impenetrable screen** between you and that money.

Intermediary

If your buyer refuses to cooperate with your exchange, you have to do the exchange with an intermediary who then sells the property to the buyer you find. Who you choose as your intermediary is important.

Who canNOT be your intermediary?

Legal eligibility is determined by the final IRS Regulation TD8346 [Regulation section 1.1031(k)-1(k)] which took effect June 10, 1991. That reg says you can use a "qualified intermediary" if that intermediary enters into a **written exchange agreement** with you. Then the reg says who is **not** a qualified intermediary—namely:

• You

• Your agent

• Anyone who, within the two years before closing on your old property, acted as your:

• Employee

• Attorney (unless he or she was only your attorney for exchanging)

• Accountant (unless he or she was only your accountant for exchanging)

• Investment banker or broker

• Real estate agent.

• Any of the following [from IRC § 267 as modified by regulation § 1.1031(k)-1(k)]:

  • Siblings (c)4

  • Spouse (c)(4)

  • Ancestors (c)(4) (i.e., your parents, grandparents, great grandparents, etc.)

  • Lineal descendants (i.e., children, grandchildren, great grandchildren) (c)(4)

  • A corporation in which you own more than 10% in value of the outstanding stock (b)(2)

  • A corporation which is more than 10% owned by the same corporation as owns more than 10% of the corporation doing the exchange (b)(3)

  • A fiduciary of a trust of which you are the grantor (b)(4)

  • A grantor of a trust of which you are a fiduciary (b)(4)

  • A fiduciary of a trust which has the same grantor as a trust of which you are a fiduciary (b)(5)

  • A fiduciary of a trust of which you are a beneficiary (b)(6)

- A beneficiary of a trust of which you are a fiduciary (b)(6)

- A fiduciary of a trust which has the same grantor as another trust of which you are a beneficiary (b)(7)

- A beneficiary of a trust which has the same grantor as another trust of which you are a fiduciary (b)(7)

- A corporation which is more than 10% owned by a trust of which you are a fiduciary (b)(8)

- A fiduciary of a trust which owns more than 10% of the corporation which is doing the exchange (b)(8)

- A corporation which is more than 10% owned by a person who is the grantor of a trust of which you are a fiduciary (b)(8)

- A fiduciary of a trust of which the grantor owns more than 10% of the corporation which is doing the exchange (b)(8)

- A tax-exempt organization covered by IRC § 501 which is controlled directly or indirectly by you or members of your family (b)(9)

- A partnership which is more than 10% owned by the same person who owns more than 10% of the corporation doing the exchange (b)(10)

- A corporation which is more than 10% owned by the same person who owns more than 10% of the partnership doing the exchange (b)(10)

- An S corporation which is more than 10% owned by the same person who owns more than 10% of another S corporation which is doing the exchange (b)(10)

- An S corporation which is more than 10% owned by the same person who owns more than 10% of a C corporation which is doing the exchange (b)(10)

- A C corporation which is more than 10% owned by the same person who owns more than 10% of an S corporation which is doing the exchange (b)(10).

Sorry for that ridiculously long and complex list. But that's what the reg and the code say. Actually, I've put it slightly more readable form.

How to identify the new property

To do a tax-free delayed exchange, you must identify the property to be acquired within 45 days of getting rid of the old property. There are explicit rules on how many properties you can identify and how you must identify them.

How many?

Exchangers are frequently rushed by the 45-day limit. As a result, they find they aren't ready to make a final identification when the 45th day arrives. Rather they'd like to identify a **bunch** of properties then close on some on the list before the 180th day.

Can you do that?

Yes, but only within very strict limits.

The five limits:

- No more than three properties of any **value** [IRS Regulation § 1.1031(k)-1(c)(4)(i)(A)].

- Any **number** as long as their aggregate fair market value does not exceed 200% of the fair market value of the property(ies) you got rid of [IRS Regulation § 1.1031(k)-1(c)(4)(i)(B)].

- Any number **and** value as long as you receive the replacement properties before the 45-day deadline [IRS Regulation § 1.1031(k)-1(c)(4)(ii)(A)].

- Any number **and** value as long as you receive replacement properties whose aggregate fair market value is at least 95% of the aggregate fair market value of all the replacement properties you identified [IRS Regulation § 1.1031(k)-1(c)(4)(ii)(A)].

- Any number **and** value as long as each is ranked according to priority and you acquire them in priority order skipping over a property only when an event described in the agreement and beyond the control of both you and the buyer of your property occurs and prevents you from acquiring the higher ranked property [Committee of Conference Report 98-861, 6/23/84, Joint Explanatory Statement of the Committee of Conference, I., E., 3., page 866].

Don't sweat the small stuff

Reg. Section 1.1031(k)-1(c)(5) says you don't have to identify "incidental property" separately. And they define incidental property as,

> *(A) In standard commercial transactions, the property is typically transferred together with the larger item of property, and*

> *(B) The aggregate fair market value of all the incidental property does not exceed 15 percent of the aggregate fair market value of the larger item of property.*

> *Example 2. For purposes of paragraph (c) of this section, furniture, laundry machines, and other miscellaneous items of personal property will not be treated as separate property from an apartment building with a fair market value of $1,000,000, if the aggregate fair market value of the furniture, laundry machines, and other personal property does not exceed $150,000. For purposes of the 3-property rule, the apartment building, furniture, laundry machines, and other personal property are treated as 1 property. Moreover, for purposes of paragraph (c)(3) of this section (relating to the description of replacement property), the apartment building, furniture, laundry machines, and other personal property are all considered to be unambiguously described if the legal description, street address, or distinguishable name of the apartment building is specified, even if no reference is made to the furniture, laundry machines, and other personal property.*

The fact that you don't have to **identify** it does not mean that you can exchange real property for a combination of real and personal property. You still have to exchange the real property of one apartment building for the real property in your new property and the personal property in the apartment building for the personal property in the new property. Regulation section 1.1031(k)-1(c)(5) only applies to **identification** and not to any other legal requirement.

Revocation

As stated in the exchange agreement in the previous chapter, you can revoke your identification at any time before midnight on the 45th day after transfer of the relinquished property. Regulation Section 1.1031(k)-1(c)(6) says the revocation must be in the same form as the identification, that is,

> ...*a written document signed by the taxpayer and hand delivered, mailed, telecopied, or otherwise sent before the end of the identification period to the person to whom the identification of the replacement property was sent. An identification of replacement property that is made in a written agreement for the exchange of properties is treated as revoked only if the revocation is made in a written amendment to the agreement or in a written document signed by the taxpayer and hand delivered, mailed, telecopied, or otherwise sent before the end of the identification period to all of the parties to the agreement.*

Embezzlement risk

Remember that you are making an **unsecured** extension of credit to the escrow company in the amount of the deal's cash and paper proceeds **every time** you do a real estate deal. You are especially vulnerable to loss in the case of a delayed exchange.

One delayed exchanger whose money was stolen by the escrow company was able to get his money back by suing his attorney—who had selected the escrow company.

Certified Public Account Donald D. Cook was the owner of San Diego Realty Exchange, a San Diego delayed exchange facilitator. To promote his firm, he gave seminars on delayed exchanges. An investigator said the firm handled at least 125 delayed exchanges in the first four months of 1990. Steven Asrilant, a former employee of Cook's said, "He used to boast about how much money he made at the Realty Exchange, and how easy it was."

At the end of April, 1990, Cook disappeared and his firm stopped returning phone calls. Investors whose money appeared to have disappeared along with Mr. Cook came out of the woodwork:

- K. Daniel Liewer lost "almost $500,000"

- Attorney Steve Kane said he could already identify $1.47 million in missing investor funds at an early stage after the discovery that Mr. Cook had disappeared

- George Inskeep, regional manager of Marcus & Millichap said he knew of more than $1,000,000 which was missing.

- Kathleen Ball was missing $49,013 which she said was her total retirement funds

- Ruth Fuqua lost $80,000

- Judy Prout lost $130,000

- David Capron lost $285,000

- Mary Bryson lost $15,000

- John Merkel lost $28,000

According to an article in the May 3, 1990 *San Diego Union*, investors who had used San Diego Realty Exchange and got their money out **before** Cook's disappearance may still have to give it back if San Diego Realty Exchange goes bankrupt. On May 4, 1990, a group of investors who lost the delayed exchange money they had entrusted to San Diego Realty Exchange filed suit to put the firm into involuntary Chapter 7 bankruptcy. Cook appeared in San Diego that day but offered no money to any investors. By that date, at least $3 million had been identified as missing.

Just one example

Derek Reynolds, owner of Exchange Channels, Inc. of Manhattan Beach, CA did seminars promoting his delayed exchange facilitation business. He absconded taking $1.5 million. He reportedly gambled the money in a diamond investment that went sour.

Secured by a mortgage

The new regs allow you to secure the promise to acquire and deed to you new property with a mortgage. It was nice of the IRS to allow that. But it's a rather cumbersome security device for the short period of time a delayed exchange is outstanding. I do not recommend that you secure the promise to acquire your target property(ies) with a mortgage. There are better alternatives like the joint signature account.

Letter of credit

The reg also allows you to use a standby letter of credit to make sure the "sale" proceeds of your old property end up in your new property. The joint account is cheaper. But the letter of credit has the virtue of being **explicitly approved** by the regulations.

The exchange regs say the standby letter of credit must meet the test established in regulation section 15a.453-1(b)(3). That reg was written to cover the same constructive-receipt issue as it applies to installment sales. Reg § 15a.453-1(b)(3)(i) says,

> ...the term 'payment' does not include the receipt of evidences of indebtedness of the person acquiring the property ('installment obligation') whether or not payment of such indebtedness is guaranteed by a third party. A standby letter of credit (as defined in paragraph (b)(3)(iii) of this section) shall be treated as a third-party guarantee.

Here's the plain English translation of that.

> IRS will not claim that you received the money someone owes you as a result of your selling them a property just because you get an IOU from the guy. And they will take that position even if the IOU is guaranteed by some third party like a bank which issues a standby letter of credit. The definition of a standby letter of credit is in paragraph (b)(3)(iii) below.

Regulation § 15a.453-1(b)(3)(iii) says,

> The term 'standby letter of credit' means a non-negotiable, nontransferable (except together with the evidence of indebtedness which it secures) letter of credit, issued by a bank or other financial institution, which serves as a guarantee of the evidence of indebtedness which is secured by the letter of credit. Whether or not the letter explicitly states that it is non-negotiable and nontransferable, it will be treated as non-negotiable and nontransferable if applicable local law so provides...A letter of

credit is not a standby letter of credit if it may be drawn upon in the absence of default in payment of the underlying evidence of indebtedness.

That phrase "...if applicable local law provides" is one of the reasons you need an attorney if you use a letter of credit to insure the safety of your money.

Serial versus direct deeding

Serially deeded exchanges involve **two steps:**

1. Buyer buys replacement property previously located by exchanger; then,
2. Buyer exchanges replacement property for exchanger's old property.

or

1. Exchanger exchanges his old property to the owner of the replacement property; then,
2. Former owner of replacement property sells exchanger's old property to buyer previously located by exchanger.

That's the way exchanges were generally done in the old days. It's the way I did my exchanges in 1978 and 1983. But serial deeding is generally becoming unpopular for three reasons:

• Toxic liability
• Real estate transfer taxes
• Need to get around uncooperative parties.

In a direct deeded exchange, there is **no** interim title holder. Each property goes directly to its ultimate owner. That is:

• Exchanger deeds his old property to buyer, and
• Seller of the replacement property deeds it to exchanger.

It's a legal three-way exchange if the two transactions are "interdependent parts of an overall plan to effect a like-kind exchange."

Legal authority for direct deeding

Direct deeding has been approved in the following **court decisions:**

• *Haden,* 165 F 2d 588
• *Brauer,* 74 TC 1134
• *Biggs,* 632 F 2d 1171

And it has been approved in **revenue rulings** 57-244 and 90-34. And in the **exchange regulations** which were issued in the spring of 1991.

Can you get interest?

Ever since the Starker decision established the right to do delayed exchanges, many delayed exchangers and their advisers have been nervous about getting interest on their money between the two closings. I don't know why. Starker himself got interest (he called it a "growth factor"). And the court did not invalidate his exchange because of it.

However, there has been a group who had a vested interest in promoting the fear that getting interest might invalidate an exchange: **delayed-exchange facilitators**. They said they would handle the transaction and collect the interest as their only fee, thereby saving you from the danger that your exchange would be overturned because you received interest.

Mighty nice of them, huh? Until you run the numbers. For example, 6% interest on $500,000 for two months amounts to $5,000. For what? Depositing $500,000 into a bank account then asking for a cashiers check for that amount later. Nice work if you can get it. The fee for holding money in escrow for a couple months **ought** to be no more than about $25 to $50.

Delayed exchangers will probably continue to pay thousands of dollars to delayed exchange facilitators. But they shouldn't do it out of fear of getting interest. The 1991 exchange regs say it's OK to get interest on the "sale" proceeds of your old property(ies) between closings in a delayed exchange—as long as you don't have the right to it until after the deadlines expire or you close on the target properties, whichever comes first.

If you're still afraid that receiving interest on your money will kill your exchange, why go to strangers? Have the escrow company credit the interest to **me**. I'll be more than happy to save you from the danger of receiving interest in a delayed exchange. No charge.

The 45/180 day rule

Prior to the Tax Reform Act of 1984, delayed exchanges were not mentioned in the Internal Revenue Code. But one had been OK'd in the *Starker* case. The judges in the *Starker* case said they saw no limit to how long you could take to do a delayed exchange.

The Tax Reform Act of 1984 changed that. Now delayed exchanges are explicitly approved by the Internal Revenue Code. That's the **good** news.

The **bad** news is you no longer have forever to do them.

1. You must **identify** the property to be acquired by midnight of the 45th day after you close the transfer of the property you got rid of.
2. You must **close** on the new property within 180 days after you got rid of the old property.

File Form 4868 if you 'sell' after October 15th

Actually, it's 180 days or the due date of the tax return whichever comes first. But the due date of the tax return can be extended by simply filing Form 4868 (Application for Automatic Extension of Time to File Return). So if you close after about October 15th, you'll need to file Form 4868. That's because the normal tax return due date (April 15th most years; 16th or 17th some years) is **about** 180 days after October 15th (leap years also affect the end point of the 180 days).

Extortion danger after the 45th day

Suppose you identify 123 Elm Street as the only property you'll exchange into. You do that before midnight of the 45th day after closing on the property you sold. That satisfies the 45-day requirement. But now the seller of 123 Elm Street knows that you'll have to pay a lot of taxes if you don't close on **his** property. He has the only property in the world you can buy tax-free.

Will he succumb to the temptation to try to extort a higher price or other concession out of you? Probably not. But **many** sellers will. It's best not to give them the chance. So you should not only **identify** the property to be acquired before midnight of the 45th day after closing on the old property—you should also **close** on the new property before that 45th midnight. Then, if the seller of that property threatens not to close, you still have some time to identify another property.

Under the **worst** scenario, closing after the 45th day, the seller has the absolute power to kill your exchange by not closing within the 180 days. You could not force him to close through the courts that fast. Unless you got an injunction. But I've never heard of a court granting a specific performance injunction.

Maybe you could sue not only for specific performance but also for the taxes you had to pay. But that'd be tricky. You sue for specific performance in **state**, not federal court. State courts are probably not interested in trying to compensate you for federal taxes paid.

Plus, the seller/defendant's attorney would argue that an exchange only **defers** the tax. And that your **basis** in your new property was **higher** than it would have been if you had done an exchange. Which is true. In other words, you are truly damaged by having to pay income taxes on what would have been a tax-free transaction if the seller had behaved. But the amount of the damage would be a highly complicated calculation involving analysis of your tax situation for the intervening years, arguments over the appropriate discount rate, and so forth. A state court probably would not have the stomach for it.

Try a penalty clause

You might try to discourage a default by the seller with a **penalty clause**. Suppose you're going to avoid $50,000 in taxes by exchanging. And you're acquiring an $800,000 property for $160,000 down. The penalty clause might say that the purchase price **and** down payment will both be reduced by $50,000 if the seller fails to close by the 179th day after you closed your old deal.

What about if he **refuses** to agree to such a penalty clause? Ask him **why**. The clause would only kick in if he refused to close without good reason. Not if you dragged your feet.

How to word the exchange clauses

Exchange
Exchanger agrees to transfer [insert property description], hereinafter known as the Relinquished Property, to Buyer, as an interdependent part of an overall plan to effect a like-kind exchange for replacement property(ies) to be designated by Exchanger in accordance with Section 1031 of the Internal Revenue Code of 1986.

Identification of replacement property
Exchanger will identify replacement property in a written document signed by the Exchanger and hand delivered, mailed, telecopied, or otherwise sent before midnight on the 45th day after the transfer of the Relinquished Property to the Buyer, the person obligated to transfer replacement property to Exchanger or to any other person involved in this exchange other than Exchanger or a disqualified person as defined in Internal Revenue Service Regulation Section 1.1031(k)-1.

Revocation of identification of replacement property
Exchanger may revoke his identification of replacement property at any time before midnight of the 45th day after the transfer of Relinquished Property by hand delivering, mailing, telecopying, or otherwise sending a written document signed by Exchanger to the person to whom the identification of the replacement property was sent.

No actual or constructive receipt
The cash received from Buyer for the Relinquished Property will be held in a qualified escrow account as described in Internal Revenue Service Regulation Section 1.1031(k)-1(g)(3). The escrow holder will be [exchanger's neighbor or other legally acceptable person]. Exchanger may not receive, pledge, borrow, or

otherwise obtain the benefits of the cash in the escrow account before the end of the exchange period.

If not identified in time

If Exchanger has not identified Replacement Property by midnight of the 45th day after the transfer of the Relinquished Property, the escrow holder will pay the cash received from Buyer for the Relinquished Property, plus any interest earned, to the Exchanger on the first business day following the 45th day after transfer of the Relinquished Property.

If not acquired in time

If Exchanger does not receive all the Replacement Property to which he is entitled on or before the 180th day after Exchanger transferred the Relinquished Property as a result of material and substantial default related to this exchange by a person other than Exchanger or any disqualified person as defined in Internal Revenue Service Regulation Section 1.1031(k)-1(k), the escrow holder will pay the cash received from Buyer for the Relinquished Property, plus any interest earned, to the Exchanger on the first business day following the 180th day after transfer of the Relinquished Property.

Don't get the wrong idea, the courts are not that strict

I've given you many legal cautions in this chapter. The escrow agent can't be your agent. You have to meet the deadlines. The documents must prevent constructive receipt.

You might come away from that thinking, "Boy, it's really hard to set up an exchange so it meets the legal requirements." Wrong. It's easy. And although the IRS is a bit hard to please on exchanges, the courts have generally been easy to please.

The taxpayers seem to win most of the exchange cases that are published. And most exchange court cases stem from **sloppy** exchanges. That's why they're in court. I doubt you can find a single court case in which the deal was set up as I have outlined—other than the ancient cases that established such basic principles as the three-way exchange. Exchanges that are set up by people who understand constructive receipt and the need to avoid it rarely even go to trial let alone result in losses for the taxpayer.

The *Brauer* case

Take the *Brauer* case, for example. Arthur and Glenda Brauer agreed to sell their farm for cash. Then, before closing, they changed their mind. They asked the buyers to do the deal as a three-way exchange. The buyers agreed. But the Brauers didn't get anything **in writing** from the buyer about switching to an exchange! Furthermore, the buyers did not buy the target property, then deed it to the Brauers in exchange for their farm. The owner of the target property just deeded it **directly** to the Brauers.

Folks, that's a sloppy exchange if ever there was one. I think so. IRS thought so. And just about every tax attorney in the world thought the Brauers didn't have a prayer of winning.

But the Brauers won! You can look it up. *Brauer*, 74 TC 84. In the opinion, even the court said the deal was sloppy.

> *While the transaction in [this] case was not as artfully done as that in Barker [another, cleaner exchange case], we do not believe that [means we should decide against the Brauers].*

In another sloppy exchange, the *Biggs* case, the court said,

...the courts have permitted taxpayers great latitude in structuring [exchanges]...To reach a different result in the transaction before us, merely because the transaction was not so artfully arranged, would be to exalt form over substance.

'Reverse Starker' exchanges

The need to do a "reverse Starker" exchange arises when you find the property you want to acquire **before** you find a buyer for your **old** property. To do a "reverse Starker," the facilitator needs to take title to either your old property or the new one until your buyer is ready to close PLUS you need to have the money to acquire the new property before you get the "sale" proceeds from the old property. Either the facilitator buys the target property, exchanges it with you for the old property then sells the old property when a buyer is found or the facilitator buys the new property then holds it until you find a buyer for the old property.

Does the law allow "reverse Starkers?" I think so. **No one knows** because none of the pertinent cases are straightforward "reverse Starkers." Rather they involve cattle (*Rutherford*, 37 TCM 1978-505) or a gas station (*Bezdjian*, 845 F 2d 217) or *Coastal Terminals* (320 F 2d 333). Other cases that give support to the notion that "reverse Starkers" are legal include *Lee*, TC Memo 1986-294 and *Garcia*, (80 TC 491). Finding someone to hold interim title to a property is a severe practical problem especially in this age of toxic liability for property owners.

The delayed-exchange facilitators named in Chapter Four sometimes do "reverse Starkers."

For those few tax advisers who are confident that the law **does** allow reverse Starkers, the proposed exchange regs had a disquieting section. It said,

> *The proposed regulations do not apply if the taxpayer receives the replacement property prior to the date on which the taxpayer transfers the relinquished property. Comments are requested as to whether section 1031 applies to such transactions.*

Delayed exchanges cost too much

Since the Starker decision approved delayed exchanges, a number of companies have sprung up for the purpose of facilitating delayed exchanges. Unfortunately, they typically charge thousands of dollars for this service. That's too much. Exchange attorney Jack Campbell who is listed at the end of Chapter Four says it should only cost from zero to $200.

Campbell doesn't recommend it, but he and I believe a simple joint account would suffice. If you have more than $100,000, you'll need a separate account in a separate bank for each $100,000 to get full FDIC insurance coverage. A joint account is just a bank account which requires both your signature **and** that of another party in the deal. There would also have to be an agreement (drawn by an exchange attorney) between you and the other party prohibiting him from letting you take the cash instead of property. With a joint account, you just put the "sale" proceeds of the old property in the account and withdraw it (accompanied by the other signatory) when you acquire the new property. There would be no charge at all by the holder of the money (the bank).

PART NINE:
SUMMARY

25

The Big Picture

Thus far in the book, I've dealt with detail. Now let's step back and see how it all fits together.

The title of this book includes the phrase "tax avoidance." In fact, tax avoidance is **not** a proper goal.

You should **maximize after-tax income** instead.

Your goal

You invest in real estate to achieve a goal. The goal might be a certain net worth. Or a certain after-tax income. Or both. But you should not invest in real estate to avoid taxes.

Let's say you **now** have a **before**-tax income of $90,000 and an **after**-tax income of $50,000. Your **goal** is an after-tax income of $75,000.

You can achieve it two ways:

1. Increase your before-tax income enough so that after tax you get to keep $75,000 instead of $50,000.
2. Shelter part of your income so that you get to keep $75,000 of your before-tax income of $90,000.

Since I'm the author of the book, *Aggressive Tax Avoidance for Real Estate Investors*, you'll probably expect me to push using real estate as a shelter. I won't .

You may love your work. You may hate managing real estate. Bob Allen, author of the real estate book, *Nothing Down*, says that he hates real estate. If you love your work and hate real estate, you should achieve your after-tax income goal by increasing the amount of money you make before tax from the work you love.

Don't hurt yourself to spite IRS

A lot of people resent tax and the IRS so much they'd rather lose money than make money and share it with the IRS. Irrational but true.

And people resent paying tax so much that they'd rather gather deductions by doing something they hate than increase their before- and after-tax income by doing something they like.

Don't avoid taxes. Increase after-tax income. And do it in the way that you enjoy most—even if that means paying more taxes.

Paying zero taxes

A lot of books and seminars have promised that they'll tell you how to "pay zero taxes" or how to "never pay taxes again." That's not necessarily a smart goal. Not that you should pay taxes out of patriotic duty or some such. But trying to pay zero taxes is generally dumb because it puts you on the wrong side of the point of diminishing returns.

For example, you could reduce your income **tax** to zero by reducing your **income** to zero. Obviously other factors make that unattractive.

In the late sixties, a report said that many American millionaires paid no taxes. An investigation revealed that accelerated depreciation, charitable contributions, and so forth made this possible. To prevent people from paying zero taxes, Congress passed the alternative minimum tax.

The best way to raise your after-tax income in the vast majority of cases is a **combination** of increasing your before-tax income and decreasing the percentage rate at which you pay taxes.

Like conserving energy

Reducing taxes is like conserving energy. You can save the first 10% without much effort. But each additional percent requires more effort. And you quickly reach the point of diminishing returns. Tax "conservation" works the same way. The effort required to reduce taxes to zero by the most advocated methods exceeds the benefit.

Especially when you get down to the lowest bracket. Why waste time trying to stomp out the last 15% when you could be spending the same time earning more and enjoying the 85% you get to keep?

You have two resources

You have two resources: time and money. You want to use them in the way that provides the greatest return. By return, I mean both monetary and psychic return.

We tend to focus only on the **money** invested in real estate—and the **monetary** return from the investment. We tend to overlook the **time** we invest in real estate. And the psychic cost of dealing with tenants and other real estate frustrations.

Before you invest both time and money in real estate, consider whether searching for properties, managing real estate, and negotiating deals are really how you want to spend your time.

Don't become blind to the price of tax avoidance

Don't become so bitter toward the IRS, and so obsessed with avoiding taxes that you become blind to the price those efforts inflict on your finances and lifestyle.

I believe that many tax-motivated real estate investors have actually **reduced** their after-tax income by thousands just so they could reduce IRS's take by hundreds.

I believe that many tax-motivated real estate investors have taken on inordinate **risk** in order to reduce their taxes.

I believe that many tax-motivated investors have spent thousands of hours in activity they **dislike** in order to reduce their taxes.

Keep your perspective. Ask yourself if your efforts to reduce your taxes are reducing your real income even more. Ask yourself if the risks you are taking are worth the tax savings. Ask yourself if you'd do the work required by your real estate investment if it belonged to someone else and you were paid a **salary** equal to your tax savings.

If not, get out of real estate.

Should you work for taxable income or property value increases?

All your life, you've been told that responsible adults work at a job. If possible, you were also told, you should also invest on the side. Most people never question that way of life.

I question it. When you work at a job, you earn taxable income. Part of which, the government is entitled to confiscate. But if you work at increasing net worth—and refrain from selling the asset whose value you are increasing—the government has no right to confiscate any of the gain. (Actually, the **local** government can probably confiscate part of it through higher property taxes.)

It seems to me that if the taxes on work are too high—and they are—then you ought not work for a living. "Not work for a living!," you say, "That's unthinkable!"

Hear me out.

Net worth instead of income

Suppose that instead of spending your day working for a salary, commission, or fees, you created value. Suppose you worked for net worth instead of income.

But, you say, I need income to buy food and clothing and cars. No, you don't. You need **cash**—not income. How do you get cash without having income? By **borrowing**. Loan proceeds are not taxable income.

In real estate, you would structure the payments on the debt so that they would consume the building's taxable income. You would spend your day doing those things which would increase the value of your real estate. In blessed freedom from bosses as well as the tax man.

The borrowing builder who never sells

You quit your job or medical practice or whatever to become a builder. Because you own the property you build, no one pays you. As a result, you have **no income** for the IRS to tax.

But with each passing day, your efforts increase the value of the property you are building. Your "pay" comes in the form of increased net worth rather than salary, commissions, or fees. The **IRS** can't touch your increased net worth. But **you** can.

Typically, you would build income properties. You collect rents. But you also deduct interest, operating expenses, and depreciation. You should have positive **cash flow**, but negative or zero **taxable income**. You can spend the cash flow on food, clothing, transportation, and so forth. And from time to time, you can get a larger slug of cash by **refinancing** one of your properties. That, too, would be tax-free.

Ironclad protection against dealer status

If you dispose of a property by sale or exchange, IRS might claim that you were a dealer. But if you **never** dispose of the property, you have ironclad protection against being declared the owner of dealer property.

Hundreds of thousands of dollars a year tax-free

If you spend your days increasing the value of properties by building or improving them—if you obtain cash from the properties in the form of depreciation-sheltered cash flow and/or refinancing—and if you never dispose of a property—you will be virtually invulnerable to taxation.

If you owned millions of dollars worth of real estate and spent your days doing nothing but increasing its value, your "income" would be in the hundreds of thousands of dollars per year—tax-free. I would not be surprised if someone who owned ten million dollars worth of real estate told me that his depreciation-sheltered/refinancing "income" was a million dollars a year.

The notion that we all have to go to school then work for salaries, commissions, or fees began in the days before we had an income tax—before inflation. But a visitor from Mars arriving with no such preconceived notions would look at our tax structure and conclude that the government does not want people to work at jobs.

We punish such activities by taxing them. The only cash generators that are not so punished are building net worth and borrowing. Looking at our tax structure and the fact that most people work at jobs, the man from Mars would conclude that we are a nation of masochists.

I thought this borrowing builder who never sells idea was only a theory. Then, at a speech I made, a couple from Beaumont, Texas introduced themselves, thanked me for the idea which they said changed their lives, and proceeded to tell me that they had become borrowing builders who never sell—and they were doing quite well, thank you. They now live as I've just described, tax-free.

A 'real estate bum'

You've heard of beach bums and ski bums. I know a "real estate bum." He's a single guy who "worked" by dabbling in real estate. He subdivided here, renovated there, and built an occasional property. And he rented out rooms in his house to other single people. He seemed to get along OK financially—and he paid little, if any taxes. He was constantly borrowing money.

So if you still wonder if the live-off-your-appreciation approach is possible, there's another real life example. I suspect that many real estate investors have followed a similar path without being conscious of it.

I suggest that you consciously consider this approach. "Wage slaves" are slaves not only to the boss, but also to the tax man. By working for net worth instead, you escape both masters.

Dig a hole, then fill it up

The typical tax shelter seeker is a professional or businessman who earns a high income. All week long he makes money as a doctor or pilot or business owner. He pays a lot of taxes.

He figures that tax shelter is something you buy once a year to reduce your taxes. To him, it's a sort of magical "black box."

He reminds me of the overweight, heavy-drinking smoker who never exercises. Once a year, he visits his doctor and says, "Make me healthy."

The tax shelter-seeking professional also reminds me of the GI assigned to dig a hole then fill it up again. Only he earns taxable income Monday through Friday then loses it in real estate over the weekend so he won't pay any taxes.

Don't create the problem to begin with

Why not solve the problem at its source instead of trying to correct it after the fact?

The overweight smoker should quit the over-eating and smoking which is causing his health problems. And the high income individual should at least consider quitting the activity which is causing his problem—earning taxable income.

The big tax savers

I've tried to alert you to most of the ways to make sure that you aren't paying one more cent in taxes than the law requires. Much of the advice generates **small** savings. You ought to take advantage of **all** the savings opportunities available to you. But you should also keep in mind where the **big** tax savings come from:

1. **Build net worth**. The biggest tax-saving technique of all is the one I just covered— devote your day to building net worth rather than earning taxable income. Get the cash you need from depreciation-sheltered cash flow and/or refinancing.

2. **Leverage**. I told you that depreciation is the only real tax shelter because it's mostly a **paper** rather than a **real** loss. I also told you how to maximize your depreciation deductions on a given property by choosing an aggressive improvement ratio, separating personal property first, and so forth.
   But there is another step you can take to maximize your depreciation deductions—buy more real estate. You do this by using more borrowed money (leverage). The more real estate you own, the more depreciation you are entitled to deduct (in the year of disposition if not now).
   Of course, the more leverage, the more risk. I recommend you read my book, *How to Use Leverage to Maximize Your Real Estate Investment Return*, to get a good handle on how much leverage is too much.
   Of all the ways to increase your depreciation deductions, leverage is the most important.

3. **Exchange**. Need I say more on this subject?

4. **Aggressiveness**. Conservatism is a self-imposed audit which is far more thorough and severe than an IRS audit. It costs you dearly. Knock it off.
   When the law is clear cut, obey it.
   When the law is judgmental, make the judgment call as far in your favor as you can without committing negligence or fraud. As long as you have a "reasonable basis" in some cases, "substantial authority" in others, you are not breaking the law.

5. **Resistance**. Do not pay any tax demanded by IRS as a result of an audit until the 90th day of the Statutory Notice. If you think you have enough of a chance to win in court to make fighting there worthwhile, fight.

Go get 'em, tigers.

242

APPENDIXES

APPENDIX A
MY LEGISLATIVE PROGRAM

I have criticized the IRS and the Internal Revenue Code in this book. If you criticize something, you ought to say how you'd do it better. Here's how I would do it better.

THE INTERNAL REVENUE CODE

Minimize judgmental areas

Most of my aggressive advice applies to judgmental areas. Congress ought to eliminate or at least minimize those parts of the Code.

Throughout history, tyrants have used vague laws to give themselves unlimited power. The Founding Fathers knew that. That's why they made vague laws unconstitutional. Unfortunately, we get our judges from the ranks of politicians. And they are not always as eager as the Constitution requires when it comes to limiting the powers of their legislative former colleagues.

The judgmental areas of the IRC are vague. As a result, they give the IRS too much power. One example is T.J. Starker's decision to pay $300,000 in tax demanded by IRS then sue in District Court to get it back rather than fight in Tax Court where he would not have had to pay until he lost. The reason, according to Starker's attorney, was a fear that he might be declared a dealer on the property in question.

Seems to me that the **possibility** of that was quite **remote**. But the **consequences** of Starker's being declared a dealer would have been **horrible**. And the definition of dealer status is extremely vague. So Starker's attorney chose the District Court route in order to make use of its "window of invulnerability." I calculate Starker's fear of IRS and resulting decision to pay, then sue for a refund cost him millions of dollars (the opportunity cost of not investing that $300,000 in real estate for the many years it took him to get his money back).

Here's my plan for correcting this problem.

1. Abolish the dealer property concept. Instead, set a time limit. If you hold a property more than, say, six months, you can claim depreciation and exchange. Less than six months, and you cannot. Then we would have an **objective**, non-judgmental way of telling where we stood.

The time period the Congress picks does not matter that much to me. Just as long as they pick some definite period. They could pick whatever period they needed to generate the same revenue as now.

Eliminating dealer property would not only let real estate investors sleep better. It would also save IRS and court time. At present, there are numerous audits and law suits in which taxpayers and the IRS are battling over dealer property disputes. Changing the law could eliminate those time- and money-wasting disputes—without reducing the government's tax take one penny.

2. Establish a standard improvement ratio. It used to be we had to pick a useful life for each building. That was judgmental and led to many time- and money-wasting disputes. Then, Congress eliminated the useful life issue in the Economic Recovery Tax Act of 1981 by establishing standard recovery periods. Between '81 and '87, the standard recovery period was sequentially 15 years, 18 years, and 19 years. With the Tax Reform Act of 1986, we got **two** standard recovery periods: 27.5 years for residential and 31.5 years for non-residential.

The Economic Recovery Tax Act of 1981 has been roundly criticized. And largely repealed by the Tax Reform Act of 1986. But I have never heard one word of complaint about the standard recovery period versus the useful life. The recovery periods instead of useful lives were one of the smartest things ever done to the Internal Revenue Code. Yet no one but me has ever mentioned it in print.

Why not extend that concept to improvement ratios? Just pick a percentage, say, 75%. That would apply to all but properties with a lot of land. To be precise, you could say it applied to all properties where the land area to floor area ratio was 30 to 1 or less. Roughly speaking, that would allow a 3,000 square foot house on a **two**-acre lot to qualify for the standard improvement ratio. But that same house on a **three** acre lot would have to use the old appraisal method of picking an improvement ratio.

As with dealer property, Congress could pick whatever ratio gave the same tax revenue as now. And, as with recovery periods, they could even make the standard ratio a political football going up and down depending on whether Congress wanted to "encourage investment" or "sock it to those loophole-using real estate bastards."

Just pick a specific number so we know where we stand.

Write the Internal Revenue Code in plain English

Everybody's in favor of "plain English" laws. They're like motherhood and the American Flag. But the lawyers throw up their hands and say, "You can't define plain English."

Yes, you can. Rudolf Flesch defined it as text with a Flesch Readability score of 60 or higher. The formula for the Flesch Readability score is:

206.835 - [(average number of words per sentence x 1.015) + (average number of syllables per word x 84.6)]

Flesch's formula makes more sense than you might think. *Reader's Digest* has the largest circulation of any magazine in the world. It's not just a coincidence that *Reader's Digest* has a high Flesch score of 65. *The Wall Street Journal* has the largest circulation of any daily newspaper in the U.S. And a Flesch score of 43. The Internal Revenue Code, in contrast, has a Flesch Readability score of **minus 6!**

Applying the principal of plain English to income tax law is not a novel idea. In August, 1977, Oregon passed a law that said that state's income tax instructions had to have a Flesch readability score of at least 60. Flesch put examples of their new instructions in his book, *How to Write Plain English*. Here's a sample:

> *You must file an Oregon return if you have moved into or out of Oregon during the year and have income subject to Oregon tax. But you can't use the form in this packet.*

The Fog Index is another standard which could be used to accomplish the same purpose. It was invented by Robert Gunning and is explained in his book, *The Technique of Clear Writing*.

The Fog Index formula is:

(average words per sentence + number of words with
three or more syllables* per hundred words) x .4

* Not counting proper names, verbs ending in "ed" or "es," or combinations of short, easy words like "manpower."

Fog Index scores range from about 4 to about 14 and is supposed to roughly approximate the number of years of education you need to understand the material in question. The lower the better. Twelve is too high. The *Reader's Digest* scores about 10; *The Wall Street Journal*, about 11. *Atlantic Monthly* scores about 12, and had to be rescued from financial difficulty by a real estate magnate. By my count, section 1031 of the Internal Revenue Code (exchanges) scores 33.48! That's a lot of education!

Form over substance

I've explained the doctrine of substance over form to you. There is one section of the Code where the normal substance over form relationship seems to be reversed—exchanges.

The three-way exchange is a ridiculous ritual. It resembles some sort of aboriginal mating dance in its convoluted complexity.

Section 1031 should be eliminated and section 1034 (the two-year reinvestment rule) should be expanded to cover business and investment property.

Tax complexity

General Grant had a captain who was dumb on his staff. He would explain his battle plans to this captain. If the captain could understand them well enough to explain them back to Grant accurately, the plans went out. If not, the plans would be rewritten until the dumb captain **could** understand and explain them.

Congress's tax-writing staffs need Grant's captain. Lately, especially, the tax laws have become mind-bogglingly complex. For example, I have yet to find anyone who claims to understand the new installment sale rules. And I've asked some of the leading experts in the nation about them.

Congress should go back to the pre-Tax Reform Act of 1986 installment sale rules. If that would cost them revenue, they should make it up with higher tax rates or longer recovery periods.

Same thing applies to the passive loss limits and all the various surcharges that push the maximum bracket up from 28% to 33% or 57.75% or 49.5% and so forth. Why not just make the darned thing 29%?

Lower tax rates

Tax rates above 25% are too high. I believe they lower the government's take through increased cheating, use of tax shelters, and discouragement of economic activity.

According to the "Laffer" curve, there is a point at which tax revenue is optimized. When rates go above that point, tax revenue does **not** increase. It **decreases**. I believe that point is about 25%. Under current law, many people pay taxes at rates higher than 25%.

The best example I know to prove the Laffer curve theory is legalized gambling. The state takes a certain percentage of gambling revenues at racetracks, casinos, lotteries, etc. Politicians always want more money with which to buy votes. But they have learned from hard experience that there is a point they dare not go above. Because, when they do, the revenue to the state is reduced, not increased. The reason is that winning encourages the public to gamble. And if they don't win enough, they get discouraged and play less.

So it is with working and investing—which is a gamble in part. If government takes **too much**, people stop "playing" in the economy. Instead, they invest in tax-sheltered investments or participate in the underground economy or both. Or they simply refrain from economic activity at all.

Don't tax corporations

Taxing corporations is silly. There is no such thing as a corporation. A corporation is a legal concept, not a thing or a person. It cannot pay taxes. A tax on corporations is nothing but a hidden sales tax on the corporation's products.

Taxes ought not be hidden. Therefore, there should be no tax on corporations. Taxing the dividends the corporation's owners (shareholders) receive will make sure no one escapes taxation.

IRS needs more auditors

IRS auditors produce far more revenue than it costs to pay them. On average, it costs IRS 41 **cents** to collect each $100 of taxes. That's a heck of a return. Therefore, there ought to be more auditors. Too many cheaters are getting away with it. I don't cheat. So I have nothing to fear from IRS auditors. But I know that I have to pay higher taxes to make up for the cheaters. So I see the auditors as my allies in reducing both cheating and my taxes.

IRS oversteps its authority

IRS needs to quit pretending it's Congress or the courts. Too often, IRS issues regs or rulings which go too far. IRS loses credibility and what little good will it has by getting reversed by the courts. They ought to be scrupulously true to the Code and pertinent court decisions.

Adopt my program, put a tax adviser out of work

The various tax laws are often called the "Accountants and Attorneys Full Employment Act of 19__." That's because they so increase the complexity of the Internal Revenue Code that taxpayers need increased amounts of professional help.

My legislative program would put many tax advisers out of work. That's as it should be. There are too many people in our society who devote their time to economically useless activities like tax advising. If my legislative program were adopted, a great many of us tax advisers would have to do something **useful** for a change.

Don't hold your breath, though.

APPENDIX B
PERTINENT BOOKS, PERIODICALS, AND SEMINARS

Books

All You Need to Know About the IRS. Paul Strassels. Random House, Inc. 1980. Inside view of former IRS man.

Annual Report. Commissioner of Internal Revenue. IRS. Annual. Statistics on audits, court cases, and so forth.

The Appraisal of Real Estate. American Institute of Real Estate Appraisers. Solid background information on how to make the appraisals necessary to calculate improvement ratios.

The April Game. Diogenes. Playboy Press. 1973. Another IRS man. Good section on how to handle an audit.

CCIM Designation Roster Realtors ® National Marketing Institute.

Distressed Real Estate Times—Offensive and Defensive Strategy and Tactics Special Report #2. John T. Reed (same author as this book). Reed Publishing.

Dodge Manual. McGraw-Hill Information Systems Co. Continuous. Building cost manual used for component breakdowns and improvement ratios.

"Election of Small Tax Case Procedure & Preparation of Petitions." U.S. Tax Court. 1979. Good, free pamphlet.

Federal Income Taxation of Real Estate. Gerald Robinson. Warren, Gorham & Lamont. Annual. Excellent book by aggressive tax attorney. Highly recommended. Updated during the year.

Federal Rules of Civil Procedure. Foundation Press, Inc. Required reference if you plan to sue in district court.

Federal Tax Guide. Maxwell-MacMillan. Annual. Very thorough tax reference. Updated weekly. You can get the weekly updates separately. See *Report Bulletins* in the periodicals section below. Commerce Clearing House publishes a similar tax guide.

Federal Tax Litigation. Garbis, Junghans, Struntz. Warren, Gorham & Lamont.

Federal Tax Regulations. West Publishing Company. Continuous. Use in library. Also published in paperback (four volumes) by CCH and P-H.

Guide to Practices and Procedures Under the Freedom of Information Act. Maxwell-MacMillan. May be useful in suit against IRS.

How to Do a Delayed Exchange Special Report #3. John T. Reed (same author as this book). Reed Publishing.

How to Hire a Lawyer. Dell Publishing Co., Inc. 1979. Mainly an overly long list of questions to ask a prospective attorney. But a good section on what an attorney's bill should include.

How to Increase the Value of Real Estate. John T. Reed (same author as this book). Reed Publishing. Chapter on increasing the value of a property by increasing its tax efficiency.

How to Survive a Tax Audit. Mary Sprouse. Doubleday & Co., Inc. 1981. Not real estate-oriented but good coverage of audits. Ms. Sprouse has a healthy skepticism about tax advisers. This is the best of the IRS insider books. The author was an audit manager for IRS.

How to Use Interest Rate Futures Contracts. Edward Schwarz. Dow Jones-Irwin. 1979. Tough to follow but necessary in some exchange situations to deal with the possibility of increase in interest rates during long closing.

How to Use Leverage to Maximize Your Real Estate Investment Return. John T. Reed (same author as this book). Reed Publishing. Has a chapter on how to calculate the time value of money. Discusses tax ramifications of real estate finance techniques throughout.

How to Write Plain English. Rudolf Flesch. Barnes and Noble Books.

Index to Federal Tax Articles. Warren, Gorham, and Lamont, Inc. Supplemented periodically. Sort of a "Readers Guide" to articles on income taxes—mostly in legal and accounting journals. A very useful reference for researching a particular tax question.

Index to Legal Periodicals. Wilson Publishing Co. A "Readers Guide" to legal articles published by the same company that publishes the *Readers Guide to Periodical Literature* and looks the same.

Internal Revenue Code. Prentice-Hall and CCH. Extremely hard to read but necessary part of your bookshelf.

In this Corner, the IRS. J.R. Price. Dell Publishing Co., Inc. 1981. Another "insider" book on IRS. Good chapters on appeal of negligence and other penalties and on using the Freedom Of Information Act against the IRS.

Interest Rate Futures. Allen Loosigian. Dow Jones.

IRS Practice and Procedure. Michael Saltzman. Warren, Gorham, & Lamont. Excellent reference on what to do if you are in a dispute with IRS.

Legal Research. Stephen Elias. Nolo Press. 1982. Layman's guide to how to do legal research.

Office Building Acquisition Handbook. John T. Reed (same author as this book). Reed Publishing.

Pay Less Tax Legally. Barry Steiner. The New American Library, Inc. 1979. Another former IRS guy. Good section on preparing for an audit.

Real Estate Exchange and Acquisition Techniques. William Tappan. Maxwell-MacMillan. 1989. Mandatory.

The Realty Bluebook. Professional Publishing Corp. Annual. Contains a useful list showing repairs and improvements. Also one of the clearest explanations available of some of the tax laws pertaining to real estate.

Residential Property Acquisition Handbook. John T. Reed (same author as this book). Reed Publishing.

Rules of Practice & Procedure. U.S. Tax Court. 1979. Hard to read but necessary if you plan to fight in Tax Court.

The S Corporation: Planning & Operation. Schreiber and Traum. Panel Publishers, Inc.

Single-Family Lease Options Special Report #1, John T. Reed (same author as this book). Reed Publishing.

The Smart Investor's Guide to Real Estate. Robert Bruss. Crown Publishers, Inc. Bob is the nationally syndicated real estate columnist. You are probably already familiar with his work.

Tax Incentives for Historic Preservation. National Trust For Historic Preservation.

The Taxpayer's Audit Survival Manual. Jacobs and Schoeneman. Alexandria House Books. 1980. Excellent guide to the nuts and bolts of an audit.

Tax Practice Deskbook. Freeman. Warren, Gorham & Lamont., Inc.

The Technique of Clear Writing. Robert Gunning. McGraw-Hill Book Company.

Your Income Tax Professional Edition. J.K. Lasser. Simon & Schuster. Annual. Excellent, cheap, general reference. No depth in real estate. Not aggressive.

Periodicals

Internal Revenue Bulletin. IRS. Weekly. Rulings, procedures, Treasury decisions, Executive Orders, tax conventions, legislation, court decisions, "and other items of general interest." Also semi-annual *Cumulative Bulletins.* Use in library.

IRS Letter Rulings. Maxwell-MacMillan. and Commerce Clearing House. Use in library.

John T. Reed's Real Estate Investor's Monthly. Same author as this book. Reed Publishing. Broad coverage of topics of interest to serious real estate investors. Pounces on and explains new tax law developments.

Journal of Property Management. Institute of Real Estate Management. Bi-monthly.

Journal of Real Estate Taxation. Warren, Gorham & Lamont, Inc. Quarterly.

The Kess Tax Practice Report. Warren, Gorham & Lamont, Inc. Monthly.

Martindale-Hubbell. Annual. Directory of lawyers nationwide. Gives limited background information.

Professional Builder. Cahners Publishing Co. Monthly. Carries real estate CPA Kenneth Leventhal's column "Accounting and the Builder."

Real Estate Investor's Monthly. See *John T. Reed's Real Estate Investor's Monthly* above.

Real Estate Review. Warren, Gorham & Lamont, Inc. Quarterly. Academic journal on real estate in general. Regular section on tax topics as well as articles. Access through index to Federal Tax Articles.

Real Estate Tax Digest. Matthew Bender. Monthly. Aggressive but difficult to read. Your tax adviser should subscribe.

Report Bulletins. Prentice-Hall and CCH. Weekly. Good way to keep up to date, although several weeks behind.

Tax Notes. Tax Analysts. Weekly. Seems to be aimed at tax policy makers.

U.S. Code--Congressional & Administrative News. West Publishing Co. Text of new laws as soon as they are enacted. Some legislative history. Use in library.

Washington Tax Review. BNA. Monthly. Forecasts on pending laws. Use in library.

Organizations which present seminars

American Bar Association. 1155 East 60th Street, Chicago, IL 60637

American Institute of Certified Public Accountants. 1211 Avenue of the Americas, New York, NY 10036

American Law Institute. 4025 Chestnut Street, Philadelphia, PA 19104

Northwest Center for Professional Education. 13555 Bel-Red Road, C 96870, Bellevue, WA 98009

Practising Law Institute. 810 Seventh Avenue. New York, NY 10019

The Real Estate Institute, School of Continuing Education, New York University, Management Seminars Division. 326 Shimkin Hall, New York, NY 10003

Realtors® National Marketing Institute. 430 North Michigan Avenue, Chicago, IL 60611

The Wharton School. University of Pennsylvania, Executive Education, Dietrich Hall, Locust Walk, Philadelphia, PA 19104

Addresses of Publishers

Alexandria House Books
901 North Washington Street
Alexandria, VA 22314

American Institute of Real Estate Appraisers
same as Realtors® National Marketing Institute

Barnes and Noble Books
10 East 53rd Street
New York, NY 10022

Boeckh Publications
American Appraisal Associates, Inc.
525 East Michigan Street
Milwaukee, WI 53201

BNA
1231 25th Street, N.W.
Washington, DC 20037

Cahners Publishing Company
5 South Wabash Avenue
Chicago, IL 60603

Commerce Clearing House
4025 W. Peterson Ave.
Chicago, IL 60646

Crown Publishers, Inc.
1 Park Avenue
New York, NY 10016

Dell Publishing Company, Inc.
1 Dag Hammerskjold Plaza
New York, NY 10017

Doubleday Publishing Company
245 Park Avenue
New York, NY 10167

Dow Jones Books
Box 300
Princeton, NJ 08540

Dow Jones-Irwin
1818 Ridge Road
Homewood, IL 60430

Foundation Press, Inc.
Mineola, NY

Institute of Real Estate Management
same as Realtors® National Marketing Institute

IRS
Washington, DC 20224

Marshall Valuation Service
Marshall and Swift Publication Co.
1617 Beverly Boulevard
Los Angeles, CA 90026

Matthew Bender
1275 Broadway
Albany, NY 12201

Martindale-Hubbell
Summit, NJ 07901

Maxwell-MacMillan.
910 Sylvan Avenue
Englewood Cliffs, NJ 07632

McGraw-Hill
1221 Avenue of the Americas, Suite 1759
New York, NY 10020

National Trust for Historic Preservation
1785 Massachusetts Avenue
Washington, DC 20036

The New American Library, Inc.
1633 Broadway
New York, NY 10019

Nolo Press
950 Parker Street
Berkeley, CA 94710

Panel Publishers
14 Plaza Road
Greenvale, NY 11548

Playboy Press
747 Third Avenue
New York, NY 10017

Professional Publishing Corporation
P.O. Box 4187
San Rafael, CA 94903

Random House, Inc.
201 East 50 th Street
New York, NY 10022

Realtors® National Marketing Institute
430 North Michigan Avenue
Chicago, IL 60611

Reed Publishing
P.O. Box 27311
Concord, CA 94527

Simon & Schuster, Inc.
1230 Avenue of the Americas
New York, NY 10020

Superintendent of Documents
U.S. Government Printing Office
Washington, DC 20402

Tax Analysts
6830 North Fairfax Drive
Arlington, VA 22213

United States Tax Court
400 West Second Street
Washington, DC 20217

Warren, Gorham & Lamont, Inc.
210 South Street
Boston, MA 02111

West Publishing Company
P.O. Box 3526
50 West Kellogg Boulevard
St. Paul, MN 55165

Wilson Publishing Co.
950 University Avenue
Bronx, NY 10452

Woodward/White
129 First Avenue, S.W.
Aiken, SC 29801

Computer tax-related data bases

Dialog Information Services
3460 Hillview Avenue
Palo Alto, CA 94304
800-334-2564

Lexis
9333 Springboro Pike
Dayton, OH 45401
800-543-6862

NewsNet
945 Haverford Road
Bryn Mawr, PA 19101
800-952-0122

TAXRIA
292 Madison Avenue
New York, NY 10017
800-562-0245, ext. 4801

Varilex, Inc. (includes Lexis)
1 Graves Street
Rochester , NY 14614
800-828-6373

Westlaw
same as West Publishing

Computer Software

MacInTax™ Softview®.
4820 Adohr Lane, Suite F
Camarillo, CA 93010

APPENDIX C
DEFINITIONS

Accelerated Cost Recovery System Depreciation scheme instituted by the Economic Recovery Tax Act of 1981 characterized by standard recovery periods rather than subjective useful lives. Originally generally embodied more rapid depreciation methods than previous law.

Accelerated depreciation Any depreciation method more rapid than straight line.

Accrual basis taxpayer Counts income when earned and expenses when incurred regardless of when received or paid.

Active participation Participation e.g. in the making of management decisions or arranging for others to provide services (such as repairs), in a significant and bona fide sense. Management decisions that are relevant in this context include approving new tenants, deciding on rental terms, approving capital or repair expenditures, and other similar decisions.

After-tax cash flow Before-tax cash flow less income taxes paid as a result of owning the property in question or plus income taxes saved as a result of owning the property in question.

Amortization Pay down of the mortgage which occurs when principal payments other than final balloon payment are made. Also a sort of straight line depreciation of certain costs like loan fees.

Applicable Federal Rate Interest rate promulgated monthly by IRS to determine interest paid for tax purposes when the law requires that interest be imputed.

Appreciation Increase in property value.

Assessment Local tax assessor's appraisal of your property, often used to arrive at improvement ratio. Also, auditor's opinion as to how much additional tax and penalties you owe after an audit.

At-risk rules Rules which limit cumulative loss deductions to the amount which the investor can lose, i.e. his down payment in nonrecourse, seller-financing situations.

Basis The value of your property for tax purposes. Generally, what you paid for it plus improvements less depreciation. Varies according to how you acquired the property.

Before-tax cash flow Rent minus operating expenses and debt service.

Boot Non-like-kind property or cash received in an exchange.

Capitalization rate Annual net operating income divided by property value.

Cash basis taxpayer Counts income when received and expenses when paid. Can have "constructive receipt" if he chooses voluntarily not to receive income which he is entitled to.

Component method Depreciation method in which you break down the property into its component parts like roof, carpet, appliances, etc. Outlawed for ACRS property but still allowed for pre-'81 basis carried forward in an exchange.

Composite method Opposite of component method. Property is depreciated as one lump sum.

Constructive receipt A legal doctrine which states that a taxpayer has received income when he has the power to receive it even though he voluntarily chooses not to receive it physically.

Credit An amount deducted from your tax payable.

Deficiency Difference between what you said you owed on your tax return and what IRS says you owe. A deficiency alone is not an offense.

Delayed exchange Receipt of new property takes place on a date after transfer of old property.

Discount rate The interest rate you think you can earn on money you invest. Used to calculate present value.

Enrolled agent Someone who has passed an IRS test and is therefore permitted to represent taxpayers before the IRS.

Examination The official IRS term for an audit.

Excess depreciation Difference between depreciation deductions which would be claimed using a 40-year recovery period and depreciation deductions actually claimed.

Expenditure Outlay of funds.

Expense Consumption of cost in the pursuit of income. Also, an amount deducted from your income for tax purposes.

Hedge Counterbalancing positions in the present and futures markets to prevent loss or gain due to changes in price of the commodity hedged, e.g. interest rates.

Improvement ratio Total value of the property minus the value of the land all divided by the total value of the property.

Imputed interest Interest calculated according to rates promulgated by IRS monthly on installment sales in which the stated interest rate is less than the Applicable Federal Rate.

Land contract An installment agreement for purchase of real estate according to which the buyer does not receive the deed until all or a specified part of the payments have been made.

Marginal tax bracket The percentage rate at which the taxpayer's next dollar of income is taxed.

Material participation Year-round active involvement in the operations of the activity on a regular, continuous, and substantial basis.

Non-passive Derived from a business in which you materially participate or from salary, wages, commissions, fees, interest, dividends, and royalties.

Non-residential Property in which less than 20% of gross income comes from dwelling units. "Transient" use property is non-residential.

Option The right but not the obligation to buy or lease a specified property for a specified price during a specified period of time.

Passive Derived from rental property or a business in which you do not materially participate.

Personal property Property which is not land or attached to land more or less permanently.

Phase-in Period over which new tax laws apply to an increasing portion of the affected income or loss.

Present value The current value of a sum of money to be paid or received in the future. Depends on discount rate you assign to the use of the money in the interim.

Principal residence Where you live. You can only have one principal residence at a time.

Real property Land and that which is attached to it more or less permanently.

Recapture Recalculation of previous year's income taxes to reflect sale of an asset prior to the end of its originally anticipated useful life or recovery period, or the end of some statutory period. Applies to accelerated depreciation and investment tax credits.

Regulation Rule put out by the Department of the Treasury. You must abide by regulations unless they are contrary to law, exceed the Treasury's authority, or are unreasonable.

Residential property Property in which 80% or more of the gross income comes from dwelling units. Units used on a "transient" basis like motel rooms are not residential dwelling units.

Ruling A promise made by the IRS to challenge or not challenge a particular way of reporting a possibly taxable event. All taxpayers may rely on Revenue Rulings. Only the addressee may rely on Letter Rulings.

Statutory notice 90-day notice sent to you after audit and appeal within IRS. You must either pay the tax or file a petition with the Tax Court within the 90-day period.

Straight -line depreciation Depreciation by equal amounts each year.

Tax adviser Accountant, attorney, enrolled agent, or other tax preparer.

Transient Occupants usually stay less than thirty days.

APPENDIX D
ABBREVIATIONS

ABA	American Bar Association	JPM	*Journal of Property Management*
AFR	Applicable Federal Rate	LLB	Latin for Bachelor of Laws degree
AFTR	*American Federal Tax Reports, First Series*	LLM	Latin for Master of Laws degree
AGI	adjusted gross income	MAI	Member of the Appraisal Institute
AICPA	American Institute of Certified Public Accountants	M-M	Maxwell-MacMillan
AIREA	American Institute Of Real Estate Appraisers	NAR	National Association of Realtors®
ALI	American Law Institute	N.O.I.	net operating income
AMT	alternative minimum tax	non-acq	nonacquiescence
aq'd	acquiesced	NYU	New York University
atcf	after-tax cash flow	PAL	passive asset loss
BNA	Bureau of National Affairs	P-H	Prentice-Hall, Inc. (acquired by Maxwell-MacMillan)
BTA	Board of Tax Appeals (precursor to Tax Court)	PIG	passive income generator
btcf	before-tax cash flow	PL	Public Law
CB	*Cumulative Bulletin* of IRS	PLI	Practising Law Institute
CCH	Commerce Clearing House, Inc.	PV	present value
CCIM	Certified Commercial-Investment Member of the Realtors® National Marketing Institute	REIM	*John T. Reed's Real Estate Investor's Monthly*
CPA	certified public accountant	Rev. Proc.	Revenue Procedure
db	declining balance depreciation method	RNMI	Realtors® National Marketing Institute
ERTA	Economic Recovery Tax Act of 1981	s/l	straight-line depreciation
FHA	Federal Housing Administration	TAMRA	Technical and Miscellanous Revenue Act of 1988
F 2d	*Federal Reporter, Second Series*	TC	Tax Court
FNMA	Federal National Mortgage Association	TCM	*Tax Court Memorandum Decisions*
FRCP	Federal Rules Of Civil Procedure	TCMP	Taxpayer Compliance Measurement Program
F Supp.	*Federal Supplement*	TEFRA	Tax Equity and Fiscal Responsibility Act of 1982
IRB	*Internal Revenue Bulletin*	TPI	total positive income
IRC	Internal Revenue Code	TRA	Tax Reform Act
IRR	internal rate of return	U.S.	*United States Reports*
IRS	Internal Revenue Service	USC	United States Code
ITC	investment tax credit	USCA	*United States Code Annotated*
JD	juris doctor (law degree)	USCS	*United States Code Service*
		USTC	*United States Tax Cases*
		WG&L	Warren, Gorham, & Lamont, Inc.

INDEX

Your Opinion of this Book is Important to Me

Please send me your comments on this book. I'm interested in both compliments and constructive ciriticism. Your compliments provide guidance on what you want. And, with your permission, I'd like to use your favorable comments to sell future editions of the book. Constructive criticism also helps make the book's next edition better.

Evaluation of *Aggressive Tax Avoidance for Real Estate Investors*

Circle one: Excellent   Good   Satisfactory   Unsatisfactory

Circle one: Too Advanced   About Right   Too Basic

What part did you like best? _____

_____

What part did you like least? _____

_____

How can I improve the book? _____

_____

My promotional material includes brief comments by people who have read the book and their name, (company name in some cases), city, state, and occupation. I would appreciate any remarks you could give me for that purpose:

_____

_____

_____

Name _____ Occupation _____

Address _____

City _____ State _____ Zip _____

Feel free to leave blanks if you prefer not to answer all of these questions. I would appreciate receiving your evaluation even if you only fill out one line.

How long have you been a real estate investor? _____

What is the total value of your investment real estate? _____

What types of property do you own? _____

If your comments will not fit on this sheet, feel free to write them on the back of additional sheets. Please send your evaluation to:

John T. Reed
342 Bryan Drive
Danville, CA 94526

John T. Reed's Order Form

Newsletter

	Unit Price	Total
_____ one-year subscriptions to John T. Reed's Real Estate Investor's Monthly (12 monthly issues)	$121.00	$_____
_____ back issues (Please see catalog for list. <u>Minimum order is 3.</u>) 1 to 11 back issues	$ 8.50 ea.	$_____
12 or more back issues	$ 8.00 ea.	$_____
All back issues starting Feb. '86	$ 7.50 ea.	$_____

Special reports (40 pages, or more)

	Unit Price	Total
_____ #1 Single-Family Lease Options	$ 29.95	$_____
_____ #2 Distressed Real Estate Times: Offensive and Defensive Strategy and Tactics	$ 29.95	$_____
_____ #3 How to Do a Delayed Exchange	$ 29.95	$_____

Books

	Unit Price	Total
_____ Aggressive Tax Avoidance for Real Estate Investors	$ 23.95	$_____
_____ How to Increase the Value of Real Estate	$ 19.95	$_____
_____ How to Manage Residential Property for Maximum Cash Flow and Resale Value	$ 21.95	$_____
_____ How to Use Leverage to Maximize Your Real Estate Investment Return	$ 19.95	$_____
_____ Office Building Acquisition Handbook (loose leaf)	$ 39.95	$_____
_____ Real Estate Investor's Monthly on Real Estate Investment Strategy	$ 39.95	$_____
_____ Residential Property Acquisition Handbook	$ 19.95	$_____

Cassettes (Two 60-minute cassettes in a binder)

	Unit Price	Total
_____ High Leverage Real Estate Financing	$ 29.95	$_____
_____ How to Buy Real Estate for at Least 20% Below Market Value, Vol. I	$ 29.95	$_____
_____ How to Buy Real Estate for at Least 20% Below Market Value, Vol. II	$ 29.95	$_____
_____ How to Buy Residential Property	$ 29.95	$_____
_____ How to Find Deals That Make Sense in Today's Market	$ 29.95	$_____
_____ How to Manage Residential Property for Maximum Cash Flow and Resale Value	$ 29.95	$_____
_____ How to Save Tens of Thousands of Tax Dollars by Exchanging	$ 29.95	$_____
_____ Offensive and Defensive Strategy for Distressed Real Estate Times	$ 29.95	$_____
_____ Single-Family Lease Options	$ 29.95	$_____

Software

	Unit Price	Total
_____ Landlording™ On Disk software by Leigh Robinson		
IMPORTANT—CHECK ONE: ☐ Macintosh ☐ IBM 5 1/4 ☐ IBM 3 1/2"	$ 39.95	$_____

	Subtotal	$_____
Discount 5% for two or more items totaling over $100		$_____
California residents: add your area's **sales tax** (including newsletter subscriptions)		$_____
Shipping: $4.00 for first item		$ 4.00
$2.00 for **EACH** additional item		$_____
For a **Rush Order,** add $5 more to the shipping costs.		$_____
(There is **one** shipping charge for any number of newsletter back issues.)		
	Total	$_____

━━━ Satisfaction guaranteed or your money back ━━━

Method of Payment: _____ Check enclosed payable to John T. Reed _____ Visa _____ MasterCard _____ Discover

Credit card # _____ Exp. Date _____ Signature _____

Ship to: Name _____

Street Address* _____

City _____ State _____ Zip _____ Telephone _____

* UPS cannot deliver to P.O. boxes. Please allow 2-3 weeks for processing and delivery.
Please mail your order to: John T. Reed, P.O. Box 27311, Concord, CA 94527
These prices are effective January 1, 1992 and are subject to change. Source Code: 03

For faster service, ☎ phone toll-free:
800-635-5425

John T. Reed's Order Form

	Unit Price	Total
Newsletter		
_____ one-year subscriptions to John T. Reed's Real Estate Investor's Monthly (12 monthly issues)	$121.00	$_____
_____ back issues (Please see catalog for list. <u>Minimum order is 3.</u>) 1 to 11 back issues	$ 8.50 ea.	$_____
12 or more back issues	$ 8.00 ea.	$_____
All back issues starting Feb. '86	$ 7.50 ea.	$_____
Special reports (40 pages, or more)		
_____ #1 Single-Family Lease Options	$ 29.95	$_____
_____ #2 Distressed Real Estate Times: Offensive and Defensive Strategy and Tactics	$ 29.95	$_____
_____ #3 How to Do a Delayed Exchange	$ 29.95	$_____
Books		
_____ Aggressive Tax Avoidance for Real Estate Investors	$ 23.95	$_____
_____ How to Increase the Value of Real Estate	$ 19.95	$_____
_____ How to Manage Residential Property for Maximum Cash Flow and Resale Value	$ 21.95	$_____
_____ How to Use Leverage to Maximize Your Real Estate Investment Return	$ 19.95	$_____
_____ Office Building Acquisition Handbook (loose leaf)	$ 39.95	$_____
_____ Real Estate Investor's Monthly on Real Estate Investment Strategy	$ 39.95	$_____
_____ Residential Property Acquisition Handbook	$ 19.95	$_____
Cassettes (Two 60-minute cassettes in a binder)		
_____ High Leverage Real Estate Financing	$ 29.95	$_____
_____ How to Buy Real Estate for at Least 20% Below Market Value, Vol. I	$ 29.95	$_____
_____ How to Buy Real Estate for at Least 20% Below Market Value, Vol. II	$ 29.95	$_____
_____ How to Buy Residential Property	$ 29.95	$_____
_____ How to Find Deals That Make Sense in Today's Market	$ 29.95	$_____
_____ How to Manage Residential Property for Maximum Cash Flow and Resale Value	$ 29.95	$_____
_____ How to Save Tens of Thousands of Tax Dollars by Exchanging	$ 29.95	$_____
_____ Offensive and Defensive Strategy for Distressed Real Estate Times	$ 29.95	$_____
_____ Single-Family Lease Options	$ 29.95	$_____

Software

_____ Landlording™ On Disk software by Leigh Robinson

IMPORTANT—CHECK ONE: ☐ Macintosh ☐ IBM 5 1/4 ☐ IBM 3 1/2" $ 39.95 $_____

Subtotal	$_____
Discount 5% for two or more items totaling over $100	$_____
California residents: add your area's **sales tax** (including newsletter subscriptions)	$_____
Shipping: $4.00 for first item	$ 4.00
$2.00 for **EACH** additional item	$_____
For a **Rush Order,** add $5 more to the shipping costs.	$_____
(There is **one** shipping charge for any number of newsletter back issues.)	
Total	$_____

Satisfaction guaranteed or your money back

Method of Payment: _____ Check enclosed payable to John T. Reed _____ Visa _____ MasterCard _____ Discover

Credit card # _____ Exp. Date _____ Signature _____

Ship to: Name _____

Street Address* _____

City _____ State _____ Zip _____ Telephone _____

* UPS cannot deliver to P.O. boxes. Please allow 2-3 weeks for processing and delivery.
Please mail your order to: John T. Reed, P.O. Box 27311, Concord, CA 94527
These prices are effective January 1, 1992 and are subject to change. Source Code: 03

For faster service, phone toll-free: 800-635-5425